THE POCKET WATCH HANDBOOK

Frontispiece Verge watch in silver pair-cases hallmarked 1807, the movement engraved 'Jer. Wing, Braintree'. The dial, with its unusual coloured scene, is also shown on the jacket. (The seconds hand forms the rotating sails of the windmill.) The outer case has a 'Wing' watch paper.

THE POCKET WATCH HANDBOOK

M. Cutmore

BRACKEN BOOKS
LONDON

Jacket photograph by Jonathon Bosley
Line drawings by Eadan Art

Published by Bracken Books,
A Division of Bestseller Publications Ltd,
Princess House,
50 Eastcastle Street,
London W1N 7AP,
England

First published by David & Charles

ISBN 1 85170 228 8

Printed and bound in Great Britain by
The Camelot Press, Southampton, England

CONTENTS

PREFACE AND ACKNOWLEDGEMENTS

This book tells the fascinating story of pocket watches from their very beginnings, with special attention to the period from 1780 to 1850 when the verge watch was replaced by the lever watch, and to the post 1880 period when the techniques of factory manufacture brought prices within everyone's reach. As well as history and technology there is also helpful advice for the collector — to show, for example, how a little research can bring meaning to a watch that may have lain unnoticed for years.

For many people, it is this unpredictable nature of collecting which brings the excitement — and sources are quoted throughout to enable you to make your own investigations. Many of the references are to *Antiquarian Horology*, the Journal of the Antiquarian Horological Society, a first-class, high-quality product with excellent illustrations. The Society is worth joining for the journal alone.

The general importance of books, catalogues and visits to museums and collections cannot be overemphasised, but, however much reading and viewing is achieved, there is no substitute for actually handling mechanical pocket watches. They are rapidly becoming things of the past and, as such, should be treated with respect — whether they are priceless antiques or have inexpensive factory-made movements. It is unlikely that many more will be made.

Many people have assisted in the production of this book. Thanks are therefore due to museums for giving valuable time to queries and correspondence, also to acquaintances, friends, collectors and dealers who have helped by loaning watches, chatting, corresponding and advising. The line drawings were made, from the author's roughs, by Ethan A. Danielson. The photographs, apart from those accredited in the caption to Plate 20, are the work of William R. Milligan, whose contribution is gratefully acknowledged.

1
THE BIRTH OF THE WATCH

Clocks were constructed before watches, so that a history of watches logically begins with a brief look at their clock ancestry. Mechanical timekeeping devices make use of repetitive motion which, in early clocks, was the oscillation of a centrally pivoted, horizontal foliot beam pushed backwards and forwards by the teeth of an escape (or crown) wheel. With each oscillation the escape wheel rotated one tooth pitch and thus the repetitive motion of the foliot allowed the wheel to rotate in increments at an approximately constant average speed. The motive power came from a weight suspended by a cord wrapped around a drum, which supplied constant torque to the mechanism. The somewhat arbitrary nature of the friction forces in the fairly crudely engineered system made the timekeeping less exact than modern standards. Adjustment of the timekeeping through the rate of oscillation was principally by the magnitude of the suspended weight and the moment of inertia of the foliot. Finer adjustment was achieved by changing the position of small weights on the foliot to alter its moment of inertia.

Clocks of this type were probably made from about 1300, but the earliest still surviving are the Salisbury clock assigned a date of 1386 and which can be seen in the cathedral, the Rouen clock of 1389 and the Wells clock of 1392 which is now in the Science Museum in London.

Early clocks of this type did not necessarily have dials with hands to indicate the time, but were so arranged that the timekeeping section (driven by the suspended weight and controlled by the foliot) actuated another section causing it to sound a bell or bells at suitably chosen intervals. The bell section was also powered by a weight suspended from a cord wrapped around a drum. A sounded bell to communicate time to all people within audible range was far superior to the visual dial and hand indication which not only required the person to be close but also necessitated an organised and recognised manner of indicating time. The word 'clock' derives from the Latin word for bell, *cloca*, which became *clocke* or *glocke* in medieval, continental languages.[1]

Not all clocks were as large as those described above, which could be 2m (6ft) wide by 1m (3ft) deep by 1m (3ft) high. Those designed to serve a large household rather than a community are now known as domestic clocks and were up to 0.6m (2ft) high with a base of perhaps 0.3m (1ft) by 0.3m (1ft). The earliest dated evidence for their existence is a manuscript of 1364 describing the Dondi clock; the earliest surviving ones are somewhat later. They are weight powered and the weights need a clear space below to fall. These clocks indicated time on a dial for use in the room and additionally sounded bells that could be heard in other parts of the house. (If no bells are used, merely visual indication, the clock is really a timepiece since it is wrong to call a device without bells a clock — a distinction not commonly appreciated by laymen but important in the accurate description of a time-giving device.)

These big heavy domestic clocks (made of iron) could not be moved without disturbing the weights and thus stopping the clock. They were also expensive and rare, so a household would be unlikely to have more than one (even that was a luxury). Thus a ringing bell was the best way of transmitting the time to every room of the house.

When the coiled spring was introduced as an alternative form of motive power, it became possible to move a clock about without stopping it. Obviously, the smaller and lighter the clock the more portable it becomes; and the immediate advantage of a spring-driven clock was reduction in size to a drum or box perhaps 0.2m (8in) in diameter and 0.1m (4in) high. Documentary evidence for spring-driven clocks exists in a manuscript dated between 1455 and 1488[2,3]; the earliest surviving example is, however, dated 1525. A disadvantage of spring-driven clocks was that, because the torque provided by a spring is not constant, the driving force for the clock decreased as the spring unwound, giving worse timekeeping than that of the weight-driven clock. Not withstanding this disadvantage, reduction in size and portability without stopping assured their success.

In due course, size was reduced further and the watch — which might be defined as a spring-driven timepiece (or clock) small enough to be carried unobtrusively on the person — came into being, with the foliot beam replaced by a dumb-bell shaped, centre-pivoted arm or a circular, spoked balance wheel. The time lapse between the earliest clocks and the earliest watches is about two hundred years, from perhaps 1300 to 1500; although the latter date is based on documentary evidence, and the three watches referred to in a letter from Milan dated 1488 may have been small clocks. Some documents suggest watches were made in Nuremburg by Peter Hele or Henlein in the period 1500 to 1510[4]. Others suggest that they originated in Italy, Flanders or Burgundy. Probably the question as to where and when will never be answered.

The earliest existing watch, kept at the Wuppertal Museum in West Germany, is dated 1548 and initialled 'C.W.' — thought to represent Casper Werner of Nuremburg. It is contained in a gilt-metal drum-shaped (tambour) case with a gilt-metal dial protected by a pierced cover. It has a single hand indicating the time on an engraved ring with both Roman numerals (I–XII) and Arabic numerals (13–24), and also raised pins on the dial enable the time to be felt in the dark. The movement is of ferrous material with a dumb-bell balance supported by a small upper bearing (cock). It has a crude device, known as a stackfreed (see page 15), which attempts to compensate for varying spring torque.

Another early watch, in the Louvre in Paris, is signed 'Jacques de la Garde', is dated 1551 and was made in Blois. The case is spherical although the brass movement is basically cylindrical, and the small dial has the time indicated by a single hand. In this watch, compensation for varying spring torque is achieved by a device known as a fusee (described later in this chapter) which was superior to the stackfreed and replaced it completely by about 1650. A similar small, spherical clock is kept at the National Maritime Museum in London.

The two examples just described illustrate between them the features of watches for the next hundred years — a brass movement incorporating a fusee for improved timekeeping and fitted in a drum-shaped case. Watchmaking had spread into most of Western Europe by 1600, and sufficient numbers of watches survive for us to trace the pattern of development. One item to note is that early watches have a ring (bow) on the case at right angles to the plane of the watch; later ones usually have the bow in the same plane. The early examples were designed to be hung around the neck of the owner to be seen and admired since they represented rarity and expense, and were thus neck watches rather than pocket watches. They are evidenced in contemporary paintings such as the one by Hans Eworth in the Royal Collection at Windsor Castle dated 1563 which shows Lord Darnley and his brother, and Lord Darnley is wearing a circular gold-coloured watch on a cord around his neck. Further examples of the illustrations which are such an important source of data in clock and watch history are 'Il Magnifico Bartolommeo' by Jacopo Pontormo, dated 1549; 'Portrait of a Young Man' by Ludger Tom Ring, dated 1550; and an untitled painting by Tommaso Manzuoli probably c1560.[5]

Most of the essential working parts of a watch have now been men-

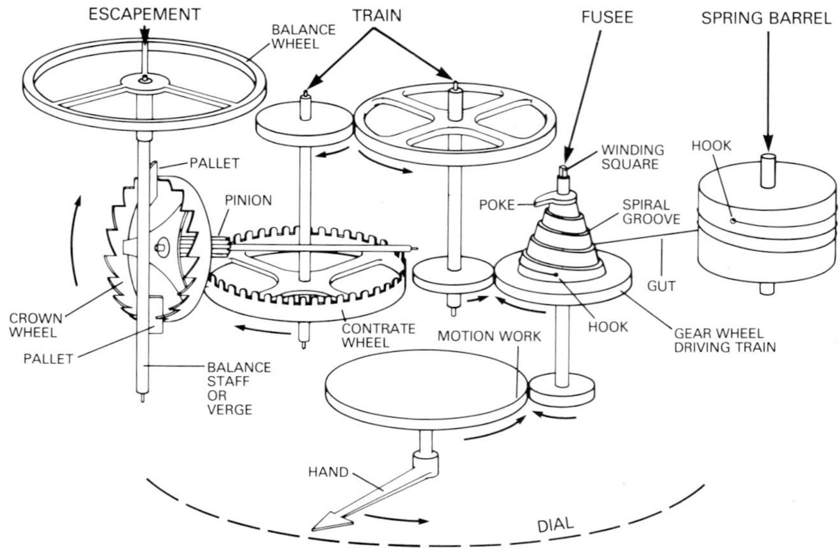

Fig 1 An early watch movement

tioned but, to summarise, a watch contains a mainspring which may be open or more usually coiled in a barrel (Fig 1). This is attached to a shaft so that, as the spring unwinds, the shaft is turned. The shaft rotation is transmitted to the escapement through a regulating device and a system of gears (wheel train) with numbers of teeth such that the ratios of the rates of rotation of the various parts are correct. The spring needs to uncoil slowly to give long running and the hand needs to rotate at the correct speed to indicate the time. The primary speed controller is the escapement with its oscillating balance wheel. This allows the escape wheel to rotate tooth by tooth and, as each tooth escapes, each wheel in the train rotates by a small increment. The hand or finger is connected to one of the wheels by the motion work and is arranged to rotate every twelve hours; as it does so it indicates the time on the dial. The regulating device is needed to even out the torque of the spring. In early watches this was a stackfreed, but the more efficient fusee had replaced it completely by the second half of the seventeenth century.

The fusee is sometimes said to have been invented by Leonardo da Vinci because there is a sketch of it in his works (cod. Madrid I, folio 32, recto). However, this is unlikely since he lived from 1452 until 1519 and an illustration in a book of c1450 shows a spring-driven clock with one.[2] To use a fusee the spring is placed in a barrel, one end of the spring being attached to the barrel and the other (inner) end to a fixed arbor (shaft) about which the barrel rotates. A length of gut is attached to and wound around the barrel, the other end of the gut being attached to the fusee. The spring is wound up by rotating the fusee with a key, which movement uncoils the gut from the barrel and coils it onto the fusee which has a spiral groove cut in its cone-shaped profile (Fig 1). When the spring is fully wound the force transmitted to the fusee by the gut acts at the smallest radius, but as the spring unwinds the gut is recoiled onto the barrel and the reducing spring force acts on an increasing fusee radius. If correctly designed, the torque (force multiplied by radius) applied to the fusee, and hence to the train, is constant.

With the exception of the hand and its driving gears (motion work) and the balance wheel of the escapement, all these watch parts are contained between two plates separated by pillars which are fixed into the plate nearest the dial. The other plate is secured in place by tapered locking pins which pass through pillar extensions protruding through it. The upper pivot of the balance is supported by a bearing held in the cock of the watch, which is itself secured to the plate — by a pin in early watches but by a screw after about 1630. These parts constitute the movement of the watch and they are normally made of gilded brass with considerable decorative detail. Steel is used for the wheel arbors (shafts), pinions, hand and various small parts. Visible steel parts are often blued.

A watch movement needs protection and is housed in a case, which is usually hinged so that the watch can be opened and the movement wound or adjusted. Watch glasses were not fitted until the second quarter of the seventeenth century. Cases could be decorated in a variety of ways.

It is worth considering the change from large clock to small watch in terms of the demand made on the tools and skills of the contemporary craftsman. It is not too difficult to envisage that a blacksmith could make a weight-driven clock of the large dimensions discussed earlier.[6] The material used would be wrought iron for the frame and most other parts; those parts that needed to be harder could be made from iron carbonised to steel, which can be hardened and tempered to suit the user.

Tools available would have included hammers and anvils, chisels, punches, crude files, saws and rasps, and crude drills, together with rules, compasses and scribers for marking out. Tools that needed to cut, such as files, would be made from steel with the teeth chiselled up and then the whole hardened and tempered. Stone was available for sharpening; thus soft materials such as iron or brass could be worked with hard, sharp tools. Joining could be achieved by soldering, riveting or hammer welding; and surfaces could be made by cold forging or case hardening.

Wheel blanks would be marked out with a radial ruler pivoted at the centre of a plate previously divided and marked out to indicate various tooth positions. The teeth could then be filed by hand to fit a profile gauge; wheel-cutting machines came later. Simple lathes had been in existence since antiquity for turning soft materials such as wood, but metal turning necessitated steel tools and much larger forces for which a simple lathe was not suitable. However, if a tool rest was fitted the lathe worker had only to steady and guide the tool rather than support the turning force as well. In larger simple lathes the power was provided by foot treadle pulling down on a cord wrapped around the workpiece, the treadle being returned by a flexible rod (attached to a fixed point above the lathe) to which the other end of the cord was affixed. Thus the work rotated backwards and forwards, and cutting took place during the appropriate direction of rotation.

With smaller clocks such as the domestic weight-driven type, the work would have been similar, but the next step to small portable clocks and even smaller watches demanded different skills which were more likely to be a feature of the locksmith's trade. The wheels in a watch — made by similar techniques to those of clocks — were perhaps 1.6cm (0.6in) in diameter with 40 teeth, and the pinions perhaps 0.4cm (0.15in) in diameter with 10 teeth. The motion of these wheels is not fast or continuous so that friction would not cause great wear or overheating, but the timekeeping would depend on the smoothness of the motion.

The lathes available would be smaller scale versions of the larger ones described above, operated by a hand-held bow moved backwards and forwards. The cutting tool would only have one hand to steer it, so that a rest was vital to work on the tiny pieces.

Finally, the spring itself, crucial to timekeeping, had to be made so that it was of even strength implying constant thickness and width with metallurgical consistency. Wrought iron would be hammered to an even thickness and then cut and filed, or drawn through fixed files, to the finished size. The end attachment holes would be made. These long strips would be cleaned, polished and coiled. The resulting soft iron spirals would then be packed into a clay box filled with carbonaceous material and heated for several days at a temperature found by trial and error until, again based on experience, it was considered that enough carbon had been absorbed to produce steel of the correct springiness. (Tool steel was made by a similar process.)[7] The springs would be allowed to cool and then be cleaned, polished, heated and quenched to become hard. These hard springs would finally be placed in a box of metal filings and heated to become tempered at a deep-blue colour, and the ends would be softened by heating. The failure rate of manufacture would be high. As the number of watches being made increased, it is likely that the iron material would be drawn and rolled as a preliminary to, or complete replacement of, the initial hammering process.

Contemporary illustrations are again useful evidence for early watch- and clock-makers' practices. One, reprinted from a late fifteenth-century manuscript, shows a clockmaker's workshop with two workers, hammer and anvil, wheels, files?, a pump drill and two clocks.[8] Another, a sixteenth-century engraving of a workshop, is far more detailed and shows a forge, anvil, hammers, pliers, vices, files, wheels, weight- and spring?-driven clocks with foliot and balance wheels.[9]

This chapter has shown how the watch developed from its clock ancestors during a two hundred year span, and has described the essential parts of a watch and their probable mode of manufacture. It suggests that by the end of the sixteenth century the pioneer work was complete and watchmaking — with its associated craftsmen watch-makers as opposed to blacksmiths and locksmiths — was an established industry in Europe. The watches that these men produced are now known as verge watches.

2
THE VERGE WATCH

The escapement of a watch allows the escape wheel to rotate one tooth at a time and thus the hand to move in small increments, the rate at which the movements occur being dictated by the time of vibration of the balance wheel. Escapements can be broadly divided into two groups: frictional rest and detached. They may also be recoil or dead beat. In a frictional-rest escapement the vibration of the balance is never free from friction due to permanent contact between the balance arbor impulse piece and the escape wheel which gives the impulse to the balance to keep it swinging. In a detached escapement there is no contact except at impulse, and the balance swings freely. Recoil is characteristic of designs in which the escapement — and hence the train, hand and mainspring — is forced backwards for an instant during the action. Dead-beat escapements have no recoil.

The earliest type of watch escapement is illustrated in Fig 1. It is known as the verge escapement and the complete watch as a verge watch. The term 'verge' refers to the staff carrying the balance wheel and pallets which engage the teeth of the crown wheel. Until new escapements were devised there would be no need to use the term 'verge watch' and this description probably dates from the nineteenth century. The verge escapement is a frictional-rest recoil design used from the birth of the watch for almost four hundred years and it is therefore very important in the history of the pocket watch.

Pre-balance-spring Verge Watches

This group of watches includes those made before 1600 mentioned in Chapter 1. Sixteenth-century watches are rare and this section is concerned with seventeenth-century examples which are still scarce but which can be seen in various museums and collections.

In a verge watch (Fig 1), the escape wheel, also called the crown wheel, is arranged in the vertical plane to engage with two diametrically opposed pallets on the verge staff, and has an odd number of teeth to avoid being locked by the pallets. As the crown wheel is driven forward by the torque from the train, it impulses the upper pallet of the verge by pushing against it and thus rotates the balance. The crown-wheel tooth slips (escapes) from this pallet and the train is free to move. As it does so a tooth on the opposite diameter engages the lower verge pallet, which is set at an angle of about 100 degrees from the upper pallet, and interferes with the rotation of the crown wheel, bringing it to rest. In bringing it to rest the crown wheel, train and hand are forced to recoil a small amount before the spring torque succeeds in pushing the bottom pallet away to restart the cycle with the balance swinging in the opposite direction. The crown-wheel teeth are undercut to ease the recoil action and the balance arc of swing is limited by a hog's bristle regulator (see page 16). As the escape wheel is in the vertical plane, a special gear wheel, known as a contrate wheel, is needed to convert the horizontal rotary motion of the escape-wheel pinion to the vertical rotary motion of the rest of the watch train. (This feature is also needed in other escapements with horizontal motion.)

Unfortunately the friction and recoil interfere with the timekeeping capabilities of the watch and from earliest days attempts were made to overcome this problem. First the spring was set up and stopped. 'Set up' means the spring was given a small amount of pre-wind using a ratchet and detent, and 'stopwork' limited the amount of winding. The result was that only the middle portion of the spring potential was used to drive the watch and it was hoped that this would give a constant rate of change of torque. The stackfreed or fusee was then used to compensate for this constant rate of change.

The stackfreed was a device which introduced a deliberately controlled amount of friction using a roller and a cam (Fig 2). The roller is

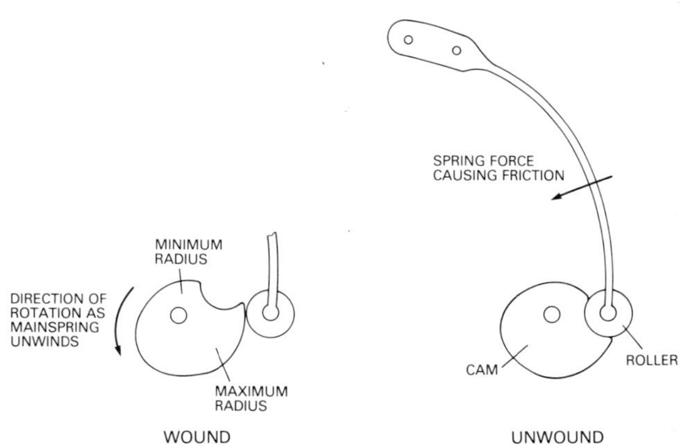

Fig 2 The stackfreed

controlled by an auxiliary leaf spring so that when the mainspring is fully wound and exerting maximum torque the cam lift and the friction torque caused by the roller on the cam are also at a maximum. As the spring unwinds and exerts less torque the cam rotates and reduces the friction torque. Since friction is a rather unpredictable effect, the stackfreed is not a very efficient torque controller. The fusee, described in Chapter 1, is a far more elegant solution to the problem and does go some way towards the desired effect so that the stackfreed was an uncommon, transient device found in early German watches.

The final device used to control timekeeping was the hog's bristle regulator. Having made the torque as even as possible, regulation was achieved by controlling the arc of vibration of the balance wheel — the shorter the arc of vibration the quicker the crown-wheel teeth would be allowed to escape and the faster the hand indicating time would rotate. Hog's bristle regulators (Fig 3) were arranged to pivot, to allow adjustment of the arc of vibration.

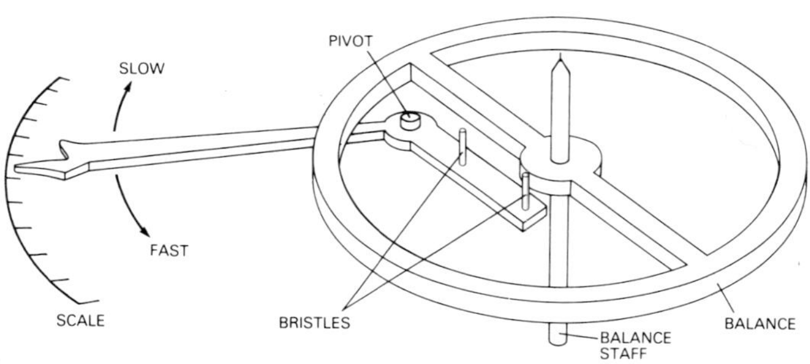

Fig 3 Hog's bristle regulator

Even if all these devices had functioned perfectly the uneven nature of the early springs, the poor quality of contemporary lubricants and the unpredictability of friction in the escapement would still have upset the timekeeping of the pre-balance-spring verge watch. This is reflected in the fact that only a single hand was fitted and the dial was marked in quarter hours. Thus, time could only be read to the nearest five minutes.

The accuracy of such watches might vary from a quarter to a half hour per day, though verifying this is difficult as continuous testing of a 350-year-old watch would probably damage it. It would also be necessary to restore the watch to its original condition to conduct a fair trial. In a lecture to the Antiquarian Horological Society in 1954, Cecil Clutton quoted a pre-balance-spring table clock driven by a spring which varied by seven minutes either way in a day. A watch would be likely to perform less well than a clock, since it was continually being moved about.

During the first half of the seventeenth century, watchmakers eliminated the stackfreed and became more skilled in making the parts for verge watches, but there were few significant technical developments. One improvement was the replacement of the ratchet and detent method of set up with a worm and wheel arrangement which gave finer control and also indicated the amount of set up on a small visible dial fitted in the plate of the watch. It is unlikely that an owner used it frequently; but it did allow a change to be made for summer and winter temperatures and for oil which thickens with age. Another improvement was the use of a chain for the fusee rather than easily broken gut, and there was a general improvement in the manufacture of fusees. An attempt was made by some makers to introduce the pendulum to the pocket watch and achieve more accurate timekeeping.[1] It seemed an attractive idea for, when the pendulum was introduced into spring- and weight-driven clocks by Christian Huygens in 1657, there was such a great improvement in clock performance that watches were made to look very poor by comparison. The pendulum in the watch was not successful even though some makers incorporated gimbals in spherical cases. The pendulums were too short with large arcs of swing. Fortunately the solution to inaccurate timekeeping of a watch was not long in coming, as balance springs appeared in 1675.

Watches of the seventeenth century were given various complications. Some were able to strike and are now known as clockwatches. Some could ring alarms and some could indicate day, date and moon phase. Each of these functions is time based and could therefore be achieved by extra gearing with phasing by pins or slots in wheels.

Apart from the mechanism, the decoration applied to the movement and to the case is noteworthy. Movements were originally functional with few embellishments, but cases were made attractive from the earliest days; during the seventeenth century decoration of both increased. Initially, the watch as a technical achievement was enough to justify pride of ownership; but as watches became more common it became fashionable to gild all the brass parts of movement and case, such gilding being not only decorative but helping to preserve the brass, leaving only the steel parts to rust. The movement had an elaborate filigree cock with filigree foot fixed to a plate engraved around the edge, with further filigree work around those ratchets or winding squares which protruded through it. Steel parts that could be seen were blued and the maker's name and place of work were engraved in elegant style on the visible plate, which thus became very attractive to look at. The under-dial plate was not elaborate although it was gilded. When viewed from the side the wheels, pillars, fusee and barrel could be seen to be gilded, and the pillars were made progressively more ornate reaching a decorative peak at the end of the century. Pillar styles can, in fact, be an aid to dating a movement.

The metal dials were usually engraved or enamelled — often with a scene. Hands were simple, robust steel or gold pointers which, with the aid of pins on the dial, could sometimes indicate time at night by touch. In early watches with no glasses, the dials were protected by a lid or an outer case.

As already mentioned, glasses were not fitted to cases until about 1630. At first they were held by tabs around the circumference of the hole in the dial cover, but a bezel split at the hinge was soon introduced. Early glasses were of rock crystal. Some early cases were made of this material and perhaps the advantage of seeing the time without opening the watch led to the idea of a clear cover over the dial.

Cases, initially of tambour form, acquired a domed back and front making them smooth-edged and more suitable as a hanging neck watch. Because the watch was thus displayed, cases reached a height of decoration in the seventeenth century which was never again achieved, their gilt or precious metal being engraved, jewelled, pierced or enamelled. Surviving examples suggest base metal was common, but this may be because precious-metal cases have been melted for scrap in times of hardship. Three particular styles which appeared in this period were the 'form' watch in which the case was made in the form of a cross, a skull, an animal or a bird; the 'puritan' watch in a very plain oval case made in England in about 1640; and the already mentioned transparent rock-crystal watch.

Enamel work came in various forms. Champlevé enamel cases were first carved out and then the hollows filled with coloured enamel. Another technique was to paint scenes in enamel on one or more surfaces of the watch-case covers, and a final variation was high-relief enamel in which the smooth enamel base had raised decorations of leaves or flowers superimposed. Translucent enamel was sometimes used to enhance an engraved case, so that the underlying design produced different light textures. Jewels were set in and around the enamel scenes to act as highlights.

Enamelling of watches began at the end of the sixteenth century and the best work was probably achieved at Blois in France in the middle of the seventeenth, with scene painting pioneered by the Toutin family. Another famous family of enamellers (Huaud) worked mainly in Geneva, but their work was later, *c*1680. Such enamelling can really be appreciated only by seeing the cases; descriptions and photographs are inadequate to illustrate the quality of the work.

Case decoration was often delicate so that an outer protective cover was required. This was often made of leather and spoilt the neck watch as a piece of jewellery. If the protective outer cover was to be seen it was itself decorated in a more robust fashion — 'Pair-case' watches, the outer case decorated with piqué work in gold or silver pins, are examples. In due course the inside case, which was not seen, lost its decoration; and at about the same time the watch started to be put into a pocket, this transition from neck watch to pocket watch coinciding with the wider use of pockets in waistcoats. One change to the case was needed in the pocket watch — the bow had to be in the plane of the case and was either fixed this way or allowed to swivel into this position.

The transition was cemented by the introduction of the balance spring which turned the watch from a piece of jewellery into a reasonable timekeeper. However, it took a considerable time for the decoration on cases to disappear, and it was perhaps another hundred years before decoration was uncommon.

Introduction of the Balance Spring 1675–1700

To quote Rees's *Cyclopaedia*[2] of 1820 on the change wrought by the balance spring:

> The small clocks and watches which were made antecedently to the time of Huygens and Dr Hooke were very imperfect performers, and professed not to subdivide the hour into minutes and seconds; the double lever, and the balance arising out of it, were very imperfect regulators of the motion, produced in the train of wheel work by the maintaining power inasmuch as they were under the influence of various opposing agents, such as friction arising from coarse workmanship, the inertia of matter, resistance of the air, etc; the consequence of which was, that the weight of the moving balance was to be determined by experiments, such as would be a proper counterpoise to the agency of the mainspring on the moving train, and at the commencement of each returning oscillation, a considerable pause took place, which made a part of the measure of time to be indicated. These inconveniences at length were obviated by the introduction of a balance spring, which became to the balance what gravity is to the pendulum; and the acceleration given to the balance during the first half of the oscillation, is thus sufficient to overcome the resistance opposed to its motion during the second half; and when the shape, length and strength of the regulating

spring are duly proportioned, its isochronal performance approaches very nearly to the regularity of the pendulum.

Allowing for the peculiarity of its style, this is a fair statement. There is still discussion as to whether Huygens or Robert Hooke was the inventor, but it does not really matter; they were both working with springs between 1660 and 1675. Hooke's law *Ut tensio sic vis* (as the tension, so is the force) was published (in code) in 1664; Huygens had a watch with a spiral balance spring in 1675 and Hooke had experimented with straight balance springs as well as having had Thomas Tompion make a watch with a short spiral spring in 1675. The short spiral spring is the one which survived. Although Rees suggests at the end of his statement that the balance spring is isochronous, it is not true. An isochronous spring has the same period of vibration irrespective of the arc of vibration. To achieve this a spring needs careful manufacture and careful installation and this was not achieved in 1675. (Similar problems occur with clock pendulums for the arc of swing affects their periodic time.) Later improvements are discussed in Chapter 8.

Hooke also developed the wheel-cutting engine with Tompion, and there is no doubt that Tompion benefited from being involved with Hooke's work, for he was able to produce excellent watches controlled by the spring. He also used a regulator which enabled the active length of the balance spring to be varied by curb pins operated by a segmental rack (Fig 4), so that the time that the balance took to make a vibration could be adjusted to give accurate timekeeping. Shortening the spring made the watch go faster, and lengthening it made the watch go slower. Regulating by Tompion's method meant that the set up lost its place on the plate and was put between the plates, the small indicator dial being retained and used to determine how the regulator was set. The action of a balance spring is to use the impulse given to the balance wheel (by the crown wheel through the pallets) to coil up the spring, so bringing the balance to rest. The spring then uncoils, returning the balance to the centre position. The impulse on the other pallet causes it to uncoil further until the balance again comes to rest. Recoiling returns the balance to the initial position.

The time taken to complete a full vibration depends on the mass and mass distribution of the balance and on the mechanical properties of the spring. As already seen, in the early days of the application it was hoped that the balance vibration was isochronous, but this was found not to be the case. Besides this it was discovered that the temperature of the watch affected its timekeeping since it altered the elasticity of the balance spring — a fault which only became apparent with the improved timekeeping of the watch. It was also found that the position (pendant up, pendant down, etc) of the watch affected its timekeeping. Thus the balance spring opened up new problems.

Notwithstanding these disadvantages, the improvement in timekeeping achieved by the balance spring was so great that watches were given two hands, and dials were subdivided into minutes. Two hands required extra gearing to provide a 12:1 gear ratio to change the hour-hand speed to the minute-hand speed. At the same time as this motion work was added, a fourth wheel was added to the train to increase the running time between windings. These changes resulted in a change in the layout of the train so that the drive for the hands came from the centre wheel rather than the fusee great wheel which was used in the three-wheel train. In the new motion work (Fig 5) the cannon pinion is a friction fit onto the extended centre-wheel arbor which rotates once every hour; it carries the minute hand and can be rotated by a key overcoming the friction fit to adjust the hands. The hour hand is fitted to the pipe of a gear concentric with the cannon pinion. This gear is caused to rotate once every twelve hours by the cannon pinion and idler gear, which runs on a pin fitted to the plate.

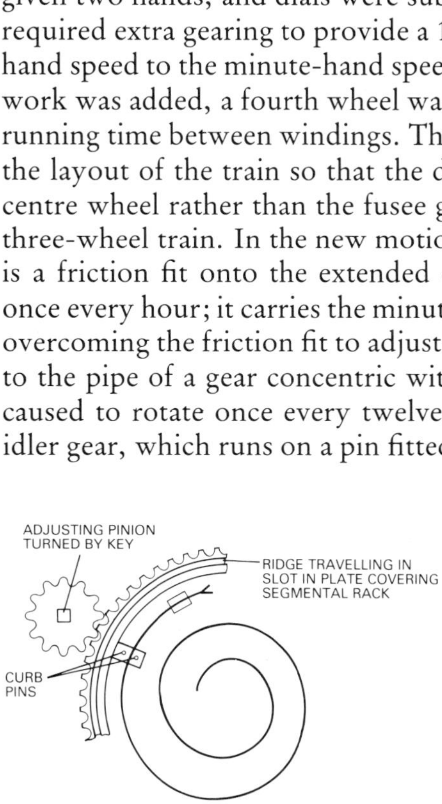

Fig 4 Tompion regulator

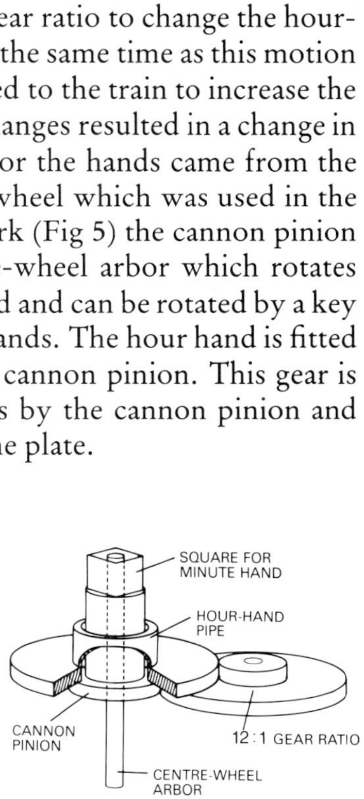

Fig 5 Motion work

The dials were marked with Roman numerals at the hour but an additional minute ring was provided with slightly smaller Arabic numbers, indicating each five minutes, around the perimeter. Before this now conventional method of indication was finalised, other experimental methods were tried, the most common being the sun and moon dial, the wandering-hour dial and the differential dial (Fig 6).

In the sun and moon dial a dark, revolving, centrally pivoted disc has a sun at one point on its perimeter and a moon at a diametrically oppo-

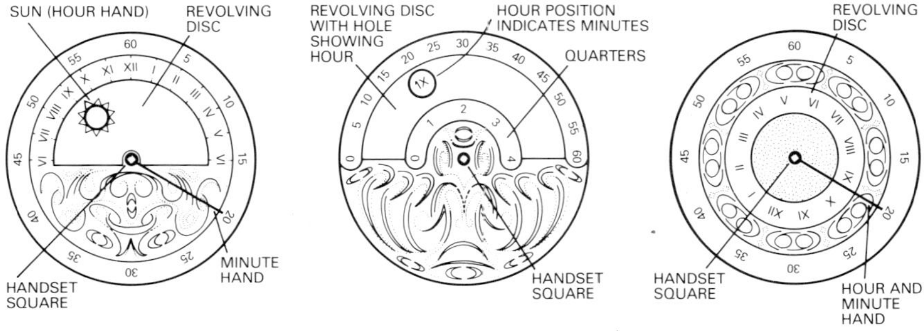

9.20 A.M.
SUN AND MOON DIAL

9.20
WANDERING HOUR DIAL

9.20
DIFFERENTIAL DIAL

Fig 6 Unconventional styles of dial

site point. The disc rotates once every twenty-four hours. The semicircular dial is calibrated for twelve hours from VI to VI with XII at the top point. The sun (day) or the moon (night) indicates the hour by its position relative to the semicircular dial. The minutes are indicated in the usual way by a hand rotating once per hour.

In the wandering-hour dial, a disc with two diametrically opposed viewing holes rotates once every two hours over a second disc marked with the hour. The hour is exposed through a viewing hole for a period of one hour during which it rotates through a semi-circle, the view-hole position indicating the minutes on a semicircular dial. At the end of an hour the view hole disappears below the right horizon, and the second hole appears above the left horizon with the next hour visible.

In the differential dial, a single hand gives minutes in the conventional manner but the hour hand is replaced by a small rotating ring geared so that the hour is indicated by the position of the minute hand above the ring. The rotating ring has to lose five minutes in an hour in order that the minute hand is over the appropriate hour for sixty minutes.

During this period of dial development the hands became more decorative. They were finer, no longer told the time in the dark by touch, and were always under glass. The minute hand was usually a straight pointer, but the hour hand acquired a scroll design towards the outer end terminating in a point to read the chapter ring. Gold and blued steel were the common materials. The need to feel the hour in the dark had been removed by the invention of the repeating mechanism by Daniel Quare and Edward Barlow in the period 1685 to 1688. Each produced different designs independently and it is said that King James II preferred Quare's design since it only needed one button to make it operate. A repeating watch sounds the time on a bell at the push of a button; it is therefore a watch which strikes at the owner's command.

This period represents a transition from poor timekeeping to good timekeeping; movement and case decoration also changed in style. In general, movement decoration became heavier but elegant, looking strong and purposeful whereas the earlier work was rather tentative in approach. Continental watches started to adopt the bridge cock secured to the plate by two diametrically opposed screws, but English watches kept the cock with a very large foot screwed to the plate. From this period English and continental watches looked different and can usually be easily distinguished, though both retain the small dial on the back plate which now indicated the regulation. The most common dials were champlevé silver or gold in which portions are hollowed out with a graver and matted to leave other parts standing smooth and proud. Normally the numerals are left proud, but are provided with slits filled with black wax to emphasise the numbers, both Roman hours and Arabic minutes being treated in this way. These dials were very elegant but are not easy to read. Dutch watches had arcaded minute bands (Plate 1) on similar dials, and French and Swiss makers introduced metal dials with enamelled cartouches inset with the numerals. They were easier to see than the champlevé type, but the watches are large with heavy cast cases and are now known as 'oignons'. There are few German watches in this period.

Plate 1 A verge watch in silver pair-cases by Stoakes, London, *c*1780. The movement has square pillars and a bridge cock, and the dial is arcaded. This style of watch is sometimes called a 'Dutch forgery'. The outer case, shown separately, is repoussé silver.

Case work started to become less decorative but there was still considerable use of enamelling. Pair-case watches with square hinges were the most common design, the outer case showing considerable variation in material and form — repoussé work (metal beaten from underneath, Plate 1), inlaid shell, leather with piqué work and fish skin.

The real change brought about by the introduction of the balance spring is summarised in the 1954 Antiquarian Horological Society lecture by Clutton. For the balance-spring verge watch he reported gains of up to two minutes per day compared with seven minutes either way for the pre-balance-spring verge. The word to notice is 'gain'; for the change is unidirectional, not either way.

Balance-spring Verge Watches 1700–1850

At the beginning of the eighteenth century, jewelling was introduced into watches. Patent 371 of 1704 granted to Peter and Jacob Debaufre and Nicholas Facio, all of whom were immigrants, was for 'An Art of Working Pretious or more Common Stones, (whether Naturall or Artificial) Christal or Glass, and certain other matters different from Metals, so that they may be employed and made use of in Clockwork or Watchwork and many other Engins . . .' In effect, it was a patent for cutting and drilling jewels for use as bearings. The patent was not extended due to opposition by watchmakers so that by 1750 the visible top bearing in the watch cock was made of a long-life, hard material. Train jewelling was not used until the end of the century when more accurate timekeeping justified the effort. Surprisingly, the technique of making holes in jewels remained an English secret until the end of the century. Indeed in Switzerland, when a competition was held in 1790[3] to produce an accurate watch, one of the conditions stated 'the use, for example, of pierced rubies is excluded, since they are imported at too great a cost from abroad'. Continental makers used a steel coqueret as a hard bearing in the cock.

In the middle of the century, Joseph Bosley devised a simpler form of regulation than Tompion's design. A lever moved by hand rotated about the balance centre-hole in the top plate (the hole was made round instead of square). The lever end indicated on a scale engraved on the plate, and two pins part-way along the lever engaged the outer coil of the balance spring to adjust its active length. Although available from 1755 it was not used in most watches until the end of the century.

In the 150 years of the verge watch, from 1700 to *c*1850, few technical developments improved its performance. However, better wheel work by use of wheel-cutting engines, more attention to pivots and more frequent cleaning and replacement of the poor quality lubricant, together with the fitting of protective dust caps, enabled the balance spring's advantages to be exploited.

It has already been mentioned that the balance spring had not solved all the problems, paramount amongst which were the effects of friction in the escapement and temperature on the spring. During the period 1700 to 1850, the number of escapements devised was enormous — over 250 — but most were never applied to watches.[4] The first successful one was the cylinder escapement developed by George Graham by 1726 (see Chapter 6), and it is important because cylinder watches were actually made and thus for the first time the purchaser had a choice. It was not a great improvement for it was still a frictional-rest escapement, but with dead-beat action; and unfortunately it was more fragile than the verge. It was made by some of the better makers in England and in small numbers in Switzerland and in larger numbers in France, where it was used to produce thinner watches. Other significant escapement designs in the early 1700s by Peter Debaufre and Jean-Baptiste Dutertre were not developed until the end of the century, when they reappeared as the Ormskirk and duplex escapements respectively (see Chapter 6).

An important factor in the search for an alternative escapement was the need for very accurate timekeeping at sea in order to navigate successfully. In 1714 the Board of Longitude offered a reward of £20,000 for a timekeeper that would determine longitude to within 30 minutes of arc of a great circle at the end of a voyage from Great Britain to the West Indies. This meant the time had to be correct to within two minutes in a two-month journey; it was, however, permissible to correct the indicated time with a *pre-stated* rate of loss or gain. Twenty thousand pounds was an enormous sum of money, and several watchmakers and clockmakers devoted much of their lives to this problem. Thomas Mudge, John Harrison, John Arnold and Thomas Earnshaw are the best known English makers involved, and Harrison eventually received the prize in 1773. The eventual products — the marine chronometer and the pocket chronometer watch — were accurate, but they did not displace the verge watch for they were fragile and costly. Both used the detent escapement (see Chapter 6) which was the first successful *detached* escapement in which the balance swings freely without the interference of friction.

The effects of temperature on the balance spring were partially eliminated by means of bimetallic compensation (see Chapter 8). A further refinement, essential to timekeeping over a long period, was the fitting of maintaining-power to ensure that the timepiece kept going whilst being wound. In its developed form maintaining-power was fitted into the fusee great wheel (see Chapter 8); verge watches did not usually have temperature compensation or maintaining-power fitted. Thus it is seen that despite all the efforts of the watchmakers to produce new escapements, new devices and compensation, the verge watch continued in its traditional form as the watch for most purchasers.

There was one aspect of design which did eventually filter through to the verge watchmaker. At the end of the eighteenth century structural changes in the plates made assembly easier. With two circular plates it was not convenient to make repairs; for example, replacing the mainspring meant taking the whole watch to pieces. By cutting a barrel-sized hole in the top plate and fitting a removable bridge, it was possible to replace springs with less effort. Similarly by putting a bridge on the dial plate to hold the bottom pivots of the third and fourth wheels, it became possible to assemble the escape wheel, centre wheel and fusee first, then the third and fourth wheels and the barrel.

The eventual successor to the verge watch was the detached lever watch (see Chapter 3), conceived and developed in the last quarter of the eighteenth century and the first quarter of the nineteenth. Because its potential was concealed by work on pocket chronometers and other escapements it was not an obvious candidate for the dominant role it later assumed. When the lever watch was recognised as a robust functional device in the second quarter of the nineteenth century, it automatically replaced the verge watch for everyday use.

Although the verge watch did not change technically there were changes in decoration and style, particularly in the dial. Champlevé dials were difficult to read and a move to white enamel dials with black numerals, used by Graham from 1720 onwards, gathered pace from about 1750. Such dials were made slightly domed because this is a more rigid structure for fragile enamel, and this had a side effect in that it precluded the use of seconds hands with a separate small chapter ring. The new accurate balance-spring verge justified the use of a seconds hand, and a flat champlevé dial was used on such a watch by Watson dated 1690.[5] Centre seconds hands only were possible with domed dials until, at the latter end of the eighteenth century, enamel techniques permitted flat dials and the now conventional seconds hand could be used. The fragility of enamel also necessitated the catch holding the watch in its case being altered from one passing through the dial to one passing under the dial.

The hands used with these new dials were the elegant 'beetle and poker' design first seen with the champlevé dial. But as the eighteenth century progressed the simpler hands used with the pocket chronometer watches were adopted for the verge watch. Pair-cases were still popular, but after mid century the use of repoussé work and horn and leather coverings became less common and both inner and outer cases were plain silver, gold or gilded copper, the general trend being towards greater elegance (Plate 2). Towards the end of the century the English verge watch had become thinner but larger in diameter; bow style had changed from a simple ring to a hinged, flattened oval one; pendants had become long, then shorter and fatter and finally bulbous; and hinges had become less obvious first by rounding and then by being hidden in the case structure. The pair case was slowly replaced by the single case in the first half of the nineteenth century, by which time there were several escapements in production so that it is not possible to take a single case watch of the first half of the nineteenth century and be sure what will be inside.

Verge movements also became progressively less elaborate in their decoration (Plate 3). Graham led the way in that he used plain cylindrical pillars, but it was a further fifty years before this design was

Plate 2 A gilt pair-cased verge watch by Jn°. Garth, London, *c*1790. The watch has subsidiary dials for time and date and the main dial is used for the sweep seconds hand (broken off short). The seconds hand can be stopped, but the whole watch is then stopped by the simple action on the contrate wheel.

Plate 3 *(Top left)* Verge movement by Cornelius Manley of Norwich, *c*1700. The movement has a large pierced cock with D-shaped foot. The figure plate is for Tompion-style regulation. *(Bottom left)* The Cornelius Manley movement showing tulip pillars, contrate wheel and spring barrel. *(Top right)* Verge movement by Jas. Dysart, *c*1820. The decoration is simple and the regulation is Bosley style. The pillars are circular. *(Bottom right)* Continental verge watch in a silver case, *c*1800. The movement pillars are five-sided and the bridge cock with steel coqueret is clearly seen. The crown wheel has adjustable bearings. The regulator indicator is clear, but there is no winding-square as the watch is wound through the dial.

common. In between, a square baluster pillar was popular. Cocks changed from large-footed designs to a smaller foot, and the foot filigree work was omitted. Filigree work remained on the cock but was not so attractive, and this too disappeared by 1840 to leave the verge cock as plain as that of other watches. However, in spite of this less complex decoration, the late eighteenth- and early nineteenth-century verge movements look entirely different to those of the new watches which were austere but very attractive.

Verge watches on the Continent exhibited a number of different features. The bridge-style cock was common with a steel coqueret bearing. The bearings (potences) of the crown wheel were adjustable (Plate 3). The outer bearing could be screw-adjusted in the plane of the wheel axis to increase or decrease the engagement of the crown-wheel teeth with the verge pallets; the inner bearing could be screw-adjusted to move the crown wheel across the verge axis to adjust the beat. This method of fine adjustment of the escapement action is credited to Julien le Roy, and is superior to that used by English makers.

Swiss watchmakers continued to make verge watches until the end of the first quarter of the nineteenth century; but in France the effect of the cylinder escapement, and in particular the work of Jean-Antoine Lepine and later Abraham-Louis Breguet, combined to produce a different design of watch which caused the earlier demise of the French verge. In the 'Lepine calibre' the top plate was replaced by a series of bars or bridges over the train, and the fusee was omitted in favour of a going-barrel directly connected to the train. It was found that the use of a long spring with correct set up and stopwork gave adequate timekeeping with a cylinder escapement. The result was a very thin, light watch compared with the traditional design. These calibres were adopted by Swiss makers from about 1830, but only rarely does an English watch use these techniques. In 1700 English watchmakers making verge watches were supreme, but by 1800 this lead was lost and the new concepts of the watch were to cause them considerable trouble in the next century.

There is evidence that verge watches were being made or finished in America at the end of the eighteenth century. These watches are rare and the following list gives some of the known makers and their approximate dates of working[6]:

Billon, 1776, Philadelphia	Campbell, 1796, Philadelphia
Carver, 1788, Philadelphia	Elsworth, 1790, Baltimore
Palmer, 1795, Philadelphia	Curtis, 1800, Philadelphia
Bond, 1800, Boston	Adams, 1800, Boston

Plate 4 A verge (sedan) clock movement made from watch parts. The shape of the plates indicates that it was purpose-built for clock use in about 1820. The engraving is crude.

American watches continued to be made in the nineteenth century in small numbers, though many makers used parts imported from Europe and complete watches were also imported. Harland made approximately two hundred watches at the beginning of the century and tariff restrictions in the period 1809–15 encouraged Goddard into production and he is reputed to have made about five hundred verge watches. As soon as restrictions were removed, imports again predominated. A new venture by the Pitkin brothers to produce machine-made watches in 1837 was not a success, and the American watch industry remained small until the second half of the century.

The English verge-watch movement was put to another interesting use at the start of the nineteenth century in that a considerable number are to be found in wooden cases as small mantel or wall clocks, sometimes called sedan clocks. Some of these movements are contained between square plates (Plate 4) and were clearly never intended for use in a watch, but most are normal circular movements with slots for hinges which, although they may never have been fitted to a watch, were made as watch parts.[7] They do need a longer centre-wheel arbor to pass through the clock dial. They were not a long-lived phenomenon for clockmakers soon produced suitable purpose-built clocks for the expanding market.

In 1797, towards the end of the life of the verge watch in England, when the war with France was four years old and there were financial problems, William Pitt imposed a tax on clocks and watches. He had already taxed many items and simple calculation suggested this new source of revenue. In 1796 nearly 200,000 silver watches were assayed in London and it was estimated that there were perhaps a million watches in the country plus a similar number of clocks. A tax of 2s 6d per silver watch would yield £125,000, not including gold watches or clocks at a higher tax rate. The tax, like that on various other commodities, was not a success; only £58,000 was collected, and the legislation was repealed, being replaced by income tax in 1799. It is not easy to assess the effects of this watch tax on verge watches, but probably it was not great.[8] The general economic situation at this time was poor in all Europe due to wars and the industry as a whole was depressed. The verge watch survived the tax and the depression to last a few more generations.

Summary

The verge watch was made from about 1500 to the latter part of the nineteenth century, though production diminished rapidly after 1850. In its developed form from 1700 onwards it was an attractive, robust watch embodying perfectly adequate timekeeping. If it had not been for the needs of navigation and man's natural curiosity there is no reason why it should not have continued in use until the present day; it is therefore worth having a verge watch restored to perfect working order and using it. Simple trials (see Chapter 11) can be conducted on any verge in good working order to assess its capability; but only if it is in this good condition can one make a fair judgement.

Chronology of the Verge Watch, 1475–1850

1475–1500	Birth as a neck watch
1548	Earliest surviving watch, introduction of stackfreed and fusee
1600	Established artifact — clockwatches, alarms, astronomical data
1630	Glasses, screws
1640	Pocket watches
1675	Balance spring
1688	Repeating watch
1726	Cylinder escapement
1770	Pocket chronometer escapement
1770–1820	Lever-watch development
1825–1850	Demise of verge watch (a few later examples do exist)

3
THE LEVER WATCH

The lever watch was the true successor to the verge watch, and any good-quality mechanical pocket or wrist watch purchased in the past thirty years will have a Swiss lever escapement. An understanding of the way in which this double-roller form of the escapement functions will give meaning to the historical developments described in this chapter.

Fig 7 shows the three components of the escapement: the escape wheel, the lever and the balance staff, arranged in a straight line. These replace the crown wheel and verge staff of the verge watch. The spring barrel, train and motion work are similar in both types of watch but modern examples do not include a fusee, for modern springs in a going-barrel with stopwork give good timekeeping. Early lever watches usually have a fusee.

As the balance swings, the impulse-pin engages the lever-fork and the safety dart enters the passing crescent on the smaller-diameter roller. The pivoted lever is unlocked by the leading side of the impulse-pin which protrudes below the larger-diameter roller on the balance staff. Unlocking causes a slight angular movement of the lever and allows the sloping face of the lever-pallet to contact the leading edge of the escape-wheel tooth. This edge slides over the lever-pallet to the position shown in the diagram, giving impulse from the lever-fork to the trailing side of the jewelled pin (and hence to the balance wheel)

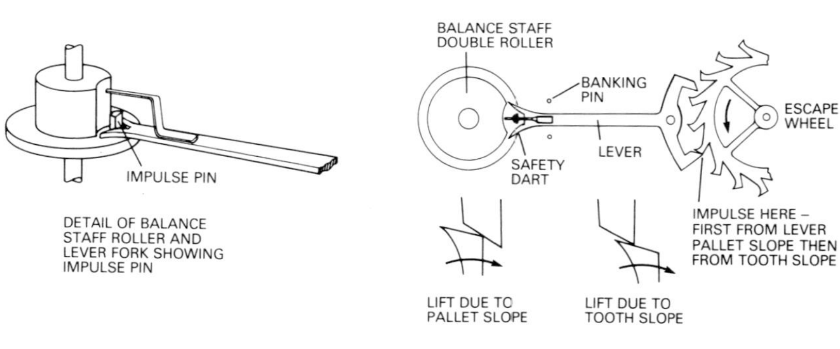

Fig 7 Swiss lever escapement

which unlocked the lever. As the leading edge of the tooth reaches the end of the lever-pallet, further impulse is given by the sloping face of the escape-wheel tooth which then escapes. During the impulse actions the lever has rotated, so that the escape wheel is only free to turn a small amount before it is relocked by the other lever-pallet engaging a tooth further round on the escape wheel. The double-impulse action is known as 'divided lift'. The lever is pulled into deeper engagement with the escape wheel by the shaping of pallet and tooth sides and comes to rest on the banking-pin. This is known as 'draw' and causes some recoil in the unlocking action. Draw is a safety measure to keep the lever out of the way of the balance which swings freely till it comes to rest under the action of the balance spring and then swings back to unlock the train again and repeat the sequence. If an accident should jerk the lever from the banking-pin during the free detached swing, the safety dart will contact the smaller-diameter safety roller and prevent any action until the passing crescent allows the correct sequence of events to occur. The small escape-wheel rotation is transmitted through the train and motion work to the hands. At each escape there is an audible tick as the lever-pallet stops the escape wheel. This escapement is therefore detached (as opposed to frictional rest) and there is no interference with the balance free swing and it is this characteristic which accounts for its timekeeping ability. Its robustness accounts for its success.

Origins of the Lever Watch

As with so many developments in watch history, just who invented the escapement is not known for certain. There are no patents involved, for at the time of its conception there was a tendency to secrecy amongst makers in the competitive atmosphere engendered by the large financial rewards which would accrue to anyone who produced a timekeeper suitable for navigation. Watchmakers were men who were rightly proud of their skills and did not wish their ideas to be copied. There are two main schools of thought, the traditional one favouring the Englishman, Thomas Mudge, born in Exeter in 1715, who discussed his new escapement with the Swiss astronomer Johann Huber when the latter visited Mudge in 1754–5.[1,2,3] The second, less well documented view, attributes the invention to Julien le Roy, working in France.

Considering the argument for Mudge first, there is a clock with a Mudge lever escapement fitted, dated *c*1760.[3] There is also a watch —

indeed the only complete watch in this debate — with Mudge's lever escapement, dated 1769. Made for King George III who gave it to Queen Charlotte, it is now in the Royal Collection at Windsor Castle and is known as the Queen's Watch. It uses a right-angle layout, ie a line joining balance, lever and escape-wheel pivots forms an approximate right angle. Mudge did not pursue the development of lever watches presumably because he felt that a constant-force escapement was more suitable for use in marine timekeepers which were his main interest (another controversial matter, for some authorities suggest that the constant-force escapement was Huber's concept).[2] Mudge used constant-force escapements in his 'green' and 'blue' marine timekeepers. There is some evidence that he did commence a second lever watch at the same time as the Queen's Watch but which was not completed until 1797, three years after his death in 1794.[1,3,4] This is known as the Flint Watch, but it has subsequently been converted from lever to chronometer escapement.

Even though Mudge had lost interest his patron, Count von Bruhl, felt sufficiently confident of the value of the escapement to persuade a reputedly reluctant Josiah Emery to take up the work, and the latter completed his first lever watch in 1782. Subsequently Emery made about forty such watches,[5] but ten valuable years had been wasted. These watches use an escapement derived from Mudge's design but which Emery improved by using a layout in which the balance, lever and escape-wheel pivots are approximately in a straight line. A model by him of his escapement is now in the Conservatoire National des Arts et Métiers in Paris. Emery lever watches maintain a rate of about six seconds per day.

It seems strange that Mudge's watch design was not developed by Matthew Dutton with whom Mudge was in partnership from about 1750; but no doubt there were good commercial reasons for continuing to manufacture the proven cylinder watch which the partnership had long produced.

Subsequent to Emery, a number of eminent English makers made lever escapements before 1800 including Pendleton (worked with or for Emery), Leroux, Grant, Edward Ellicott (the second), Perigal and Margetts.[6] Only one watch by George Margetts appears to have survived.[7] It has a three-arm compensated balance wheel and adjustable banking-screws. Rees has a diagram and description of Margetts' watch escapement which appears to be a straight-line crank-lever design with safety roller (he also shows Mudge's clock escapement).[8] Possibly, if von Bruhl had not persuaded Emery to try the lever escapement, Mudge's design might have disappeared as just another unsuccessful escapement. As it was, interest in the lever watch appeared to fade in the early years of the nineteenth century.

The argument for Julien le Roy as inventor proposes that he conceived a lever escapement at about the same time as Mudge (or even a little later), but that his design was executed earlier since le Roy died in 1759, ten years before the Queen's Watch was made. To support this view there is an incomplete watch movement which has been investigated,[9] restored[10] and of course debated,[11,12] one of the most important points being to decide if the lever escapement is original to the movement. There seems to be agreement that it is original, and further that the watch had gridiron temperature compensation of some sort. However, it may have been partly the work of Pierre le Roy (Julien's son) at a later date. Pierre could have seen an Emery lever, and either Julien or Pierre could have heard of Mudge's work. It is possible that two eminent watchmakers designed lever escapements at similar times, since this was a period of intense effort towards marine timekeeping both in England and on the Continent. It is curious that no other examples have been found, and no other makers tried the escapement if it was executed before 1759, but perhaps this single effort failed to convince Julien le Roy of the value of the escapement and he discarded the idea.

The problem is not clarified by Breguet, who could have seen a le Roy lever when he came to Paris in 1762 although his career is not clear until 1782.[13] Breguet is significant because he started producing lever watches in 1787 and continued to do so in small numbers — perhaps twenty or thirty a year — until about 1800. His work was disturbed by the French Revolution and he left Paris in 1791 for four years during which time he was both in his native Switzerland and in England. Not only could he have seen a le Roy lever, but also an Emery lever between 1782 and 1787, so that his lever could have been from Mudge via Emery, from le Roy or his own concept. There were other continental makers before 1800, notably Robert Robin and Jean Moïse Pouzait, but their work does not appear to derive from le Roy.

Irrespective of whether Mudge or le Roy was the first maker, the continuation of the lever was mainly along the Mudge–Emery line. The lessening of interest in the lever escapement at the turn of the century in both England and France is curious, but both groups of watchmakers seemed to have virtually abandoned it for about twelve years. The reason for the lack of interest may have been that marine timekeeping problems had been largely solved. After the pioneer work by Harrison and various other attempts in England and on the Continent, Arnold (1782 patent) and Earnshaw (1783 patent in the name of Wright) devised practical marine chronometers and pocket chronometer watches which were relatively easy and cheap to produce (see Chapter 8). Thus the great financial rewards for producing a successful marine timekeeper were gone, and watchmakers could concentrate their efforts on earning a living by selling watches with established escapements — verge, cylinder, duplex, pocket chronometer. Experiments with levers were not necessary if the customer was satisfied with the choice already available. With a knowledge of developments to come in the first quarter of the nineteenth century it is possible to realise that the work of Mudge, Emery, Leroux, Grant, Perigal, etc was not wasted, but in their own time they did not really succeed in their attempts. They were dead by the time the lever watch was established.

In the period 1812–16 the lever watch returned, never to look back. On the Continent, Breguet, and later Leschot, were the significant makers; in England, Peter Litherland, Edward Massey and George Savage made important contributions. But before following these later more successful approaches, some consideration of the pre-1800 levers is necessary.

Pre-1800 Lever Watches

The terminology used is that given in the description of the modern Swiss lever escapement at the beginning of this chapter, and watches made in England are considered first.

The Mudge lever watch (Fig 8) looks complex and cramped.[2] Each component is composed of separate pieces. The lever is in two parts — one part with two pallets which receive impulse from the escape wheel, and one part to transfer impulse to the balance. There are three rollers on the balance staff, one for safety with a slot to allow passage of a horn on the end of the part of the lever which receives impulse, and two separate rollers which engage with pallets on the other part of the lever. These rollers work as a pair so that on one swing of the balance the upper roller unlocks the escape wheel and the lower roller receives impulse, and on the other swing the lower roller unlocks and the upper receives impulse. The work of the two rollers could have been done by a single-impulse jewel with action on either side of the diameter (as in the later Swiss lever escapement described earlier). There is no draw as the escapement is dead beat. It is clear that the escapement was almost in the research and development stage and it was possible to change

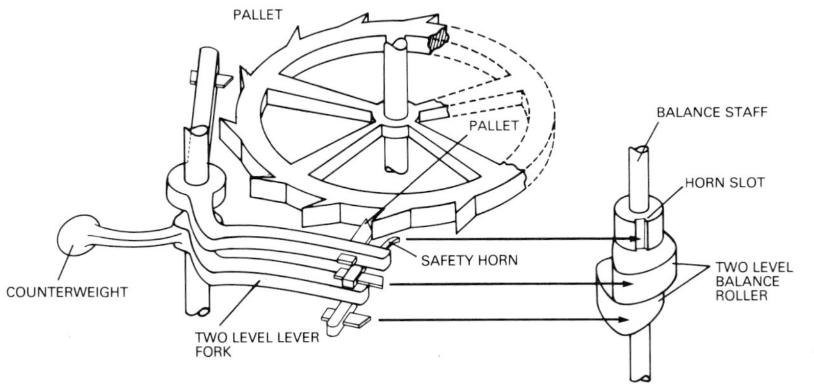

Fig 8 Mudge lever escapement

parts, to adjust the angular positions of the rollers and to adjust the pallets till the action was satisfactory. This is not surprising for it was the first lever to be fitted into a watch, though Mudge had had experience with a lever escapement in a clock which was perhaps eight times as large.

The developed Emery lever[14] which, as we have seen, changed Mudge's cramped looking right-angle layout to a straight-line layout, dispensed with the double lever by arranging the safety device as a screwed on dart which protruded below the lever-fork (Fig 9). The lever-fork is in one plane which is all that was needed to engage either side of the pivoted steel roller which replaced the two-plane, two-roller Mudge system. Emery levers did not have draw and were therefore dead beat. The whole product was lighter than Mudge's work, but this was a result of steady development work since in his early levers Emery retained the Mudge roller system in a straight-line layout. He used a free-sprung balance with S-shaped bimetallic temperature compensation (Chapter 8).

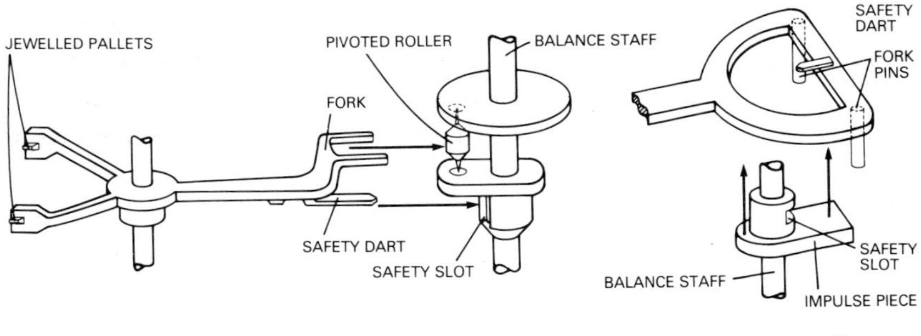

Fig 9 Emery and Pendleton lever escapements

Richard Pendleton, who worked with or for Emery, also used a straight-line layout in his own levers.[15] His movements look similar to those of Emery for they both used bridge cocks, but his lever design is different at the balance-staff end. The Pendleton lever tail has a D-shaped hole surrounding the balance-staff roller. Two pins protrude vertically from the back of the lever tail to engage the impulse-piece on the balance staff for both unlocking and impulse. There is no draw. Safety is achieved by a dart which also protrudes from the back of the lever tail, but on the opposite side to the impulse-pins. The dart passes through a slot in the roller. Pendleton, too, used a free-sprung balance with S-shaped bimetallic temperature compensation (Fig 9).

John Leroux was the man who first introduced draw in about 1785,[14] anticipating the next watch to use it by perhaps twenty years. Makers probably preferred no recoil. Leroux used a right-angle Mudge layout but in a form which is a forerunner of the later English levers with the lever arm tangential to the escape wheel (Fig 10). The balance has a double roller: one for safety and one for unlocking and impulse. A free-sprung balance with bimetallic temperature compensation was fitted.

Francis Perigal also used a right-angle layout but with a simplified Mudge-style lever rather than the Leroux type. The lever has a simple fork and safety dart, and there is no draw.[16] Temperature compensation is by a straight curb, and the balance spring has a regulator.

John Grant made various forms of light escapements.[17] He used both double-plane and single-plane forks, safety darts and both straight-line and right-angle layouts. It would seem that he was continually experimenting to find the right combination but was never satisfied that he had the answer to all the problems. He does not appear to have used draw, but he did use free-sprung balances with temperature compensation.

All the makers above except Leroux had their lift on the lever-pallets; Leroux had his on the teeth of the escape wheel. There is also a movement by Taylor[18] which has lift on the teeth, but it is undated. It is very similar to a lever watch by Ellicott[18] and there is mention of a partnership between Ellicott and Taylor in a trade directory. There is also a pocket chronometer by Ellicott and Taylor in the Clock Room of the Guildhall Library (see Chapter 12). The Ellicott lever watch (Fig 10) is dated 1805 and is worth noting since the escape-wheel teeth are shaped like those in the later pin-lever watches discussed in Chapter 4; in fact this watch could be the ancestor of those designs. The layout is a straight-line lever whose circular end passing round the balance staff

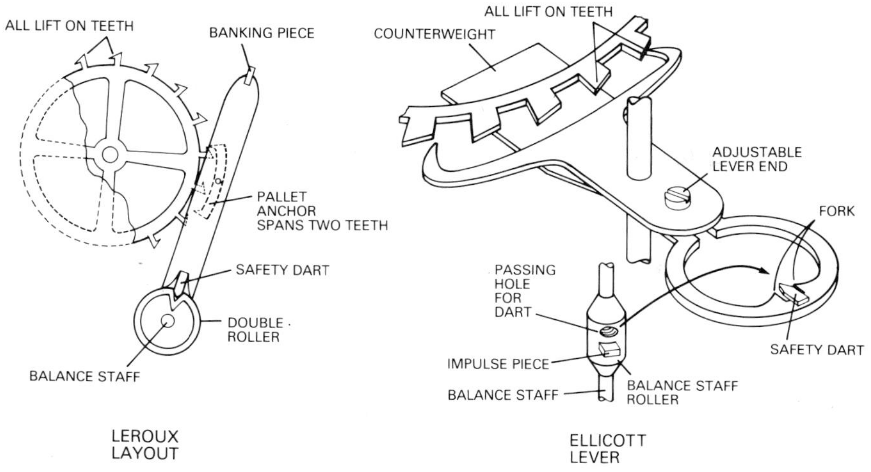

Fig 10 Leroux and Ellicott lever escapements

acts in a similar way to the Pendleton lever. It has no draw and has a well-developed compensation balance.

All these makers used one of two forms of temperature compensation to allow for the fact that a balance spring becomes less 'springy' as temperature increases and therefore the watch goes more slowly. The first is the straight or bent curb in which a bimetallic strip influences the active length of the balance spring as temperature rises, and so speeds up the vibrations to compensate for the lack of 'springiness'. The second is to arrange for some mass on the balance to be transferred inwards as temperature rises, thus speeding up the vibrations to compensate for lack of 'springiness' (see Chapter 8). Transference is achieved by making some balance parts of bimetallic strips. All these early levers were fitted with maintaining power in the fusee so that they did not stop whilst being wound.

The style of the watches, as opposed to the detail of the escapements, was elegant and simple. Mudge's watch was traditional 1770 style with a white enamel dial, Roman numerals on the chapter ring, Arabic numerals for minutes on the outer ring, beetle and poker hands, etc. Other makers used white enamel dials with spade or pointer hands and a conventional seconds hand with a subsidiary dial over the 6 o'clock mark. However, Emery, Leroux, Pendleton and Grant used regulator-style dials in which the hours and minutes were indicated unconventionally — the hour by a single hand over a small subsidiary dial under the 12-hour mark, the minute by a single hand rotating normally about the watch centre, and the seconds by a conventional subsidiary dial above the 6-hour mark.

The cases used were either plain pair-cases or, later, single cases which looked like pair-cases. This latter style was an intermediate stage between the pair-case and the conventional double-backed pocket-watch case of the nineteenth century. The glasses fitted to the cases started to change at this time from the thick glass with a flat at the centre used for the past two hundred years, to a thinner curved glass with no flat so that vision was not distorted.

The movements became increasingly devoid of decoration; most retained engraved cocks but little else. Grant made some plain gilt cocks. These watches were in the style of pocket chronometers rather than verge pocket watches. They were designed for accurate time-keeping (albeit they had temporarily lost the battle to the pocket chronometer) and decoration was not needed. Pendleton and Emery, as mentioned above, used bridge cocks; but the other makers used simple spade-shaped cocks which did not completely cover the balance as had the traditional verge cock.

Turning now to continental makers, the earliest is possibly Julien le Roy.[9] The already mentioned watch fragment has a right-angle layout with its lever-pallets in the form of pivoted cylindrical rollers. Another pivoted cylindrical roller acts as the balance-staff roller to receive impulse from two pins standing up from the lever tail to form a fork

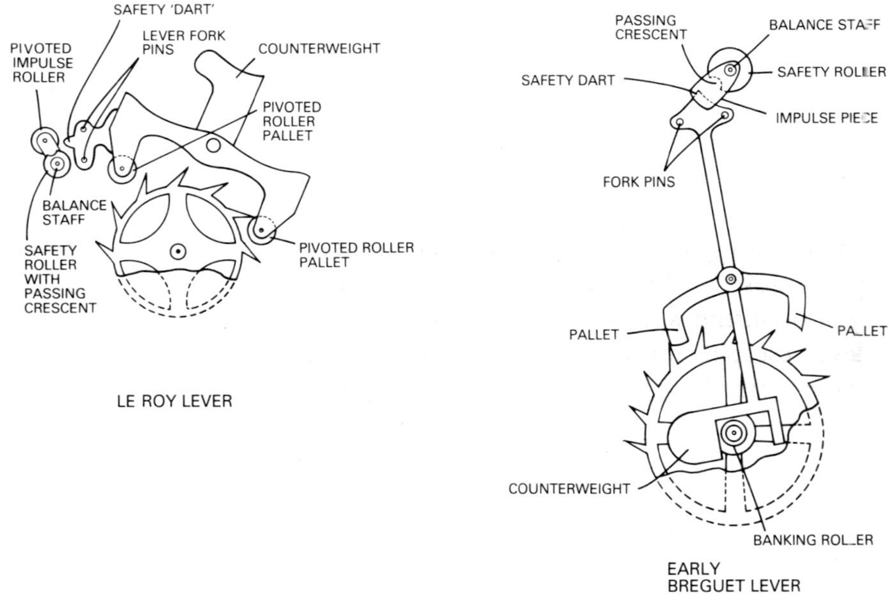

Fig 11 Le Roy and Breguet lever escapements

(Fig 11). A safety piece on the lever-end passes through a crescent in a second, conventional balance-staff roller. Because the design uses pivoted cylindrical rollers and straight-faced teeth, draw is present on only one pallet and the impulse given to the pallet with draw is much less than that given to the other. These oddities suggest that, whatever the provenance, this escapement is still in the experimental stage and had it been developed these defects would have been corrected. This lends support to the possibility of le Roy abandoning the design.

The most important continental lever maker of the pre-1800 period was Breguet. In 1787 he made at least thirty levers so that by this time his experimental work was over; indeed by 1793 he had produced over two hundred. He used straight-line levers without draw, presumably feeling a dead-beat design was preferable (Fig 11). It is not known whether or not Breguet saw the work of Mudge, Emery or le Roy, but all his levers were light and well developed. There is circumstantial evidence that Lepine may have collaborated with Breguet during the development of the characteristic lever shape.[19]

In these early watches Breguet used standing pins to form a lever fork and a simple impulse-pallet on the balance staff to engage the pin. There was a safety roller, and a pointed end to the lever to pass the slot on the roller. Banking was on the balance staff by extended arms which also acted as counterbalances for the long lever tail, all the lift was obtained from the lever-pallets and temperature compensation was used for the balance (in some watches Breguet used a curb). Whereas all the English makers used a fusee, Breguet used going-barrels for his lever watches and many were self-winding — an interesting step when most watches were still key wound, self-winding being invented by Perrelet between 1770 and 1780. Breguet's slim movements were usually of the barred Lepine calibre and his dials were usually white enamel or light metal. His hands were styled as pointers with a circular piece close to the extreme end with an offset hole in the circle. His workmanship was first class and it is unlikely that he would have made lever escapement watches when other escapements (see Chapter 6) were available unless he felt that the lever offered advantages.

There are other continental lever escapements worth a brief mention, though they are not classical levers in the sense that they follow any particular line of development. In the Pouzait lever watch (1786)[20] the escape-wheel teeth or pins project upwards from the rim of the wheel and interact with the anchor which passes over the rim (Fig 12). Impulse is transmitted to the balance in the usual way by a fork and impulse-piece and there is a safety pin: draw is not used. Pouzait levers

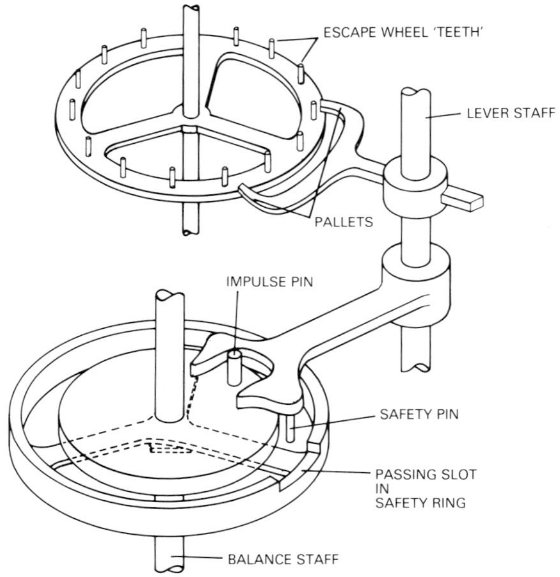

Fig 12 Pouzait lever escapement

were designed to beat seconds and used a large-diameter slow-swinging balance, often equal in diameter to the whole movement. Breguet made some Pouzait lever watches and others were made in Switzerland in the nineteenth century.

Robin[21] made several lever watches in the last decade of the eighteenth century. In one Robin lever escapement (1790) the lever is used solely to lock and unlock the escape wheel which gives impulse to an impulse piece on the balance staff on alternate swings of the balance. This impulse method is similar to that used in the pocket chronometer watch, and the escapement was 'reinvented' several times during the nineteenth century to produce 'chronometers' that were more robust than the detent design (see Morton's Patent, page 156 and Fig 42). Tavan in Geneva was also involved in lever escapement work.[22, 31]

The history of early lever watches is by no means complete in spite of a considerable increase in published information in the period 1955–65, much of which is reported in Clutton and Daniels[13] making it essential reading for the early lever enthusiast. The position is similar to that of the sixteenth-century watch in that although there is more documentation available there are only about twenty-five pre-1800 lever watches that were made in England in existence. Twelve of these emanate from Emery, five from Grant, and the remainder from the other makers. Most are in museums or collections which make them inaccessible to the average person except from the outside of the glass case in which they are displayed with the watch case open or closed as the curator wishes. Some are not displayed. With earlier or later watches which are more plentiful than these few early levers, the average enthusiast can buy specimens and take them carefully to pieces for examination and measurement. Early levers may only be examined internally by photographs or drawings made by the fortunate few privileged, and skilful enough, to take them to pieces. Thus all the information above is at least secondhand, and the lever watch enthusiast should make his own research of the literature and view the watches displayed so that he can better do justice to these pioneer makers.

Rack Lever Watches

Although interest in the development of the detached lever watch waned around the turn of the century a related, but not detached, lever escapement was made in England during this period, retaining a tenuous foothold for the lever design. In 1791 and 1792, Peter Litherland, born in Warrington in 1756, took out patents for what is now known as the rack lever escapement. (There were no patents with the other early makers.) Patent No 1830 of 1791 is the original concept, and patent No 1889 of 1792 develops this in specifying a large thirty-tooth escape wheel with inclined teeth. The design is not completely new having been conceived in 1722 by Abbé de Hautefeuille but never used, but the rack lever escapement is very significant because of the considerable number of watches that were made in England during the early years of the nineteenth century.

In the common rack lever escapement with right-angle layout, the pointed-tooth escape wheel gives impulse to the pallets on the lever in

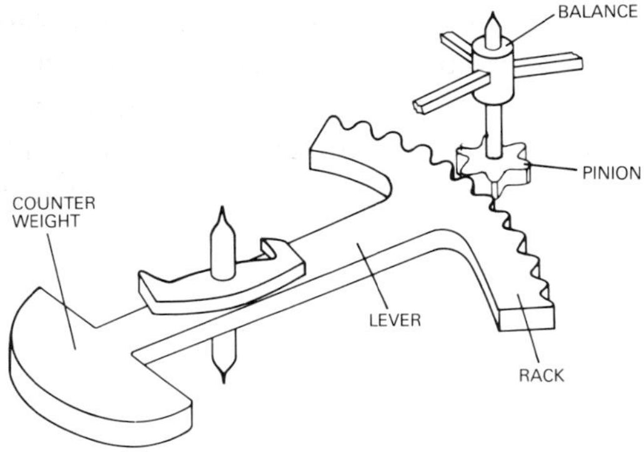

Fig 13 Rack lever escapement

the normal manner described for the earlier levers, all the lift being on the lever pallets. This impulse is transmitted to the balance by a rack (Fig 13) on the end of the lever engaging a pinion on the balance staff. A D-shaped rack counterweight is formed at the other end of the lever. There is no draw so that the escapement is of dead-beat, frictional-rest design. Compensation balances are rarely used and the normal regulation is of Bosley type on a balance spring fitted below the balance wheel. Most rack levers have fusees but not always with maintaining power. Dust caps were usually fitted. The patent, supplied by the Patent Office, is not particularly clear.

> An entire new escapement to be applied to watches or clocks, or dials called watches or clocks, for the use both of sea and land, which acts upon an entire new principle, producing greater certainty of time than any hitherto invented, being more simple and less liable to be out of repair etc.

Fortunately it is accompanied by diagrams illustrating a segmental rack on a lever which engages a pinion on the balance staff to transmit the impulse obtained by the lever anchor pallets from the escape wheel with radial teeth. Both right-angle and straight-line layout are shown and some 'dimensions' are given — fifteen teeth on the escape wheel 'laver [lever] three-tenths of an inch long or less'. There is also a rack winding system in the patent; Litherland obviously liked racks. In the second patent a diagram shows the fifteen-tooth layout and a thirty-tooth layout with inclined teeth which would work with a three-wheel train. There is also provision for a pirouette for gearing up the balance to obtain a seconds-beating watch. A compensation curb and further method of winding are added for good measure.

Litherland also covered himself for marine uses, hoping perhaps to have produced a rival to the chronometer. This is borne out in an article[23] in which the writer quotes from the Letters Patent to Litherland. These are more detailed than that supplied by the patent office quoted above which ends 'etc'. In particular the 'etc' included the words 'and which he considers will be of very great public utility especially for ascertaining the Longitude at sea at much less expense than those now used . . .' But it is hard to believe that in 1791 any watchmaker could have been unaware of the trials and tribulations of Harrison, Mudge and Emery and the work of Arnold and Earnshaw to obtain a detached escapement with temperature compensation. Thus either Litherland was completely out of touch or was merely making sure that if his escapement did prove a winner he would be the beneficiary. He cannot really have expected longitude-quality timekeeping. Litherland was 35 when he took his patent. If he had spent all his life in North West England he could have been ignorant of London affairs. His second patent does mention a compensation curb so he did have ideas about timekeeping. However, most rack lever watches have plain balances and although there may be some with compensation balances, there are few with curbs.

Even if Litherland's marine hopes were naïve, his rack lever watch was a good design in that it is simpler than the cylinder, the duplex and the pocket-chronometer watch and, given patience in setting into beat, it functions well and keeps reasonable time. It was, besides, the first cheap, robust alternative to the verge watch. The setting up is difficult because the balance is directly geared to the lever and hence to the escape wheel; therefore, unless the lever-pallets are absolutely central in the dead position of the balance, it has a tendency to run out of beat and lock. (The same is of course true of the verge but verges do not lock easily.) It is also essential that the escape wheel and pallets are engaged to the correct depth so that the balance-swing frees each pallet on each vibration. Many rack levers have adjustable slides to enable the engagement of the pallets and wheel to be varied, some also enable motion along the lever axis to adjust the engagement of the rack and balance-staff pinion. Although such adjustments are useful it would seem better to plant the parts correctly in the first place. Rack levers without slides seem to work well, but perhaps the slide allowed adjustment for wear.

The 30-tooth escape-wheel design with a 3-wheel train produced a fast-moving seconds hand. Watches of this period had balance springs giving 4 vibrations per second (14,400 per hour), which with 30 teeth gives 1 revolution in 15 seconds. With the smaller 15-tooth escape wheel and a 4-wheel train, the seconds hand fitted to the fourth wheel could be arranged to rotate once per minute.

Some time before 1804, when he died, Litherland must have gone into partnership with Whiteside. Apparently[23] his son was not a watchmaker, and perhaps the father sold out. Although Litherland appears in the trade directories till 1803, Litherland, Whiteside & Co also appear from 1800 to 1813 as patent lever watchmakers. From 1816–76 Litherland, Davies & Co appear first as patent lever watchmakers and, from 1832 on, as chronometer and watch makers. It is recorded that in 1841 a chronometer by Litherland and Davies came first in the Greenwich trials.[24] It is also reported that Litherland sold his patent rights to Robert Roskell.[25] Roskell certainly 'made' large numbers of rack lever watches; he could have bought movements from

Litherland, Whiteside & Co. In fact it is possible more were sold in his name than in Litherland's (in all forms and partnerships), since by 1825 his serial numbers were up to 39,000 whereas the Litherland sequence had only reached 12,000. The table from which these totals derive is useful for dating purposes.[26]

One of the most significant factors about Litherland and Roskell is that they were Lancashire makers (though Roskell also worked in London) and this period saw the rise of the Lancashire and Liverpool watch industry. This developed an attractive style of its own with deeply chiselled cocks, many of which were duplicated; very large clear or ruby-coloured train jewels now known as Liverpool windows; and distinctive 'crow's feet' engraving on the plate for the scale of the Bosley regulator. Some watches were made with the lever on the opposite side of the escape wheel to that normally chosen. These reversed lever watches usually had the mainspring stopwork on the top plate with additional chiselled decoration. Many watches were fitted with a stop device which could have been for timing or transport. The cocks were often engraved 'patent' and in the case of rack lever watches were

Plate 5 An early nineteenth-century silver pair-cased watch, hallmarked 1810, which has a rack lever escapement by Rt. Roskell, with thirty-tooth escape wheel and three-wheel train.

often of a distinctive shape. The Liverpool style lasted from about 1800 to 1845 and was used on all types of lever watch made during this period.

Rack lever watches (Plates 5 and 6) are most commonly found in pair-cases with enamelled dials and hands appropriate to the period. Occasionally they are found in more elaborate cases, and later examples appear in single cases. Rack levers are found with London makers; but examination of the movement usually suggests a Lancashire product and that the 'maker' is, in fact, the seller. Most assay marks on rack lever watches are those of Chester. There are very few continental examples.

Massey Lever Watches

The most significant step in the development of the English lever watch in its final practical form (as opposed to the pioneer work of Mudge, Emery, et al) was arguably due to Edward Massey who was born at Newcastle-under-Lyme in 1768. He was the son of a clock- and watch-maker and was apprenticed to his father from 1783 to 1790. He was then a freeman of Newcastle but moved several times, probably being in Coventry from 1814 to 1819, Prescot from 1819 to 1830 and London from 1831 until his death in 1852. These moves are not haphazard in the light of the geographical distribution of the watchmaking industry and his other interests. Massey took out patents for depth sounders and logs in 1802, 1806, 1834, 1844 and 1848; for taps in 1808; for clocks and watches in 1812, 1814, 1820, 1838 and 1841; and for pens in 1833 and 1834. His important watch patent is No 3854 of 1814 for 'Improvements in chronometers and pocket watches', a very short statement containing five different ideas spelt out in detail over eight pages and seven drawings, the five ideas being his escapements, his pump winding, a grid-iron compensation balance, compensation curbs using the regulating lever and moonwork for a watch.

It is not easy from this long statement to completely relate the patent to the watches that exist. However, the diagrams clearly show his ideas. It is also apparent that he must have made watches before 1814 to designs which were the predecessors of those shown in the patent, and that he had ideas about a seconds-beating watch, which seems to have obsessed makers of this period (see Chapter 6). Leaving aside this watch with its special lever-fork (known as Type IV), it is possible to identify four common variants of the Massey escapement (Types I, II, III and V). Type I may well have been developed from the rack lever,

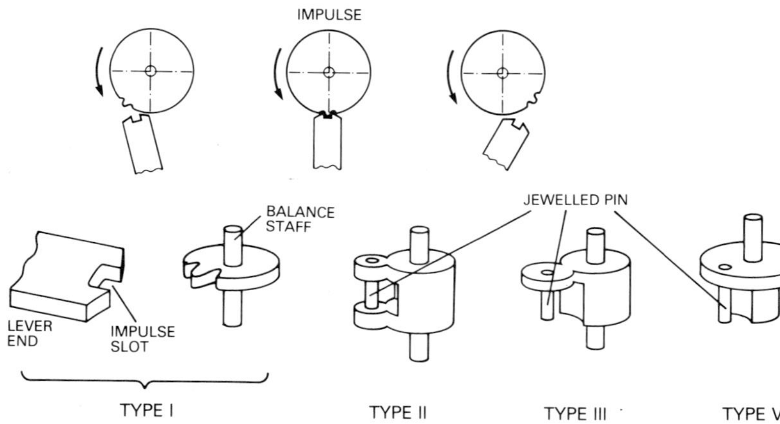

Fig 14 Massey lever escapements

the rack and pinion being replaced by the lever-fork (rack) operating with a single-tooth steel pinion which unlocks the train and receives impulse for the balance. It is a clever idea incorporating safety, because the escapement action can only occur when the pointed ends of the lever-fork engage the slots on either side of the single tooth. It is most important to realise that in this form the lever is again *detached* (Plate 6). Massey used a right-angle layout with either thirty- or fifteen-tooth escape wheels with inclined straight-faced teeth, similar to the rack lever wheel. There is no mention of draw in the patent and all the lift is on the lever-pallets. However, some Massey lever watches do have draw from about 1820, its existence revealed by the fact that a lever with draw will snap back onto the banking pin if the lever is displaced slightly by moving the fork with the balance removed. Maintaining power is usually fitted. Types II, III and V are developments of Type I (Fig 14) involving changes to the balance-staff roller. In Type II the metal pinion tooth is replaced by a cylindrical jewel supported at either end by extensions to the roller. Type III simplifies Type II by dispensing with one of the supports for the jewel, and Type V simplifies manufacture by using a two-part roller in which the jewel is suspended from a disc and the safety action is achieved by a separate roller with a passing curve or flat. Some Type V rollers are in one piece.

The action is similar in all forms. As the balance swings through the centre arc, the roller tooth or jewel engages with the slot in the end of the lever and unlocks the escape wheel. The jewel then receives impulse from the slot (transmitted from the escape wheel) and the balance becomes detached for the remainder of the action, the escapement being locked by one of the pallets on the lever during the detached portion of the vibration. On the return swing the roller tooth or jewel again picks up the lever slot, unlocks the train and receives impulse. While the balance is in the detached portion of the vibration, the lever should remain drawn into the escape wheel. Should it move from this position because of the absence of draw, or the failure of the draw action, the curved surfaces of the outer sides of the lever's slotted end (lever horns) will rest on the cylindrical surface of the balance roller, preventing the train from unlocking and damaging the escapement. This safety action will introduce friction and destroy the advantage of the detached balance as regards timekeeping ability, since for the faulty part of the action the escapement is frictional rest in character. When the return swing of the balance brings the roller tooth or jewel back to the appropriate position, the engagement with the lever slot will restore correct action so that the friction is only temporary.

It is not easy to arrange Massey levers by date and type. The order I, II, III, V seems a logical sequence of development, but if watches are examined the spread of types and dates does not yet give a clear pattern. One problem is that, as late as 1965, the escapement was stated to be 'extremely rare'; however, this supposed rarity is probably because not many people knew what to look for, and only recently has the work of Alan Treherne drawn attention to Massey. A personal examination of twenty watches revealed the following data where M = movement:

Type	I	II	III	V
Date	1824	1828	1823	1821
	M	1829	1828	1834
	M	M	1831	1840
		M	1832	
		M	1833	
			1835	
			1840	
			M	
			M	
Total	3	5	9	3

Another sample gave results as follows:[27]

Total	4	10	66	6

It is clear that Type III is the most common, but Type V is easily confused with a table-roller lever unless the safety pin on the table-roller design is sighted. The dated Type I was in a pair-case. This sample lacks early examples dated before 1820; this might be conclusive. The case hallmarks were almost exclusively Chester and if it is assumed that crow's feet engravings for regulation represent Liverpool origins, thirteen of the twenty watches in the first sample came from that area. Those that are not Liverpool were all hallmarked later than 1828. None of the twenty was signed by Massey himself. It is possible to identify the basic movement maker,[28] but this is not of great help since the finisher who fitted the escapement will be the 'maker'. Even Massey himself would not have made the whole watch, but merely fitted his escapements to bought-in movements.

The shape of the spokes in wheels (wheel crossings) can help in deciding if a movement is late or early — earlier movements have rounded crossings and later ones have angular form. In the sample above, the only watch with round crossings was the 1821 Type V; one of the undated Type I movements had round crossings and a three-wheel train with thirty-tooth escape wheel. None of the watches had compensation balance, but the 1823 Type III had a curb. No conclusions about draw were made as all the dated watches had draw.

The movements exhibited eleven chiselled Liverpool cocks — ten with the word 'patent' and one with 'detach'd'. Eight of the cocks were plain and one had no cock. Five movements had Liverpool-window jewelling.

Evidence exists of further experiments with Massey-type escapements. At least four variations are known, but the improvements are imaginary except in one case where manufacture may have been simpler.[29] They all involved adjustment to the impulse jewel either by using a cylindrical rotating roller, two pins, or a projecting radial jewel. There is much need for the painstaking collection of data from both watches and movements.

The general conclusion about Massey's escapement is that it was detached, robust and simple. Once draw had been introduced — with recoil to ensure safety — it could be improved only by transition to the table-roller lever. Massey himself is very close to this design in his Type V, and it only required a simple change in the safety arrangement to arrive at the English table-roller lever escapement.

Savage Lever Watches

This safety arrangement was already in existence in the Savage two-pin lever which was being made concurrently with the Massey lever. It was invented by George Savage at about the same time as the Massey lever (*c*1814) and again uses a right-angle escapement, but the arrangement for locking and unlocking the train and for impulse and safety are different. As shown in Fig 15, the balance staff is fitted with a roller which has two pins protruding from its surface. Situated centrally between these pins is a slot. The lever end has a wide opening with a jewelled pin just below the centre point of the bottom edge of the opening. As the balance swings, one of the pins on the roller enters the jaws of the wide lever opening. This unlocks the train, and impulse is transmitted from the escape wheel to the balance roller as the pin on the lever engages with the slot in the roller. The train is then locked by one of the lever-pallets in the usual way. The balance becomes detached for the remainder of the vibration except for the repetition of the action on the return swing, when the second pin on the roller effects the unlocking of the train. Should the lever become displaced during the detached portion of the vibration, the lever jewel will rest on the side of the balance roller giving a safety action with frictional rest until normal unlocking and impulse restore the situation. All lift is on the lever-pallets, and examples can be found with and without draw. Compensation balances are seldom fitted, but maintaining power is usual.

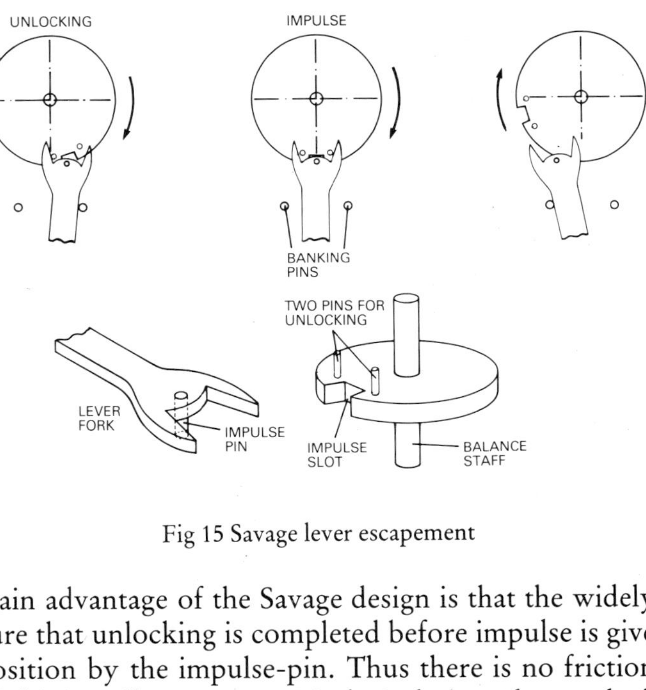

Fig 15 Savage lever escapement

The main advantage of the Savage design is that the widely spaced pins ensure that unlocking is completed before impulse is given at the centre position by the impulse-pin. Thus there is no friction during impulse. This is really a return to Mudge's design where unlocking and impulse were performed by three separate rollers. In order to be successful the pins have to be very precisely planted, which is probably why Savage lever watches are scarce compared with Massey levers.

Table-roller Lever Watches

The most important part of the Savage lever is the safety action of the vertical pin which also acts as the impulse-pin. If such a pin is fitted to the Massey lever at the base of the lever-fork and a passing crescent is put into the upper roller of the Type V escapement, the lower roller can be removed and there is no need to shape the lever-fork with special concave safety ends. The resulting balance roller with jewel and lever-end with pin form a table-roller lever escapement which is simple to make and therefore relatively cheap, but nevertheless strong and effective.

It is not to be suggested that the table-roller lever escapement was specially designed in this way. It evolved and there is no patent; indeed Breguet had used a similar design in about 1810. It is unlikely that Massey and Savage ever worked together as Massey did not go to London until 1830–1, whereas Savage went there from Huddersfield in 1821 and then emigrated to Canada. They probably never met. The fact that the table-roller lever was made by a number of good makers from about 1825 or perhaps a little before — including Pennington, Penlington, Earnshaw, Hornby, Barwise, Cummins, Roskell, Viner, Mairet, Jump, Dent and Frodsham — shows that it was quickly realised that this escapement was the one to replace all others (Plate 6).

Some idea of the success of the table-roller lever is given by a survey of lever watches hallmarked between 1820 and 1840, found in sale-rooms and markets. The ratio appears to be 1 Savage: 5 rack: 25 Massey: 40 table-roller levers. Nearly all rack levers are signed Litherland or Roskell, virtually no Massey levers are signed Massey. The table-roller levers are signed by a variety of makers and come mainly from two areas — Lancashire or London — though it is doubtful whether the movements all originated at the place of signature. It would seem that Massey levers represent a change in methods of making and marketing compared with rack levers which was emphasised by the table-roller lever. Both the rack and the Massey lever were patented devices enjoying some degree of protection, but whereas Litherland and Roskell probably allowed watches to be retailed with their names on them, Massey allowed his watches to be sold under other 'makers' names or 'subcontracted' the whole work and collected a royalty. Of course by the time that the unpatented table-roller lever was in production, makers of Massey escapements no longer needed to worry about his 1814 patent which would be out of date. There is scope for investigation here.

Plate 6 *(Top left and right)* A rack lever movement by Thos. Savage, London, *c*1820. Although marked 'London', it appears to be a Lancashire product with typical cock, jewelling and crow's feet regulator index. The lever has adjustable bearings. The watch is pair-cased and has a fusee with maintaining power, a stop-piece and a four-wheel train. *(Bottom left)* A Massey lever movement with a Type II balance roller and a straight-sided lever. The watch is shown in Plate 30, and Fig 47 shows the case hallmarks to be 1828. The movement again appears to have Lancashire origins and has a fusee with maintaining power, a stop-piece and a dust cap. *(Bottom right)* Another, later, movement of Lancashire origin, *c*1860. This has a table-roller lever escapement, a lever with curved edges, a compensated balance, smaller jewelling and less elaborate cock decoration. It is of good quality, but by 1860 many watches were using three-quarter plate movements.

English Lever Watches

It is now possible to describe the evolved form of the English lever-escapement watch. It uses a fusee with maintaining power, a four-wheel train and a right-angle layout with the lever tangential to the fifteen-tooth escape wheel. This escape wheel has pointed teeth with draw so that all lift is on the pallets. It is a detached, recoil escapement (Fig 16). The lever-fork engages the D-shaped impulse-pin protruding below a disc-shaped balance-staff roller which has a passing crescent to allow the vertical safety pin sited below the bottom of the lever-fork to pass. The lever has a simple rectangular slot with protruding horns on either side to reduce the necessary balance arc. The horns are not essential in the single-roller design, but if safety is achieved by a second roller and dart similar to the Swiss pattern described at the beginning of this chapter, the horns are necessary to complete the guard action. This is called the double-roller design and is not common in English lever watches. Detailed dimensions of this escapement (and others) can be found in specialist books.[30]

In English table-roller levers made after 1825, a full plate movement — with dust cap, barrel bridge and third and fourth wheel bridge — was used. The movement was thick. Balances were usually plain steel or gold without compensation, but on better quality watches compensation was fitted. At this time continental makers were making thin going-barrel watches with barred movements, and by mid-century the English lever had been thinned by the use of three-quarter plate movements which allowed the balance wheel to be fitted below the level of the top plate. This required a change in the layout of the watch using separate cocks for balance staff, lever and escape wheel with the train,

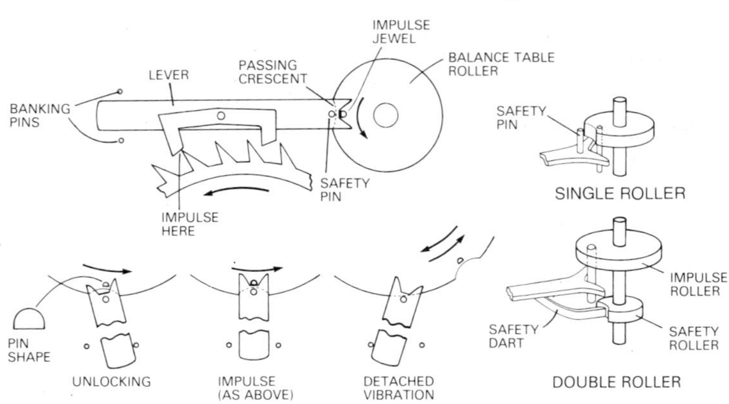

Fig 16 English lever escapement

Plate 7 An English watch with table-roller lever escapement in a silver case hallmarked 1827. The silver dial has raised gold numerals. The movement has a fusee with maintaining power, an oversprung balance, cylindrical pillars and a dust ring; and *(right)* Plate 8 English watch with table-roller lever escapement in a silver case hallmarked 1873. A typically robust mid-Victorian example, of moderate quality. With good care and attention a watch like this should last indefinitely.

fusee and barrel under the three-quarter plate. The fusee had a finer pitch and a thinner chain to reduce height.

Dials on these watches were gold, silver or more commonly enamel which was off-white from *c*1830 to *c*1840 but white later (Plate 7). Initially the chapter ring for the seconds hand was large and flush, but from 1850 it became smaller and was sunk into the dial so that the seconds hand was flush with the dial surface. Early levers had straight sides, but from about 1860 they were changed to a scalloped form. Some early levers exhibit oddities in banking, such as a single pin with a circular hole in the end of the lever. The rate of vibration was increased from 14,400 per hour to 18,000 per hour from about 1860. The case, too, changed. In 1830 it was as elegant as the watch with thin curved (but fragile) glass and fine bezel; by 1860 the bezel was bulky and the bevelled glass thicker, flat and stronger as appearance was sacrificed to robustness. With proper care and attention, watches made between 1860 and 1900 will last indefinitely.

Technically there was little change in the design of the English lever watch between 1830 and 1900. Even the development of button wind on the Continent and in America hardly changed its design although some makers, notably Dent, used button wind and Burdess produced a system for fusee winding without a key. Most watches continued to use key wind, which suited the method of manufacture (with specialist makers for each part) used in England at this time (see Chapter 5).

The Swiss Lever Watch

We now turn to the Continent at the beginning of the nineteenth century to see how the Swiss form of the lever watch developed. The story again starts with Breguet who, after the disturbances of the French Revolution, became re-established in Paris as a maker of quality watches and, by 1814, was again producing lever watches, but to a different pattern from those he had ceased making twenty years earlier. These later watches used divided lift, partly due to the shape of the escape-wheel teeth and partly to the shape of the pallets. He used a single roller with passing crescent and a safety pin, he introduced draw, he also used a double roller with safety dart. Thus he had effectively produced the Swiss lever described at the start of this chapter. One special Breguet feature was the use of conical pivots for his balance staff. These were more robust than conventional pivots, but less consistent in performance since the whole arbor can tilt (with the necessary clearances) when the watch position is changed from dial up to pendant up. However, since his work was of such high quality, this slight inconsistency in rate was not significant. He made use of temperature compensation and jewelling.

Other makers on the Continent did not greet the revived lever with great enthusiasm and preferred the cylinder escapement as an alternative to the verge watch. The watches produced with going-barrel and barred movements in slim cases with double backs were key wound and, in general, were half the bulk of English watches of the same period. Dials were metal or enamel, and little or no movement decoration was used.

In Switzerland, problems with train wheels and balance springs hindered watch development, and a competition was announced in 1833 for a successful method of making balance springs.[22] This was won in 1836 by Quartier, who in 1833 had made a gear-cutting machine for wheels. However, his springs were not completely successful and it was another twenty years before the Lutz process for balance springs was perfected. Notwithstanding these problems, George Auguste Leschot introduced draw to early Swiss levers in about 1830 and, with Lechaud, supplied lever movements to Swiss 'makers'.

Leschot was interested in making parts, including escapements, by machine. His work attracted the firm of Vacheron and Constantin who were seeking standardisation; and in 1839 they sought Leschot's help to organise manufacture of watch parts, backing him financially to devise a machine to make lever or cylinder movements in all sizes. Leschot succeeded with a pantograph-based machine which used a six times full-size template of the watch plates so that the holes could be drilled directly. He also devised other machines, his success making it possible for Vacheron and Constantin to produce so many movements that they were able to supply some to other 'makers'. This was not however machine manufacture as we understand it today but simple jig aided production, and although it set the lever watch on an equal footing with the cylinder in Switzerland, it blinded the Swiss to the possibilities of machine-made watches (see Chapter 5). However, since England was even more blind to the way forward, Swiss industry was gradually able to dominate European watch manufacture. It took a further half century or more for the lever watch to oust the cylinder, but the verge watch was finished on the Continent. It should also be emphasised that, parallel with these developments, good quality hand-made watches were being produced on the Continent which compare favourably with those from English craftsmen.

American Lever Watches

So far there has been no mention of non-European lever watches; but for the period 1840–60 we must look at America where European ideas of machine production were developed for factory manufacture (see Chapter 5). The new methods then spread back to Switzerland.

The vogue for international exhibitions was one way in which ideas were disseminated. In 1851, the Great Exhibition was held in London and this was followed by exhibitions in Paris (1855), London (1862), Paris (1867) and Philadelphia in 1876. Further exhibitions followed, but it was the Philadelphia Exhibition which caused the Swiss to realise the magnitude of the American challenge and to start appropriate action towards gearing their industry to similar mass-production methods.

Before 1850 few watches were made in America, though some early watchmakers are listed in Chapter 2, and mention was made of Pitkin's early unsuccessful attempt to produce machine-made watches. Both England and Switzerland exported watches to the New World,[22] but after 1850 the position changed, the breakthrough coming from Aaron Dennison, Edward Howard and Samuel Curtis who, perhaps realising the superiority of the Swiss methods, sent Dennison to Europe to learn all he could. In 1850 they founded the American Horologe Company in Roxbury, Mass, which became in turn the Warren Manufacturing Company, the American Watch Company (1859), the American Waltham Watch Company (1885) and, in 1906, the Waltham Watch Company which continued in business until 1957 — a hundred-year span. From the beginning their products were lever watches wound by key, button wind being introduced in 1870; and eventually they had no less than thirty factories. The Waltham Company was basically a producer of quality watches and was joined in this field by the E. Howard Watch Company (1857), the National Watch Company (1864 — after 1874 called the Elgin National Watch Company) and the Hamilton Watch Company (1892). Other nineteenth-century American companies included the Illinois Watch Company (1885–1925), Rockford Watch Company (1873–1912), Seth Thomas Watch Company (1883–1915), Columbia Watch Company (1883–1903), Hampden and Dueber-Hampden (1888–1930); but none were as long-lived as those of Waltham, Howard and Hamilton. Illustrations of many of the movements made by American firms can be found in Chamberlain.[31]

A peculiarity of American watches is the variety of names used on dials and movements. The personalised names came from partners of firms, and the many company names from amalgamations, financial problems, changes of site, etc. There was also a tendency to use monograms instead of names on dials. The better quality American watches of this period were lever watches, and they often had elaborate methods of regulation control with fine screw adjusters of various designs, and attractive engine engraving on the movements.[31] They did not use the fusee, which would not have been suitable for machine production even if it had been considered. Movements had differing amounts of jewelling; some used very large numbers, up to 28 being recorded. It is also interesting to note that many movements were sold as such to retailers who also sold empty cases — a facility made possible by factory production. One movement would suit a variety of cases. The latter were also available in various qualities — gold, plated gold, silver etc; so that it was possible to choose a movement and case to suit one's purse, desire for a good movement or for a good or good-looking, plated case. A typical catalogue of the period shows, for example, a range from an 18-carat gold case at $218 down to a nickel case at $3.50, and a 20-jewel movement at $120 down to 7-jewel at $7, all for an 18-size watch.[32] These are all American-made Swiss-lever escapement movements, not cheap pin-lever ones.

Cases were double-bottomed or hunter in European fashion (but not style) for key wind or button wind; but there was also an interesting style with a screw-on front with button wind. The button had to be partially removed to allow the movement to be hinged out of the case if access to the regulator was needed.

It is thus clear that in America during the period 1850–1900 the quest for volume production at a price and quality to compete with Swiss products led to the formation of a large number of watch companies. Many of these failed to survive and were sold, combined or taken over. There was no signing of movements by individual makers as in Europe, since from the very start the concept was one of a machine-made factory product. There were a few specialist watchmakers making quality watches — notably Potter and Fasoldt — but they were rare men.

Lever Watches from 1925

It is difficult to understand how the Swiss and the Americans could see the market potential of machine-made watches when England, where the Industrial Revolution was born, could not. The annual export figures achieved in the twentieth century by Switzerland (24 million in 1950, 41 million in 1960 and 63 million in 1967)[22] show the magnitude of the missed opportunity. These watches were of course mainly wrist watches.

It was probably England's social structure which led to the strongly conservative attitude of the skilled craftsman who refused to admit that machines could produce work of similar quality to his, and more cheaply. There were, however, at least two unsuccessful attempts to produce machine-made lever pocket watches. The first, on the part of Ingold from 1843 to 1845,[33] did not really get underway and the second, the Lancashire Watch Company producing Swiss lever escapement watches,[34] lasted from 1889 to 1910 (see Chapter 5).

Whatever the reasons for the demise of watchmaking in England, there is no doubt that the table-roller English lever watch (Plate 8) was virtually dead by the end of the first quarter of the twentieth century, and deserved to be so for the failure of its makers to advance with the times. The only quality lever pocket watch from this time on has been the Swiss lever watch made in the factories of Switzerland and America. Just after World War II, Smith's made an attempt to produce pocket watches in Britain with Swiss lever escapements, but the day of the pocket watch was over by then and production was only for a limited period.

Although this book is not about wrist watches it is worth noting that early examples of these used the cylinder escapement, presumably because it was available in suitable sizes from fob watches. However, the superior quality and performance of the lever escapement led to its replacing the cylinder in this role and, as we saw at the beginning of this chapter, any good mechanical pocket or wrist watch purchased in the last thirty years will have a Swiss lever escapement.

Chronology of the Lever Watch

Date	*English Maker*	*Continental Maker*
1769	Mudge (1715–1794) lever watch	Julien le Roy (1686–1759)
	Emery (1725–1796)	Pierre le Roy (1717–1785)
	Leroux (1744–1808)	Lepine (1720– ?)
	Pendleton (? –1808)	Breguet (1747–1823)
	Grant (? –1810)	Pouzait (1743–1793)
	Margetts (1748–1808)	Robin (1742–1809)
	Perigal (? –1794)	Tavan (1749–1836)
	Ellicott (? –1835)	Leschot (1800–1884)
1792	Litherland (1756–1804)	
1814	Massey (1772–1852)	
	Savage (? –1855)	

4
INEXPENSIVE WATCHES

In the third quarter of the nineteenth century, most of the watches being made in England and the USA used the lever escapement, while European watches used either the cylinder or the lever escapement. These were all basically good quality watches, and the Swiss cylinder watches were probably the cheapest.

During this period, society was changing from a rural to an industrial base and, as a result, patterns of work were also changing. Industry was concentrated into factories rather than using outworkers. Whereas the agricultural worker's day had been dictated by daylight and darkness, and the outworker could work as he saw fit, the factory system required that everyone should start and finish at the same time. It was therefore desirable that clocks and watches should be cheap enough for every house and person to possess one. Hooters or whistles on factories could give an indication of time, rather as clock bells always had, but this was a poor substitute for a personal timepiece.

Railways were also developing rapidly during this period, and anyone using trains really needed a portable timekeeper. Fortunately, most travellers who could afford to use a train could also afford a lever watch, but this was not necessarily so. The populations of the Western World were also rising, as shown in the following table.

Populations of the Western World (millions)

	UK	Switzerland	USA
1800	16	—	5
1850	27	2.5	23
1900	42	3.5	93

Thus, the situation was ideal for the introduction of cheap mass-produced watches and in both Switzerland and the USA this was soon recognised but it hardly appears to have been considered in England.

To make a cheap watch by factory methods, the watch must be designed specifically with this in mind and use techniques to keep costs low. In particular there are four requirements: a simple escapement, a

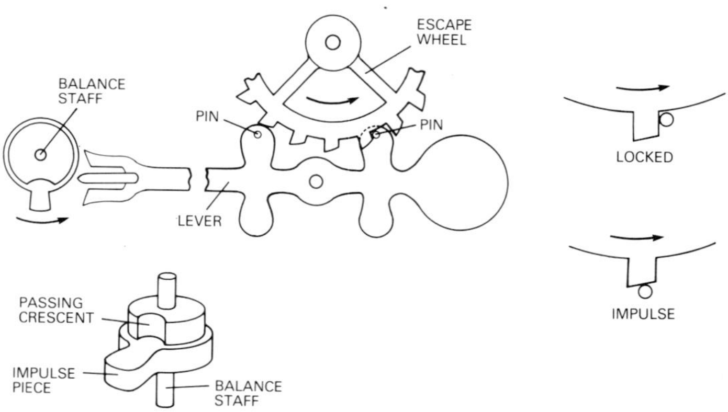

Fig 17 Pin-lever escapement

simple train, ease of assembly and minimum material costs. These will be considered in turn.

A simple escapement needs a simple escape wheel, and should be detached. The cylinder escapement is not suited on either of these counts, and the predominant Swiss lever escapement was a complex shape. If a lever escapement is chosen as robust and reliable, it needs teeth and pallets. The simplest concept for lift on a tooth is a ramp, and the simplest pallet is a cylindrical pin. The pin-pallet or pin-lever escapement uses this principle (Fig 17). The lever has two circular pins spanning the escape wheel with ramp-shaped teeth, similar to the Ellicott lever of 1805 discussed in Chapter 3. These pin-pallets take impulse from the escape wheel and transfer it to the balance in the normal way through a lever-fork with safety arrangement. Various fork-and-safety systems were used: double roller with dart, single roller with pin and passing crescent, and other variations. Both straight-line and right-angle layout were used. Banking was arranged in a variety of ways. Examination of escapements shows that much thought went into the designs to save costs. For example, it is easier to stamp out a complex lever shape which includes banking than to make special banking arrangements.

A simple train perhaps implies a return to a three-wheel design, but four-wheel trains and some unusual arrangements were used to enable a conventional seconds hand to be fitted. The gear wheel blanks were stamped out. The train was often driven by an open spring (like an alarm clock), so saving the barrel. The spring was often fairly strong, to overcome any crudity of the train work. Spring winding and hand set was by button in most cases.

It was essential to have the smallest possible number of parts to give easy assembly in jigs, and once assembled, the watch movement was screwed or nutted together. The balance and lever are best under separate cocks, and balances may sometimes use conical pivots for ease of assembly. Assembly is easy in a factory's special jig, but it is not always so easy to dismantle such a watch and reassemble it without the jig. However, since these watches were not designed to be constantly repaired, but rather to be discarded when broken, this was not important. Dials were often printed on paper and hands were stamped out.

To use the minimum amount of material, the plates of many movements were stamped as skeletons connecting the necessary pivot-points and pillars. This made some attractive forms. Gilding was sometimes used and the finish of the movement was simple. Nickel plating was preferred to gilding in later designs.

Having made a cheap movement it then had to be given an attractive looking case to encourage potential customers. Ideally, the case had to prevent the casual observer from discovering that the watch was cheap. Pin-lever watches can therefore be found in a wide variety of cases: brass which was nickel or chrome plated, blued steel etc. Initially, not all watches embraced all the principles discussed above but, by the early twentieth century, competition ensured that only companies making watches to these principles would survive.

The pin-lever escapement had three clear lines of development. The first began in Switzerland in 1860, when G. F. Roskopf decided that he would design a watch which could be bought by the ordinary workman at a reasonable price.[1] The watch would have a base-metal case and a paper dial, but the movement would be made of high-grade materials by skilled workers to ensure accuracy. Although he envisaged a cheap watch, the quality he chose made his price the equivalent of about £15 today, which was really too high for the market.

Roskopf did his development work and produced a watch with a pin-lever escapement, using a right-angle layout with fork-and-safety dart (Plate 9). He patented it against use outside Switzerland (presumably to benefit Swiss industry), but the new concept met with resistance from the traditional Swiss craftsmen, and Roskopf had difficulty getting satisfactory production in his lifetime (1813–99). The escapement was driven by a train with no centre wheel, which gave space for a larger spring-barrel to pass over the centre of the plate and drive the (third) wheel pinion. This eliminated one wheel. The movement was constructed with half-plates: pillars were riveted to one plate and the other plate was screwed down. The escapement was completely separate from the plates and could be fitted last of all. The hands were driven from the barrel-arbor through motion work. Keyless winding was used, but the hands were adjusted with the fingers, rather like a clock. The printed paper dial was abandoned because there was a danger of the ink reacting with the movement and staining the dial. Cases were made of German silver.

The first watches appeared in 1867 and Roskopf exhibited one at that year's Paris exhibition where he received a bronze award. After modification to allow button set of the hands, it was put into production in 1870. Only limited numbers were made because of the opposition mentioned earlier and because the outworker system was not suited to mass production. After the Philadelphia Exhibition in 1876, the Swiss turned to the idea of factory-made watches, and Roskopf watches were made in large quantities in the twentieth century. However, these later makers did not adhere to Roskopf's high-quality watch which, as we have seen, was not really cheap enough. Instead, they had to produce the right looking watch at the right price.

(left) Plate 9 Swiss Roskopf movement with large going-barrel and three-wheel train, *c*1900. The escapement is pin-lever with right-angle layout. *(right)* Plate 10 German 'Fearless' watch by Thiel *c*1895. It has a long mainspring behind the movement, the train is shown in Fig 18 and it runs for fourteen hours only. The paper dial is held to the movement by pins sticking up from the wedges holding the movement together. The pin-lever escapement has a lever-fork incorporating impulse and safety.

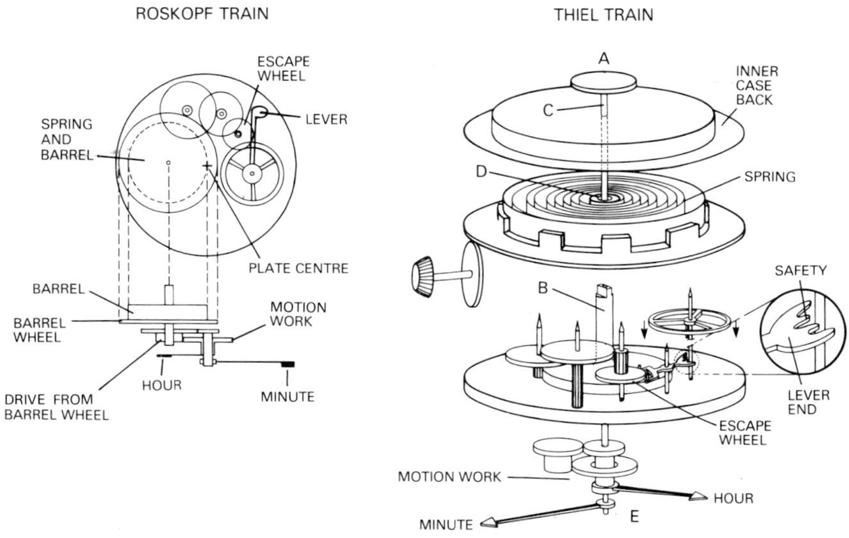

Fig 18 Roskopf and Thiel trains. Hand drive from spring through D to B, C, E. Hand set by knob A through C to E.

The Roskopf design (Fig 18) can be recognised by the large barrel with no centre wheel. It has no seconds hand. Some makers abandoned button wind for cheapness, and others inserted an extra wheel in the train to allow the use of a seconds hand. These trains look very cramped and depart from Roskopf's principles, but they supplied a demand (Plates 12 and 13).

A second line of development used Roskopf's concept of a three-wheel train, but with a large centre wheel driving the third-wheel pinion. Gearing in this design allows for a seconds hand. To save a wheel, the mainspring drives the centre wheel directly, using an arbor extended through the back plate. The long spring is arranged centrally and is wound by a button turning a pinion engaging with a wheel equal in diameter to the movement. Thus, the spring is in an open 'back barrel' which is closed by the rear of the case (Fig 18). One watch of this design (Thiel), using a paper dial, is held together by wedges (Plate 10). Many of the parts are stamped out, and the lever-fork incorporates safety in a three-valley design. Whereas Roskopf's design was conceived as a good-quality watch, this design is obviously cheap. The hands are adjusted by a button in the back of the case which passes through the centre-wheel arbor. (Not all watches with a large rear spring have pin-lever escapements. The early Waterbury watches with a duplex escapement and some eight-day watches also use rear springs.) This early Thiel was not a long-lived design, probably because the running time of the watch was only about fourteen hours.

Plate 11 Large Ingersoll 'Yankee' watch made *c*1896, probably by the Waterbury Clock Company. The winding button is false and the winder can be seen inside the case at the back of the watch. Hand set is by the central knob. Underneath the dust cover, the watch is like a small clock with lantern pinions, an open spring and cut-away plates held together with nuts on the pillars. There is a paper dial and pin-lever escapement. The case is of thin plated metal.

The makers changed to a more conventional train layout — with open spring or going-barrel, seconds hand, button wind and hand set — which also offered easier assembly for their workers (Plates 12 and 13).

The third line of development is due to Robert and Charles Ingersoll in the USA.[2] They were salesmen rather than watchmakers, and their first watch (Ingersoll 'Universal') was made by the Waterbury Clock Company and sold wholesale to dealers in 1892. It was really a small clock put into a watch case about 3in (76mm) in diameter and over 1in (25mm) thick. Later that same year they produced a mail-order catalogue and sold direct to the public; then in 1893 they marketed the Ingersoll 'Columbus', which was slightly smaller than the 'Universal', but still clock-like. Perhaps in retaliation, the Waterbury Clock Company also started to sell directly, but the Ingersolls then negotiated a sole agency agreement. In 1896 their watches were reduced in price to $1 and renamed the 'Yankee' (Plate 11).

All these early clock watches used pin-lever escapements, and had paper dials with a seconds hand. The clock-like features included lantern pinions (which are made from wire rods held between two end discs), fold-away winding keys in the back connected directly to the open spring-arbor, and skeleton plates held together by nuts on threaded pillars. The 'Yankee' had a false winding button fitted to make it look like a watch, but it was still a small clock. Stem wind was introduced in some Ingersoll watches in about 1896.

These watches represent the start of the cheap pin-lever watch industry in the USA. From about 1900, the Ingersoll brothers produced machine-made, full-plate, pin-lever watches in conventional sizes, with conventional winding and hand-set arrangements, and paper dials. These were marketed in the USA and Britain, and eventually (in 1911) they were also assembled in Britain. The design was so successful that similar watches (though not Ingersoll) could be purchased in Britain until 1980 (Plates 12 and 13). The early watches are marked with progressive lists of patents indicating that detail improvements were being made, but they all look similar. Many of them also have their guarantee paper inside the back of the plated case and it may read as follows:

> This watch is GUARANTEED to keep good time for one year and if without misuse it fails to do so will be repaired by us FREE or (at our option) exchanged for a new one for 25c. Robt. H. Ingersoll & Bro., Makers, 315, 4th Ave, New York.

British watch warranties were similar:

> . . . for 2/- . . . Robt. H. Ingersoll & Bro., Makers, Ely Place, London E C.

In 1922, the Ingersoll brothers were bought out by the Waterbury Clock Company. The Ingersoll name was retained, but in 1930 the British operation became a separate company — Ingersoll Ltd. The watches that could be seen in Britain recently were made by Smith's in Wales even though they had Ingersoll on the dial. Previously, the only

Plates 12 and 13 Three watches, with their movements. *(Left to right)* Roskopf-style watch of about 1930, an Ingersoll watch of about 1916 and a Thiel watch of about 1930 — cheap, factory-produced pin-lever watches from Switzerland, America and Germany respectively. The Swiss and American watches have paper dials and the German a painted one. Each uses many stamped-out parts. The Roskopf watch has a three-wheel train, but the others have a four-wheel train allowing the use of a seconds hand. The watches originally cost about 5s or $1. Each would have a guarantee and the Ingersoll one is shown in the back of the case. The cases are plated with nickel or gilt. The movements are mainly brass.

pin-lever pocket watch made in Britain was the 'John Bull', produced in small quantities (5,000 in all) by the Lancashire Watch Company, between 1905 and 1911.[3]

The success of the Ingersoll machine-made, pin-lever pocket watches led to other designs, deriving from Roskopf (Switzerland) and Thiel (Germany), being made by machine throughout Europe in the first forty years of the twentieth century. It is clear from an examination of the movements that there were several different types of machine involved, as distinct patterns can be seen. There is a considerable variety of watches available which use the Roskopf pattern: three- and four-wheel trains, double-roller, single-roller, full-plate, three-quarter plate, etc. Many use paper dials, and all have button wind. The general impression is that cheapness was the most important factor in the movement (provided it lasted the usual one-year warranty), but that the case had to be attractive and up-to-date.

The cases used show considerable variety: they include plain brass, nickel or chrome plate, embossed metal etc. Cast or stamped repoussé cases with railway engines, ships, cars and other designs abound. The watch lent itself to the free-gift and souvenir trade and the cases often commemorated some international or national event. Some idea of the distribution of pre-1939 pin-lever watches can be obtained from the following survey of 100 watches and movements:

2 Early Ingersoll (1895)
4 Early Thiel (1890–1900)
4 Roskopf (pre 1900), 2 key wind
30 Roskopf (post 1900)
20 Ingersoll (post 1900)
6 Other American design
20 With combined impulse and safety fork
14 Dart safety of continental origin (not Roskopf)

Although the pin-lever is a cheap watch and was not designed for repair, it is possible in some of the better quality designs to make repairs.[4] In general, since they were machine-made, spare parts from other movements may be transferred.

Although the design of the pin-lever pocket watch survived from 1867 to about 1980, there was an alternative produced in the USA in the nineteenth century. This design was specifically for machine production, whereas the Ingersoll watch was derived from clocks and the Roskopf was designed for the outworker system.

The American watchmaker D. A. A. Buck exhibited at the 1876 Philadelphia Exhibition and was approached to design a cheap watch

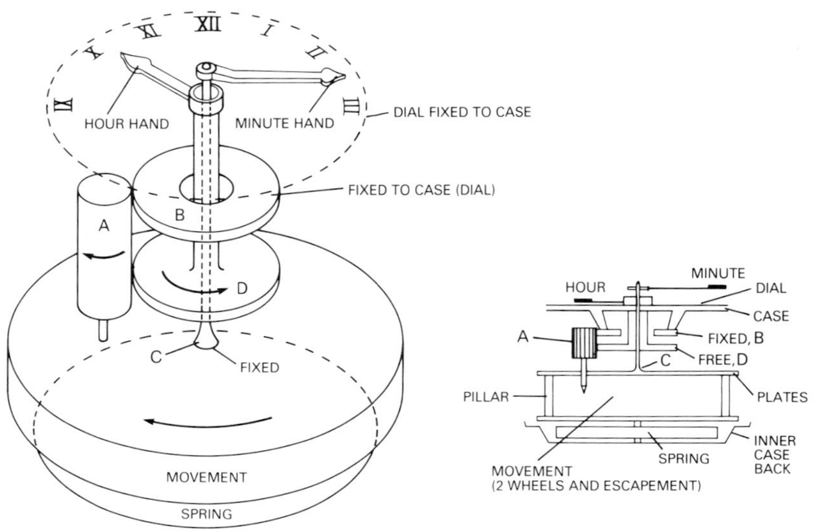

Fig 19 Waterbury rotary watch. Pinion A, 8 teeth; Wheel B, 44 teeth; Wheel D, 48 teeth. One revolution of movement gives 1/12 revolution of wheel D.

suitable for machine manufacture. His amazing design had about fifty-seven parts, which is roughly half the number of parts in a conventional lever watch of the period. It had a mainspring, 3m (10ft) in length, in the back of the case as described on page 65. This spring needed about thirty winder turns and it drove the whole movement complete with the minute hand round a fixed centre wheel once per hour. The motion work was arranged by having two wheels with slightly different numbers of teeth engaging the same pinion, so that their rates of rotation were different (Fig 19). This is almost impossible to believe since all gears should have the same pitch. In effect, the rotating watch was a crude form of tourbillon (see Chapter 7), which Breguet had designed to combat positional error. The tourbillon needed very precise workmanship and was only fitted to very expensive watches. Buck's movement was designed for cheapness and the rotating action saved parts. It is doubtful if he was concerned with positional error. Not satisfied with this unusual approach, Buck also used a duplex escapement (see Chapter 6) which had a partially stamped-out escape wheel. This escapement is also associated with very precisely made expensive watches, but, again, it needs less parts than a lever watch.

Buck's patent is dated 1878, and Benedict and Burnham started production in 1880 at the Waterbury Watch Company (no connection with the Waterbury Clock Co) — it became known as the Waterbury watch. The dial was paper and button wind was used. The long-wind rotating movements ran through series A to E between 1880 and 1890. Series F to W used the same duplex escapement, but a conventional

Plate 14 Waterbury model 'J' in an original purple rayon lined box. There is a guarantee printed in the lid of the box and a view of the factory on the bottom. Model 'J' is a conventional wind watch with a partly pressed out duplex escapement, *c*1895. The small movement piece shows the escape wheel.

barrel between the plates with a normal-length mainspring and normal train (Plate 14). The layout varies throughout the series, some being full-plate, some three-quarter plate, and the quality also varies, as a few were jewelled.

The company changed its name to the New England Watch Company at the turn of the century, but Ingersoll bought it out in 1914. Waterbury watches were supplied in attractive lined boxes with a guarantee similar to Ingersoll's. The rare first Waterbury model 'A' has a skeletonised movement (to save material?); the later non-rotary varieties are more common. There are about three rotary models to every twenty non-rotary ones in the salerooms. The total numbers produced are obviously far less than the number of pin-lever watches, since production was from one factory for thirty years rather than several factories for about sixty years. In 1888 about half a million were produced, which would suggest that the total number of Waterbury duplex watches made would exceed the total number of conventional duplex watches.

It also seems possible that the total number of pin-lever watches made (including wrist) is second only to the total number of Swiss lever watches produced, which proves that the concept of a cheap watch was of vital importance to the watch industry. However, the English watchmakers missed out on this opportunity, perhaps because of their reluctance to make watches in factories, as discussed in Chapter 3.

5
WATCHMAKING

The very first watches may have been made by one 'maker' or more probably by a small group of people who worked with one maker. However, if a number of similar objects are to be made containing, amongst other things, wheels, pinions, staffs, plates, springs, balances etc, it is probably more efficient to allow one man to specialise in the manufacture of one particular part. However, since the parts have to fit together, there must be a coordinator. Extending this system of specialisation leads to the method of manufacture used from *c*1650 to 1860 (Plate 15, overleaf).

The makers became organised in 1631 when the Worshipful Company of Clockmakers was formed by charter from Charles I.[1] The objectives of the guild were to ensure quality of work and the correct training of apprentices, whose number was controlled. It was only as a member of a guild that a person could practise a trade, and the progression from apprentice to journeyman to member was a long one. This sounds straightforward but a watch had parts which were made by members of a different company.

The actual details of the work done, the tools available and the methods used changed as more devices were invented, but the principle of specialisation remained. For example, wheel-cutting engines were introduced in the seventeenth century and improved as time passed, jigs for drilling plates were made and lathes were developed.[2] The materials available also changed: for example, early work required a great deal of hand cutting and shaping, but the development of wire-drawing techniques in the early eighteenth century reduced the effort needed to produce complex shapes for pinions, clicks etc.[3]

Rees[4] lists all the workers needed at the end of the eighteenth century to complete a rough movement before it was taken to the finisher, and then lists the workers needed to finish the watch — thirteen for the first stage, and twenty-one for the second. He also mentions briefly the similar system in Switzerland, pointing out that the subdivision of labour was greater in that country. Some detail of Swiss work can be found in Jaquet and Chapuis.[5] It is clear that the name on the watch

(left) Plate 15 A partly finished verge movement of about 1820. It is not an ébauche since work has started on finishing, but it is far from being completed: the cock is unpierced and the fusee is not cut nor is the crown wheel finished. Other work is also required. *(right)* Plate 16 A factory-made American movement of good quality with compensated balance, seventeen jewels and fine regulation. The escapement, as with all good quality American factory-made watches, is a Swiss lever (see Plate 31).

plate is not the maker, but the coordinator or final finisher. Some idea of the methods of movement-making in Lancashire in the nineteenth century can be found in an article about Prescot, which was a well known centre for watch movements.[6]

Each of the items made by this system of specialist workers was an individual unit in that it belonged to one particular watch, and as the watch parts were made they were added to the movement which was gradually being built up. The movement would travel from worker to worker starting as a pair of plates and gaining a cock, barrel, wheels etc to become an ébauche where all parts were still in a rough state and no escapement had been fitted. The watch would then be finished including fitting of the escapement and gilding of the parts.

The fact that the finished part for one watch would not fit another meant that any breakage during manufacture or use needed individual replacement by a repairer, involving considerable work and expense. If any real volume of production was to be achieved, it was necessary that the finished parts be made so accurately as to be interchangeable.

One specialist worker could then make a batch of 1,000 wheels, another could make 1,000 plates, and so on, until eventually all the parts could be brought together to make 1,000 watches. This concept is familiar to anyone involved in a modern factory, but in 1850 it was an ideal not yet achieved in the watch industry. The reception of the ideal differed in different parts of the world.

In America, where there was no traditional watchmaking industry, the idea of factory methods with interchangeable parts assembled on the same site was accepted and introduced (Plate 16). In Switzerland, makers accepted the idea of interchangeability but continued to use the outworker system of manufacture with a central assembly location rather than bring the whole process into a single factory. In England, with few exceptions, the new ideas were eschewed, for the English watchmaker believed that quality work required his individualistic methods and that quality work would always be required. He was convinced that factory methods produced cheap, poor quality goods.[7] The result of these attitudes was to build strong American and Swiss watchmaking industries and to end the historical superiority of English watchmaking. Because of the size of the market for mass-produced watches, it is worth looking briefly at the history of the machine-produced watch from 1850 to 1930.

The story might be considered to start in Switzerland in the period 1839–43 when Leschot, under contract to the firm of Vacheron and Constantin, devised pantograph machines to make 'identical' plates for watches. He devised other machines to make other parts which, although not interchangeable, were machine made. Later, in 1851, Antoine Lecoultre exhibited six movements which could be taken to pieces, mixed randomly and reassembled. These movements had no escapements but at least the plates, and the wheels and pivots, were identical. This, however, was not a breakthrough in factory production, merely a demonstration of the principle of interchangeable parts.

A step forward came when P. F. Ingold, a Swiss, designed machine tools for the manufacture of watch parts. The designs are not the same as those used today, but they could produce identical watch parts. In particular, patent No 9993 of 1843 states:

> . . . the nature of my said invention to consist of such improvements in machinery for making, first what are called the top and bottom plates of watches and other timekeepers, whereby I am enabled to bore the necessary holes, make the taps and countersinks, and give all the various elevations of the surface, both at the back and front of the plates, with such accuracy as greatly to improve the article manufactured.

This describes the renowned 'plate' machine which is a lathe with a hollow mandrel and eccentric chuck. The chuck holding the plate was able to set the latter at various repeatable positions, so that operations carried out along the centre line of the lathe would always be at the same place on each plate (provided the operator set it correctly). Torrens[8] states 'it was possible to produce a watch pillar plate or top plate complete *at one chucking*, with all holes drilled, the screw holes tapped and hollows and turnings finished *on both sides of the plate and at the edges*'. He also suggests how close Ingold was to the modern jig-boring concept. Merely by using master plates to set up the coordinates, he would have made an enormous advance in design. A full description of this machine can be found in Carrington.[9] The patent above also gives details of a fly-press for wheel blanks.

Ingold, together with other backers, founded the British Watch and Clockmaking Company in Soho, London in 1843, so that his machinery could produce two to three hundred watches daily at low cost. He expected to save 30 per cent over traditional methods. For various reasons —opposition by the trade[9] and eventually by Parliament — the company was forced to close, and few of the small number of watches produced survive. For Ingold this rejection followed similar discouragement in Switzerland and France, and he went to America in 1845. His ideas were not taken up there and he returned to Switzerland.

The next stage of development was in America, and it is difficult to know if Ingold spurred it on. Dennison was experimenting in about 1850 with methods different from those of Ingold, and based on techniques used in the Springfield Armoury. He was not entirely successful. However, Moseley, a toolmaker from the armoury, did design some automatic machines between 1855 and 1860, a description of which can be found in Torrens.[8] Some of these early American machine tools were exhibited at Philadelphia in 1876 when they impressed the Swiss, and in London in 1885. A few English firms showed interest, including Rotherham and Sons, Coventry who purchased and installed some in 1880 and the Lancashire Watch Company who incorporated a considerable number when they opened their factory in Prescot in 1890.

The Lancashire Watch Company, with T. P. Hewitt as managing director, was set up to make complete watches, including cases, in a single factory at Prescot (Plate 17). This was traditionally a great watchmaking centre, and the availability of skilled labour was no doubt an attraction; but this tradition in itself became a fundamental problem in that the workers were not completely in favour of the

Plate 17 A Lancashire Watch Company, three-quarter plate, Swiss lever watch with seven jewels and a going-barrel. The movement is engraved 'VIGIL'. The watch looks American in concept but was made in the company's factory at Prescot *c*1900, using mainly American machinery. The company existed from 1889 to 1910.

methods used. By 1893 a thousand workers were employed and about 50,000 watches per year were being produced. The style of movement can be seen by examining some watches marketed by J. G. Graves or H. Samuel during the 1890–1910 period; they clearly come from the same source although few carry the Lancashire Watch Company logo. The company made a large range of watches in various sizes and qualities to satisfy all potential markets, but its selling techniques were not adequate to defeat the Swiss and American manufacturers and it closed in 1910. The company and its machinery are described by Smith.[10]

When, in the late 1870s, the Swiss realised that the Americans were ahead of them, they took steps to redress the balance. Some attempts to produce a cheaper watch for the working man had been made by Roskopf in 1867 (see Chapter 4) but his were not factory-made watches. However, by the time the Swiss had solved their machine-tool problems there was a market for cheap watches, and Roskopf's design was adapted as an addition to the lever (Plate 18) and cylinder types.

Swiss machines developed along different lines to American ones even though the concept came from America. Nicholas Junker invented a machine with a sliding headstock in about 1880, and the design persisted. Although there was resistance from the traditional Swiss watchmaker, it was overcome and by 1910, when jig-boring was introduced, Switzerland was set on the path to success in the very year the Lancashire Watch Company closed. Descriptions of Swiss machines can be found in Torrens,[8] Indermuhle[11] and Jaquet and Chapuis.[5]

Some idea of the real capacity of watchmaking machinery at the end of the pocket-watch era can be found in the *Encyclopedia Britannica*[12] where, in the section on mass-production of watches, a breakdown of the time taken for each operation is given. If all these times are added together, the equivalent time to manufacture a single watch is about 20 minutes. Some of the times, in seconds, are: making a case 36, as-

Plate 18 A Swiss factory-made watch of about 1925 having a straight-line Swiss lever escapement with going-barrel. The three-quarter plate movement has fifteen jewels and a dust cap; the case is silver. This is the type of watch that English makers refused to produce in factories, thus eventually losing their markets.

sembling a movement 72, putting into case 117, putting on hands 36, poising the balance 19, timing 170. This might mean that the 1,000 workers in the Lancashire Watch Company could have made nearly 7½ million watches per year rather than the 50,000 they made in 1893. Quite an increase in a 30-year span of machinery development.

Although it was clear by 1920 that American and Swiss manufacturers held the major part of the world market in pocket-watch manufacture, there was one final British effort to regain a position in this lucrative field — the attempt made by Smith's from about 1932 mentioned in Chapter 3. The development of suitable machinery was started before the war but not completed. After the war a factory was opened to produce pin-lever pocket watches, and higher quality watches were made elsewhere. However, the pocket-watch era was over; and although Smith's also produced wrist watches the venture was not completely successful, production ending completely in 1980.

Mechanical watches are now largely being replaced by factory-made electronic watches. It is most likely that, by the end of the twentieth century, mechanical watches will only be made to order by individual craftsmen or specialist firms. Indeed this is already true today if a particularly complicated watch is required; for example, only a few firms — such as Patek Philippe — now produce pocket watches with perpetual calendars, repeating work and chronograph included. In terms of mechanical watches, we are returning to the sixteenth century.

6
ALTERNATIVE ESCAPEMENTS

In earlier chapters the three most successful types of pocket watch were discussed in some detail — watches using the verge, the lever and the pin-lever escapements. These were not the only escapements devised, indeed Peate suggests that between 1700 and 1850 over 250 were recorded.[1] Many of these were not pursued, but the most common of those that were are considered below.

The most important was patented in 1695 (No 344) by Booth (also known as Barlow), Houghton and Tompion. The patent reads:

> A new sort of Watch or Clock with the Ballance Wheele or Swing Wheele either Flatt or Hollow, to Worke within and Crosse the Center of the Verge or Axis of the Ballance or Pendulum, with a new sort of Teeth made like Tinterhook, to move the Ballance or Pendulum withall, and the Pallett of the Axis or Verge of the Ballance or Pendulum are to be Circular, Concave and Convex, or other Teeth or Pallett that will not goe but by the help of the Spring to the Ballance, which will make such Watch or Clock goe more True and Exact, and be of greater use to our subject both at Sea and Land, than any other heretofore made or now used.

This is a vague description and there are no drawings. No watch is known to survive, but there were rumours a few years ago of a possible fragment and in Rees[2] there is a diagram purporting to show the escapement. What is certain is that in 1726 Graham, who was married to Tompion's niece and worked with Tompion, introduced the horizontal or cylinder escapement — 'horizontal' implying that the escape wheel was horizontal rather than vertical as in the verge. This escapement had a long life which, on the Continent, lasted until the wrist watch era. It was not made in such great numbers in England, and it was not the successor to the verge because it was not detached. It ranks, however, as the fourth most successful escapement.

The escape wheel has a vertical arbor and teeth which project vertically from the rim of the wheel (Fig 20 and Plate 19). These teeth engage with, and pass through, a special slot cut in a hollow cylinder fitted into the balance-wheel staff. The working portion of the hollow cylinder has approximately half its circumference removed so that a

Plate 19 Two views of an English cylinder escapement watch by Thos. Farr, Bristol. It is in a silver case hallmarked 1815. The fusee has maintaining power and the movement has a stop-piece operating on the balance. The side view shows the form of the escape-wheel teeth.

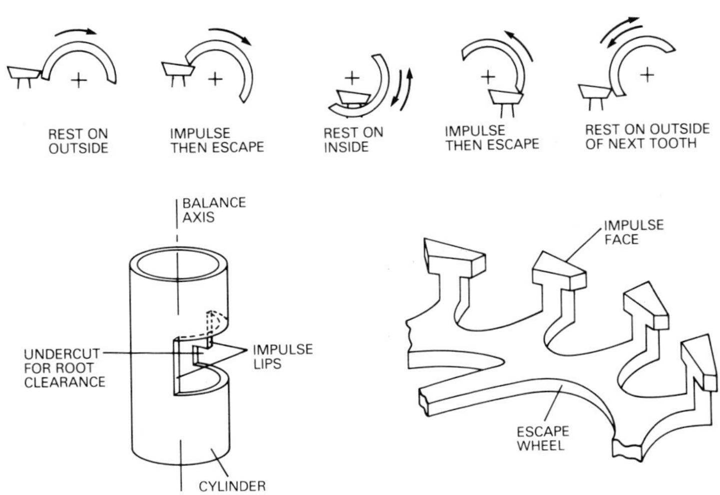

Fig 20 Horizontal or cylinder escapement

Plate 20 *(Left)* A full-plate English duplex escapement movement of 1817. The impulse teeth standing up on the escape-wheel rim can be seen. The fusee has maintaining power. *(Right)* A barred continental movement of about 1840 with duplex escapement. This is not common in continental watches and it is possible it was fitted later or finished in England. The locking-teeth on the escape wheel can be seen.

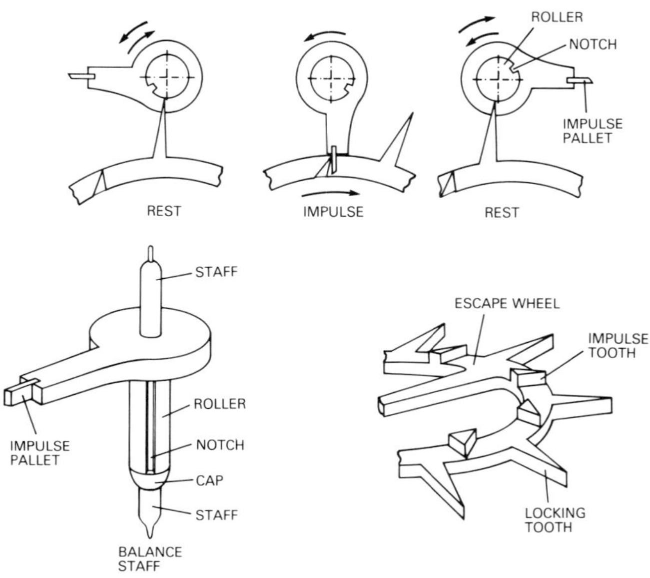

Fig 21 Duplex escapement

tooth may escape by passing through the cut-away portion of the cylinder at the appropriate moment during the balance vibration, but may rest on the outside or inside of the cylinder during the remainder of the vibration. The retained half of the cylinder is undercut to allow the tooth-root clearance when the tooth rests on the inner surface of the cylinder. The escapement is of frictional-rest, dead-beat design in which impulse is given to the balance twice per vibration by the sloping surface of the escape-wheel tooth acting on the edge of the hollow cylinder.

Another escapement which had reasonable success is the duplex (Fig 21 and Plate 20). It was conceived by Dutertre in about 1720 as a double-wheel escapement, but was modified and patented by Thomas Tyrer in 1782, and finally the two wheels were combined into one. It was made mainly in England until about 1850 as a high-quality alternative to the verge escapement. In the more common form with two sets of teeth on a single escape-wheel rim, one set of teeth locks the train and the other impulses the balance, the teeth being set alternately around the rim. Impulse is given once per balance vibration, since the locking-teeth only escape when the balance is rotating in the opposite direction to that of the escape wheel. The impulse is given by the inner ring of raised teeth on the rim of the wheel striking the impulse-pallet which projects from the balance shaft or staff. The outer, pointed teeth projecting from the escape-wheel rim are allowed to escape by passing through a vertical slot cut in a roller fitted around the balance staff. Escape is in two steps: a very small movement as the tooth slips across the width of the slot, and a much larger movement as the tooth escapes from the slot. This motion is stopped as the next pointed tooth comes to rest on the roller surface. On the return swing of the balance the slot slips past the tooth resting on the roller without permitting it to escape. This tooth is pressing on the roller for almost the complete vibration, and the escapement is frictional rest with single-beat action.

The practical escapement developed by Arnold and Earnshaw for the marine chronometer (see Chapter 8) was also applied to watches. Pocket chronometer watches were made in small numbers from about 1780 until the beginning of the twentieth century, when it was finally accepted that the lever watch could give equal performance at smaller cost and with considerably greater robustness. English pocket chronometers usually used the spring-detent escapement (Fig 22), and continental pocket chronometers (Plate 21) the pivoted-detent. In the former, the detent is sprung about one end and it holds the escape wheel and train locked by means of a jewel (known as the locking-

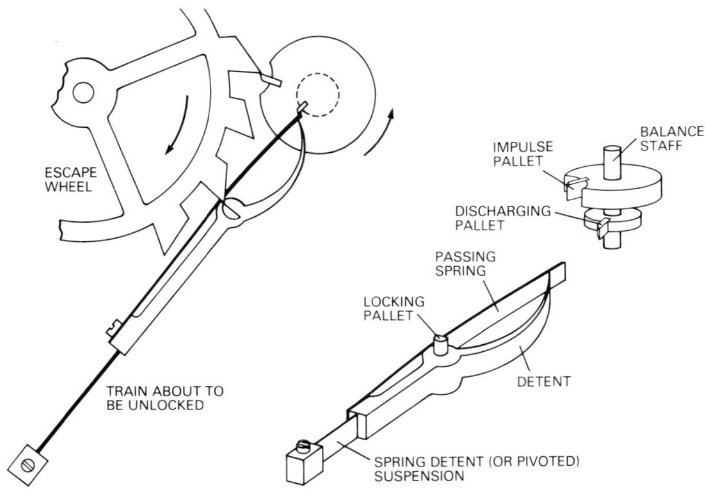

Fig 22 Spring-detent escapement

Plate 21 Early twentieth-century pivoted-detent pocket chronometer by Maurice Dreyfus, Chaux de Fonds, Switzerland. The three-quarter plate movement has helical balance spring, going-barrel and cut-compensated balance. The gold hunter case is engine-turned all over to achieve the quality the movement deserves. The lever adjacent to the 4 o'clock mark is pulled out to allow the hands to be set by the winding-button.

pallet) standing up from its surface. The balance staff carries two pallets and, as the balance swings, the discharging pallet momentarily pushes the passing spring against the detent which moves to release the escape wheel. The rotation of the latter allows impulse to be given to the impulse-pallet on the balance staff by an escape-wheel tooth, before the train is again locked by the locking-pallet on the detent. On the return swing of the balance the passing spring merely flexes as the discharging pallet passes, and does not unlock the escape wheel and train. Thus escape only occurs once per vibration. During the vibration the balance is detached except at the instant of unlocking and impulse, and the escapement is of detached, dead-beat design with single-beat operation. A full description of all types of chronometers can be found in Gould.[3]

An escapement invented by Debaufre *c*1700, used two escape wheels giving impulse to a single pallet on a balance staff. It was taken up in various forms during the eighteenth century,[4] the most common type being the Ormskirk or chaffcutter escapement (Fig 23 and Plate 22) made in Lancashire for a period of about thirty years from 1780. All 'Debaufre' escapements use a contrate wheel and can at first sight be taken for a verge watch. However, closer inspection will reveal that the crown wheel and verge have been replaced by various arrangements involving one or two pallets attached to the balance staff with an

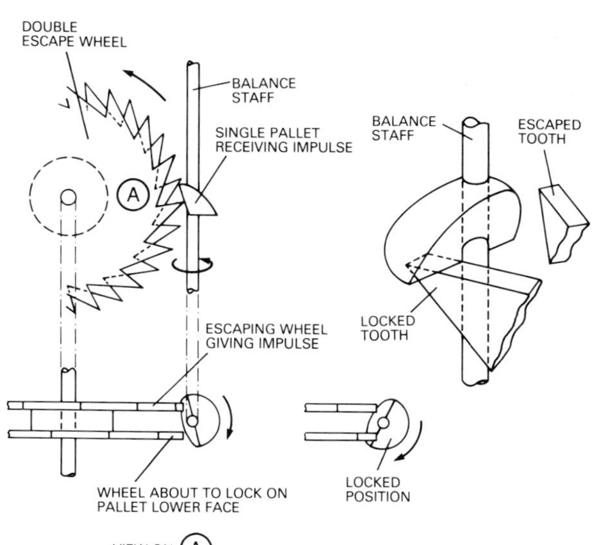

Fig 23 Ormskirk or chaffcutter escapement

Plate 22 Ormskirk or chaffcutter watch in gilt pair-cases made by James Ryland of Ormskirk *c*1785. It has an open mainspring driving a three-wheel train and an escapement with two saw-tooth wheels (Fig 23). The watch is a typical Ormskirk product with continental bridge-style cock and Bosley regulation. The escapement is one of the Debaufre group.

escape-wheel system comprised of a single or a double crown wheel, or a single or double saw-tooth wheel.

The pallets are horizontal, D-shaped and have inclined edges. They alternately receive impulse from an escape-wheel tooth on the inclined edge, and lock the train on the horizontal surface. If two escape wheels are used, the single pallet receives the impulse as one wheel escapes and then locks the other wheel. If two pallets are used, the single escape wheel gives impulse to the one pallet before being locked by the other. All the escapements are frictional rest.

There are many other escapements to be seen in museums and collections, but the above four are the commonest alternatives to the verge, lever or pin-lever. Two other groups, however, merit mention. The first is characterised by a widespread desire to have a watch with a seconds hand which would move in discreet jumps once per second. In the period between 1790 and 1830 a number of designers attempted this feat including Pouzait and Litherland and Massey (who both allowed for seconds-beating watches in their patents, and some were made).

Patent No 3620 to Samuel Smith in 1812 is for a 'dead-beat seconds' design, and a three-quarter or seconds-beating design by Wall and Frost is described in Chapter 11. None of these designs could be considered a great success; Pouzait's was probably the best. It is difficult to understand the fascination of seconds beating, but perhaps the longcase clock inspired the cult. Later, in 1846, Yates (see Chapter 11) attempted a half-seconds-beating watch, but this was again unsuccessful. In all cases the slow swing of the balance was liable to be disturbed by the violent motion of the watch when it was worn.

There were at least two successful designs of watch in which the seconds hand did move at second intervals, but these used conventional rates of vibration for the balance and a delay device for the hand. In the Chinese duplex[5] design the outer ring of locking-teeth of a duplex escape-wheel (Fig 21 and Plate 23) was modified to give each

Plate 23 Chinese duplex watch movement which is, as usual, highly decorated. The escape wheel can just be seen with the double ends on the locking-teeth enabling the seconds hand to move once every two complete balance-swings and so indicate complete seconds. The stopwork is fitted to the top of the going-barrel and the movement is enclosed in a double-backed silver case.

tooth a double end. Thus instead of escape occurring every other vibration of the balance, it needed four vibrations to escape past the double locking system. The train was a normal 14,400 design which allows 3,600 escapes per hour, ie once per second. Chinese duplex watches were produced mainly on the Continent at Fleurier in Switzerland, but there are English examples. They were a moderate success.

An alternative approach was to use a second train driving an independent seconds hand triggered once per second by the normal watch train. The triggering device is known as a whip.[6] This design was successful but was used as a precursor to the stop-watch (see Chapter 7) rather than as a pseudo seconds-beating escapement. It is a development of an original Pouzait design of 1777.[7]

The second group of escapements that merits a mention are sometimes misleading in that some lever-escapement watches appear to have unusual layouts but, when examined closely, are seen to be conversions. When the lever escapement became established, broken verge, cylinder, duplex and chronometer watches were not always repaired but the original escapement was replaced by a lever escapement. In the verge watch such replacement is very obvious, but in the cylinder and duplex designs clues are the train layout and the unusually small lever and escape wheel that have been fitted. If the watch is dismantled it is sometimes possible to find wording such as 'leverised in 1864' under the dial or on the plate, which is confirmation of conversion. It is also possible by close examination to see old holes in the plates that have been filled in and gilded over. The presence of an extra potence or bridge between the plates supporting the lever or escape wheel is another indicator. These watches should not be regarded as fakes, but as genuine contemporary updating of a broken watch.

The large number of escapements not discussed here can best be investigated by reading the literature. A considerable number are illustrated in Chamberlain.[8]

7
MECHANISMS

Striking watches, normally known as clock-watches, have been made from the very beginnings of watch history. This is not surprising since, as we have seen, the watch was developed from the clock which is itself a striking device. The design of early striking watches followed the pattern of clocks, using two trains with a slotted locking-plate to sequence and arrange the number of strikes, and a lifting-piece which set the strike in action once each hour. The watch contained a bell and the case was pierced to allow the sound to escape. Alarm-watches were also made which released the strike train at some predetermined instant. Both clock-watches and alarm-watches were made in small quantities throughout the life of the pocket watch.

Astronomical data, calendar work and moonwork were also fitted to watches from the earliest days. These indications were achieved by pins attached to wheels which turned another wheel one notch or tooth at the appropriate interval in a similar way to motion work. For example, date work (Fig 24) needs a 2:1 gear ratio to translate the rotation of the hour wheel to the rotation of a day wheel, with a pin to move the date ring forward one notch every 24 hours. The date ring can operate a month indicator every thirty-second day, and hand correction can be used to compensate for short months. Weekdays are based on the date-pin operating a 7-notch wheel and moonwork requiring a 29½-day cycle uses a 59- or 118-notch system.

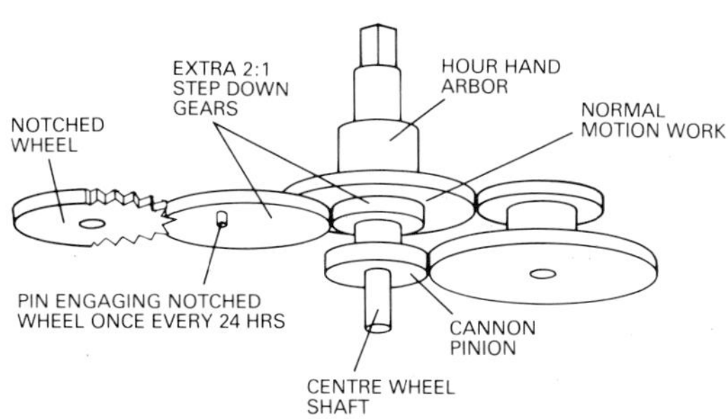

Fig 24 Date work

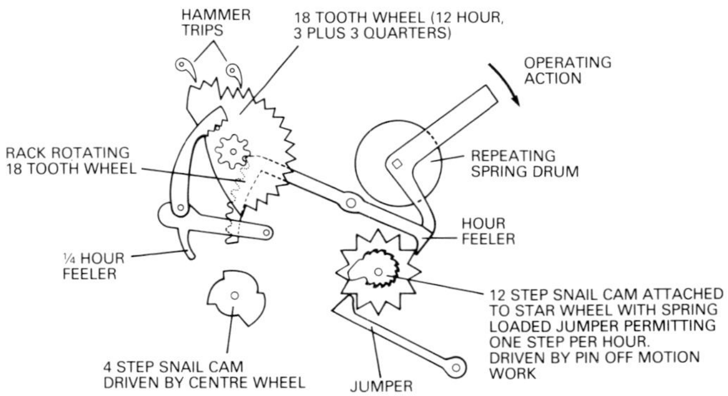

Fig 25 Repeating work

Although to know the day, date and moon state was helpful, striking after dark was probably of more use. The concept of a repeating watch which would strike to indicate the time at the command of the owner was an attractive proposition, and the design was achieved separately in 1685–8 by Quare and Barlow (see page 22). The general principle of repeating work is to actuate a button or lever so that it performs two functions: firstly, it winds a spring to run the repeating mechanism and, secondly, it positions feelers on stepped snail cams that indicate the time to the repeating mechanism. A 12-step cam for hours and a 4-step cam for quarter hours is the most common quarter repeating form which enables time to be indicated on bells (or gongs) to the nearest quarter of an hour (Fig 25). When the actuating button is released the mechanism sounds one ring for hours and two rings for quarters. Some watches give time to the nearest 7½ minutes, these are half-quarter repeaters, others to the nearest 5 minutes and others to the nearest minute. All these types were available before 1800. There are a variety of designs of repeating mechanisms, for example those of Stogden (Stockten) 1725, Elliot (1804) and Berollas (1810); the latter two designs involving hand operation rather than spring power.[1] A full history of repeating watches can be found in Wadsworth,[2] and a description of later repeating mechanisms and their maintenance in specialist texts.[3,4]

The gong replaced the bell in the nineteenth century because it enabled the new, slimmer watches to have repeating facilities. There was also a form of silent repeating where the hammer struck a pulse-piece felt by the finger, which was useful for deaf or blind people or in situations where the noise of the strike would be disturbing.

In the same way that the repeating watch was an improvement on the striking watch, a watch which would automatically allow for variable-length months and leap years would be an improvement on simple day and date work. The perpetual calendar watch made by Breguet in 1795 incorporates a 48-notch wheel for the 4-year cycle of the calendar. This notched wheel is fixed to a 4-year cam which has a land for a feeler for each month, the height of the land determining whether a 31, 30, 29 or 28-day month is indicated. A full description of this mechanism can be found in Britten.[5] There is evidence that Mudge may have made the first perpetual calendar watch in about 1764.[6]

It is also possible for a watch to have a hand which indicates equation of time, so that the watch can be set with a sundial without recourse to tables (see Chapters 8 and 11). For this, the equation of time is incorporated into a kidney-shaped cam, rotating once per year, which draws the hand across the chapter ring indicating the equation of time. Equation clocks were made from about 1700 and were probably invented by Joseph Williamson[7,8]; watches came later. Certainly Breguet and Robin[9] were making equation watches at the end of the eighteenth century. Wenzel's description of equation work (for clocks) gives a clear indication of the mechanisms used and shows the layout of the special cam.[8]

The construction of an equation-of-time mechanism in a watch needs considerable skill. The average daily variation in difference between sun time and mean time is of the order of 10–15 seconds. This is accommodated on a cam with a base circle diameter of about 12mm (½in), whose average daily change in radius would need to be about 0.1mm (0.004in). It is not surprising that equation watches are rare and that only the finest makers would undertake this work and then only on their best watches.

Pocket watches were also used to discover how long it took to perform some action — a general term for these is stop-watches. Sometimes they are called chronographs but, since this implies a written record of the time, the term is not correct. The first stop-watches had a lever which literally stopped the watch by interfering with the train. They are quite a common feature of verge and lever escapement watches made between 1800 and 1900, the use of the stop device no doubt due to the general use of seconds hands on watches by this time. This was obviously a very unsatisfactory method for obtaining elapsed time since the starting time was arbitrary and the stopping caused the watch to be wrong as a timepiece. To overcome this problem some watches used two trains: one for the conventional timepiece, and one which could be stopped and started at will which drove a separate seconds hand. This hand sometimes moved in one-second jumps (Plate 24).

This type of watch was an improvement, but still lacked two vital ingredients of the modern concept of a stop-watch — the ability to count elapsed times of greater duration than a minute, which necessitated a minute counter to be successful, and the convenience of starting the counting hand from zero each time to avoid the need for arithmetic, which necessitated a reset device. These two functions were both achieved in the mid-nineteenth century. In 1842, Nicole patented a reset system for a seconds hand which could be independently stopped and started; and in 1862 the now familiar three-press button system was patented (Plate 25).

(left) Plate 24 Swiss lever watch with two trains, *c*1870. The left-hand train drives the normal hands and the right-hand train drives a centre seconds hand which moves forward at one-second intervals controlled by a 'whip' mechanism. It can be stopped and started at will without stopping the normal hands, and is therefore an early form of stop-watch. *(right)* Plate 25 Watch with Swiss lever escapement, made *c*1920. The normal hands are supplemented by a centre seconds hand and minute counter. The start, stop and reset action is operated by pushing the winding-button. The normal hands are set by depressing the small push-piece (to the right of the button). There is also a scale for determining vehicle speed.

In this system the starting and stopping is achieved quite simply by bringing a wheel (with extremely fine teeth or serrations) into mesh with another wheel which rotates permanently with the main train of the watch. The engaging and disengaging is achieved by pushing the winding button, or a special button, which operates a spring-controlled lever system. The lever-ends not concerned with engaging or disengaging feel their way into, and out of, slots in a column-wheel which rotates one step at each push of the button to control the stop, reset, start sequence. A third push on the button is used to reset the seconds hand. This is achieved by a special heart-shaped cam pivoted in such a way that, when the heel of a spring-loaded piece presses against it, the torque will bring the cam around to the starting position. It is held in this position, with no overshoot, by the foot of the spring-loaded piece applying the pressure which rests on a flat surface on the cam profile (Fig 26). This profile is such that if the watch is stopped before the seconds hand has completed half a revolution, it will return in an anticlockwise direction; but if more than half a revolution has been made, the return is clockwise. The hand returns by the shortest route.

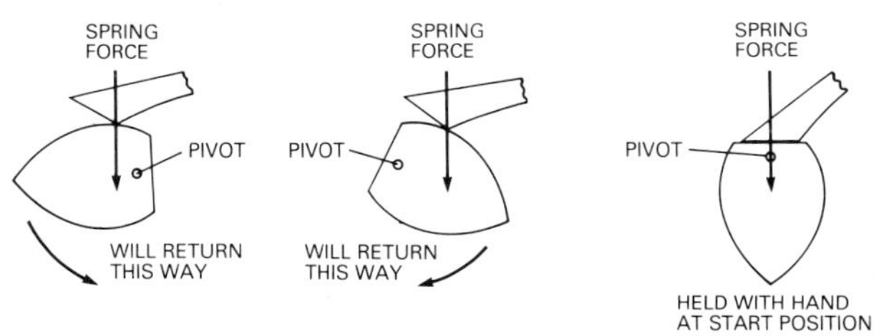

Fig 26 Stop-watch heart-piece

Watches[3,4] were also developed with two seconds hands, each of which could be stopped and started independently, which allowed the difference in two elapsed times to be observed directly (split-seconds watch). At the same time, despite the availability of these proper stop-watches, some quite elegant looking watches (usually with 'chronograph' on the dial) were made with the simple stop device which interfered with the train. Cheap versions were also sold; presumably the early stop-watches were too expensive.

Each of the complications described so far has been functional in that it improved the amount of information that could be obtained from a watch. Other complications were more fanciful, for example the incorporation of a musical box into watches at the start of the nineteenth century. At first these used the familiar pinned cylindrical drum acting on a tuned comb to produce the music. Later a flat, pinned disc operated the comb which was so arranged as to use both sides of the disc, giving a thinner movement. Another non-functional complication, used in repeating watches, was to put automated figures on the dial apparently striking bells in time with the real repeating gong-ringing action inside the watch. These figures are known as 'jacquemarts'. A third non-utilitarian complication was the use of the oscillating motion of the balance to provide a visual display on the dial, or under the rear watch-cover if the display was erotic.

Parallel with such complications, improvements to the mechanism made the watch more accurate. Chapter 8 deals both with errors caused by the temperature of the environment, and therefore largely out of control of the watch owner, and with errors due to the position of the watch in the owner's pocket which can be partially compensated for by attention to springing, or alternatively by allowing the escapement to rotate so that the error is averaged and the rate of loss or gain is constant. This method is used in the tourbillon and karrusel watches[4] (Fig

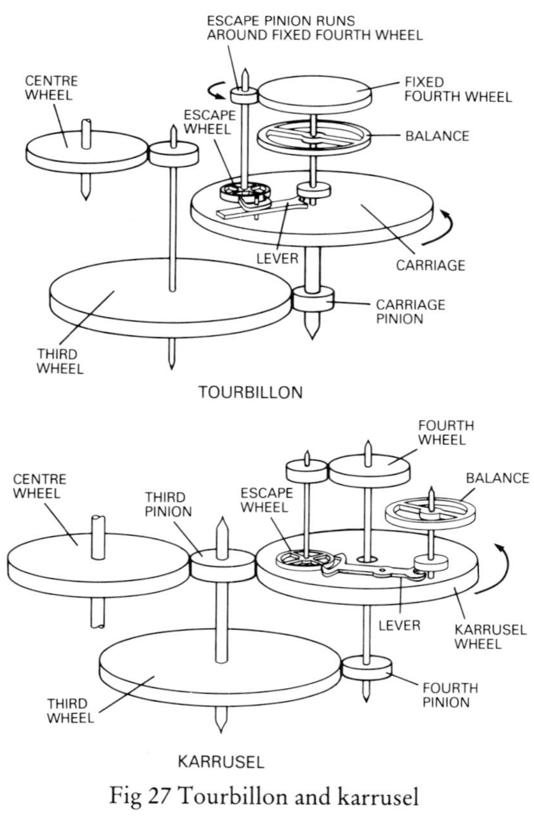

Fig 27 Tourbillon and karrusel

27). In the tourbillon, invented by Breguet in 1795, the escapement (balance, escape wheel etc) is mounted on a carriage which carries a pinion driven by the third wheel. The fourth wheel is fixed and is concentric with the carriage shaft. The escape-wheel pinion meshes with the fixed fourth wheel. Thus, as the carriage rotates, the escape-wheel pinion will roll around the fixed fourth wheel, causing the pinion to rotate and operate the escape wheel and balance in the normal way. In the karrusel by Bonniksen (patent No 21421 of 1892), the carriage is mounted on a karrusel wheel driven by the third-wheel pinion. The fourth-wheel staff passes through the centre of the karrusel-bearing to allow the fourth-wheel pinion to mesh with the third wheel, and power is transmitted to the escapement in the normal way rather than through the carriage rotation as in the tourbillon. The rate of rotation of the karrusel is about once per hour compared with the tourbillon which may rotate once per minute. Both these designs demand considerable manufacturing skill, and are only found in watches of high quality.

Some makers produced watches with combinations of complications. Thus it is possible to see a watch with a perpetual calendar, moonwork, minute repeating and split-seconds hands. A few very high quality complicated watches are still made (Plate 26).

From the point of view of convenience, the most annoying part of operating a watch is winding and hand setting by key. This was long recognised, and many makers produced solutions. One of the earliest of these was the self-winding watch in which the motion of a swinging weight wound the spring. This was invented by Perrelet in 1770, patented (No 1249) by Recordon in 1780, and used by Breguet from about that date. It did not become popular, however, until wrist-watch days, possibly because the pocket watch did not get sufficient motion.

During the final years of the eighteenth and early years of the nineteenth centuries, several makers patented push-or-pull forms of winding devices, including Leslie (No 1790 of 1793), Massey (No 3854 of 1814) and Berollas (No 5586 of 1827).[10] In these the pendant, or a button passing through the pendant, is pushed (or pulled) to operate a rack or similar device which rotates the square at the centre of a going-barrel to wind the spring. Massey's patent mentioned using a fusee, but in general the fusee was not chosen for keyless winding. Another worker of this period — Thomas Prest in patent No 4501 of 1820 — approached the present-day concept when he used a simple button-wind system for a going-barrel (Fig 28). The hands, however, had to be set with the fingers. Prest worked for John Roger Arnold, and there are a number of Arnold watches with Prest winding.

Plate 26 Four photographs showing a modern complicated watch with grande sonnerie or petite sonnerie chiming (which can be set on or off), perpetual calendar with moon phases, split seconds chronograph and minute repeating on three gongs: *(top left)* the watch in a 1965-style case; *(bottom left)* with dial removed to reveal the calendar mechanisms; *(top right)* watch-back removed to show the chronograph mechanism, escapement and repeating hammers; *(bottom right)* calendar mechanism removed to reveal repeating and striking work. Such watches can still be purchased today. *(By courtesy of Patek Philippe)*

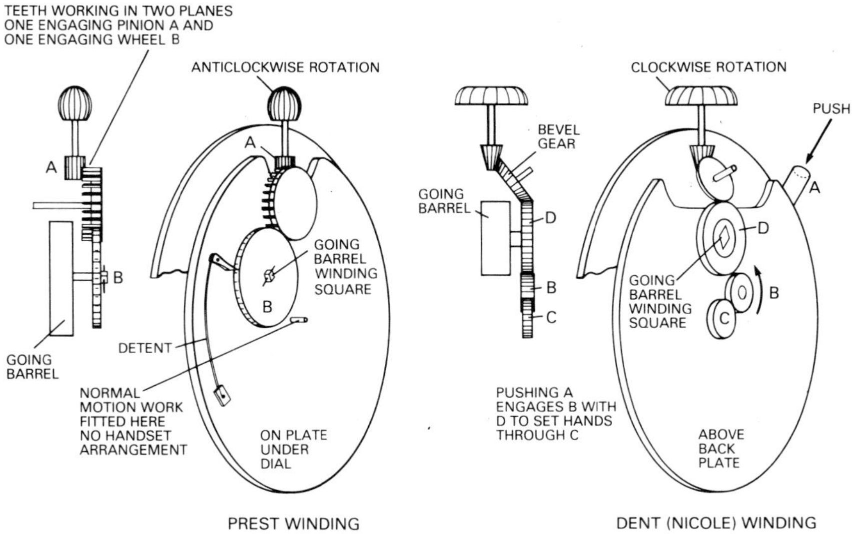

Fig 28 Early keyless winding by Prest and Nicole (Dent)

The first man to devise both winding and hand setting by button was the Swiss maker Louis Audemars, in 1838. He was followed by other makers, notably Adolphe Nicole who took out English patent No 10348 in 1844, Phillipe, Lecoultre and Huguenin. Nicole's method was used by Dent from 1846 to 1862 as the 'sole licensee', and his watches are engraved 'patent'. The button winds the watch and the hands are moved by pushing a piece to engage the motion work at the same time as the winding. Thus if the watch is fully wound the hands can only be moved backwards through a slipping device (Fig 28). Adrien Phillipe was responsible for the shifting-sleeve design which was the final form of keyless winding, and Lecoultre and Huguenin for rocking-bar designs. In the early forms of both, the change of mode from wind to hand set was by means of a small push-piece at the side of the winding-button, but this extra piece was not required in the design in which pulling the winding-button itself effected the change of mode. Fig 29 shows four arrangements of later keyless winding systems. There are other varieties involving different layouts in which mode was engaged by button pushing or pulling, and it was years before the pull-button shifting-sleeve form became the norm.[3,4] In a period of twenty-five years spanning 1900 there were over a thousand patents concerned with winding and hand setting.[11]

The keyless winding and hand-setting system brought change in case design. It was not necessary for the front to hinge open for hand setting, and so a snap-on bezel was introduced. Similarly, it was only necessary to open the back for regulation or servicing, and as this was

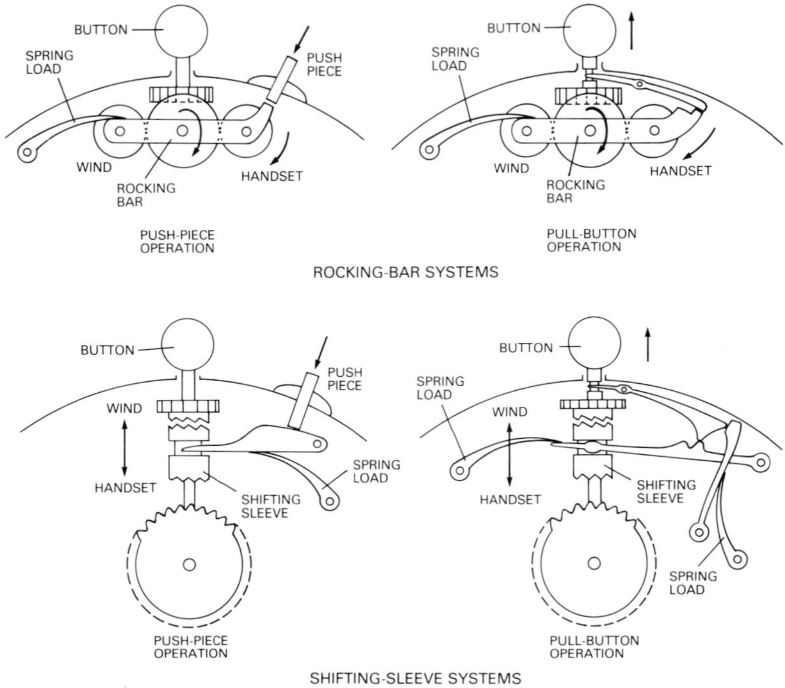

Fig 29 Later keyless winding systems

Plate 27 Movement of an English lever watch from a case hallmarked 1905. The watch has Burdess patent winding (No 2286 of 1869). The lever attached to the fusee passes through a slot in the inner dome of the case. When the back of the case is opened the watch is wound by moving the lever. The hands are set by opening the front of the watch to reveal the small wheel (adjacent to the cock) which may be turned by finger.

normally the job of a watchmaker the double bottom to the case was abandoned. Instead the hinged back was snapped firmly shut, with a small lifting-piece to allow it to be opened. The dust cap on the movement was no longer required and was replaced by a small, hinged cover fitted inside the case back. The movement was no longer hinged to the case but was held in place by screws and, when the bezel and screws were removed, could be passed out through the front of the case.

In English watches keyless winding was rare in this period mainly because most of the systems discussed were only suited to use with the going-barrel watch, and English makers still used the fusee. A system to avoid the need for a key was devised by Adam Burdess (patent No 2286 of 1869). This design (Plate 27) has a lever attached to the fusee winding-square which protrudes through the back of the conventional inner part of the double-bottom case. The lever can be moved backwards and forwards through a small arc to wind the watch; hand set is achieved by a wheel under the bezel of the watch. Burdess included instructions on a paper inside the back of these watches, quaintly spelling bezel as 'bizzel'. These watches were made till the turn of the century by which time the fusee watch was almost finished. Winding systems must have contributed to its demise.

This chapter has introduced a large number of mechanisms which improve the usefulness and operation of a pocket watch. It is a field where a great deal more detail can be found in specialist texts, patents etc. It is also an area in which examination of the complications is the only way to get a clear picture of their operation; but great care should be taken if any complicated watch is dismantled for study.

8
TIMEKEEPING

The basis of man's concept of time is the apparent motion of the sun. A day and a night constitute a natural unit as does a year. Day and night are caused by the rotation of the earth about its axis, and the year by the orbit of the earth about the sun. During night-time observations the rotation of the earth causes the stars to have apparent motion; it is thus possible to have a sidereal (relative to the stars) day used by astronomers and a solar day used by the ordinary person.

Unfortunately the motion of the sun relative to the earth is not constant, due partly to the shape of the earth's orbit which is elliptical rather than circular and partly to the fact that the plane of the orbit is inclined to the equator at an angle of 23½ degrees. Thus a solar day does not occupy a constant amount of time. It is not convenient to have a unit which is not constant as the basis for time measurement, and this gave rise to the concept of a mean day which is constant in length.

The cumulative difference between mean time and apparent solar time is called the 'equation of time'. For some of the year the real sun is slow and sometimes it is fast relative to the mean time, the maximum difference being about sixteen minutes at the beginning of November. On four days of the year there is no difference. Nowadays the equation of time is of no interest to the average person, although it is still of interest to navigators and astronomers concerned with observations of heavenly bodies at times indicated by mean-time clocks or watches which have to be corrected. This was not always so. The invention of the pendulum for clocks and the balance spring for watches brought the concept of the equation of time to the notice of any serious timepiece owner.[1]

Prior to the invention of these devices the poor timekeeping abilities of the foliot clock and pre-balance-spring watch would make any real difference between indicated time and sundial time disappear. Whenever the sun was shining clocks and watches could be checked and put right according to the local sundial which would be assumed to be correct. Since everyone would be using *local* sundial time there would be no problems — the dial was correct and the watch wrong if there was a difference. With the advent of the balance spring, the difference between sun time and mean time became apparent and every owner needed a table of the values of the equation of time so that he could read the sundial, obtain the equation of time, calculate the mean time and set the watch right. What 'right' meant could be debatable. If the local community had a village clock which kept mean time this might be 'wrong'. There was also the problem of the accuracy of reading a sundial. The tables of equation of time were sometimes engraved on the watch case or printed on a circular watch paper kept in the back of the watch case; but such tables contained a selection of values rather than a full day-by-day table for a year which could be kept indoors near a clock.

Sundials were normally fixed in position, but portable ones were made so that a traveller could check his watch anywhere whenever the sun shone. For this purpose the portable dial was fitted with a compass. (Early dials using sun altitude rather than sun direction needed no compass, but were not so convenient to use.) The portable dial would be unlikely to give such accurate values of sun time as the fixed dial, but it did prevent the watch being very far from correct. Sundial work is discussed further in Chapter 11.

The year is the other natural unit of time which gave mankind problems. From early days man was able to work out the approximate length of a year, but small errors in his organised counting system were cumulative. If 360 days were thought to be a year, mid-summer would become mid-winter in 35 years. An error of this magnitude, however, quickly became apparent and could be corrected. Thus, in 46 BC, Julius Caesar established the Julian Calendar based on a year of 365 days with one additional day every fourth (leap) year. Probably most people imagine this is the system we use now, but that year is in fact too long — even by 1580 the calculation was about ten days in error. Therefore, with the superior astronomical knowledge of that period, the New Style calendar was drawn up by Pope Gregory XIII with leap years omitted at the century years unless the century itself is divisible by four. Thus 1700, 1800 and 1900 were not leap years but 1600 was and 2000 will be. This calendar needs a small adjustment every four thousand years, but this is not significant.

The Gregorian Calendar which proclaimed the day after 4 October 1582 to be 15 October 1582 was accepted at once in Italy, Spain, Portugal, France and Poland; in 1583 by Catholic states in Germany, Holland and Flanders; and in 1587 by Hungary. Non-Catholic countries were slower to accept the change. German and Dutch Protestant states and Denmark chose 1700, Britain 1752, Sweden 1753, Japan 1873, China and Albania 1912, Bulgaria 1916, Russia 1918, Rumania and Greece 1924, and Turkey 1927, dates causing chaos throughout this period. In Britain in 1752, when the Calendar New Style Act of 1750 came into force, the day following 2 September was called 14 September. This caused disturbances as many people thought they had lost eleven days of their life! The 15 October 1982 was therefore the quater centenary of the Gregorian Calendar and in the previous four hundred years one cycle was completed. This means that the days and dates now repeat — in 1986 we could use a 1586 diary or calendar.

Even today it is possible to see references to the change from the Julian to the Gregorian Calendar. Each day *The Times* newspaper carries a list of anniversaries in which entries such as that for 30 October: 'Births: Fyodor Dostoyevsky (New Style Nov 11), Moscow, 1821' and 11 November: 'Births: Fyodor Dostoyevsky (Old Style Oct 30), Moscow, 1821' may be seen.

The mean-time system and the Gregorian Calendar organised time satisfactorily for the ordinary person, but timekeeping has other uses. To understand why there was a continuous drive to make more accurate clocks and watches which would need new escapements, it is necessary to consider the problem of navigation at sea in so far as it is relevant to the pocket watch.

The sun appears to move from east to west so that, for example, noon at Greenwich is 17 minutes before noon at Plymouth. There is a relation between longitude and time. During a single day the sun traverses 360 degrees of longitude in 24 hours, thus 1 degree of longitude is equivalent to a 4-minute change in noon time and Plymouth is 4¼ degrees west of Greenwich.

The determination of latitude and longitude is vital to navigation. The former is not difficult nor, in theory, is determination of the latter. The principle is simple. A timekeeper is set correct at the port of departure of a vessel and must then keep correct time. A determination of local noon at any subsequent geographical position will enable the difference in time between the port of departure and the present position to be found by subtraction. This can then be converted to the longitude of the position using the 4-minute time equivalence to 1 degree of longitude. The problem is to obtain a timekeeper that will keep correct time throughout the voyage.

In 1714 the British government appointed a committee to consider the problem. One piece of evidence was given by Isaac Newton who stated 'That for determining Longitude at Sea there have been several

Projects . . . One is, by a Watch to keep time exactly: But . . . such a Watch hath not yet been made'. In Chapter 2 when the verge escapement watch was considered it was seen that observation suggests that the balance-spring verge watch could keep time to within about two minutes per day. This represents an error in longitude of up to thirty miles. As the watch error is cumulative and random, there was no way of navigating with the ordinary verge watch. Navigation was achieved by travelling until you were 'certain' you were either east or west of your goal, then getting to the correct latitude (simple enough) and then travelling due west or east to reach your destination. Shipwrecks were frequent and exploration was hazardous. The 1714 committee recommended, and the government agreed, an Act offering large financial rewards for any 'practical and useful' methods of finding longitude at sea. The test was to be a voyage from Britain to the West Indies at the end of which, if the longitude was in error by less than 60 minutes of arc of a great circle, the reward would be £10,000; for 40 minutes of arc, £15,000; and for 30 minutes of arc, £20,000. The Act also set up the Board of Longitude to administer the competition and to advance small amounts of money to promising leads. It took about fifty years for the award to be won and a further nine years for the government to pay. By this time the method of lunar distances had been developed and brought into use by the publication in 1767 of the *Nautical Almanac* by Nevil Maskeleyne, the Astronomer Royal. Unfortunately, the calculations with lunar distances were so complex that the results obtained were often in error.

In 1714 the only watch escapement available was the verge, and the fusee was the accepted method of achieving constant torque. Set up and stop work existed to avoid using the ends of the spring. Mainsprings had been manufactured for nearly two hundred years and were therefore a reasonable product; the spiral balance spring had been used for thirty years. Pendulum-controlled clocks were also available and such weight-driven devices had constant torque. The anchor escapement for a clock was well established, and in 1715 Graham produced the deadbeat form of this escapement. This list represents the armoury for the prospective prize-winner.

There were a considerable number of varied attempts by makers from various countries to gain the prize.[2] The winner was John Harrison (1693–1776) who spent virtually the whole of his working life producing marine timekeepers. His first, completed in the period 1729–35, was a very complex machine but it worked. The next two were simpler but still complex and required considerable skill and time to make. The fourth, 'No 4', was the timekeeper which won the prize by making a voyage from Portsmouth to Jamaica, leaving on 18 November 1761 and arriving on 21 January 1762 (fifty-six days) with an error of five seconds slow — less than one nautical mile. The error is deduced by the indicated time corrected by a *pre-stated* rate of loss or gain known as the 'rate of a watch'. The Board also required a second trial in 1764 before accepting 'No 4' as the winner. This winning timepiece was basically a verge watch made to very high standards. It was fitted with a remontoire system of applying constant torque in which the mainspring winds up a smaller auxiliary spring every 7½ seconds at the *balance end of the train*. It had maintaining power so that it would not stop during normal winding, and a bi-metallic temperature-compensation curb acting on the spiral balance spring. The four timekeepers can be seen in the National Maritime Museum at Greenwich, London.

In satisfying the conditions of the trial the timekeeper was a remarkable achievement; but it was not really a very practical solution to the problem as the time and skill needed to build it precluded its being reproduced in sufficient quantity for the ships of the world. It was left to others to produce a more practical device. The Board of Longitude was not dissolved. It offered a new prize (never won) and continued to give support to other inventors.

As far as watches are concerned, the only item retained was the maintaining power which was in future fitted to all fusee watches with any pretence to timekeeping ability. A going-barrel watch does not need such a device. Maintaining power is achieved from a leaf-spring in a recess in the great wheel below the fusee, and tensioned by a steel ratchet wheel operated by the mainspring against a detent. This thin ratchet wheel is sandwiched between the fusee and the great wheel. When the watch is wound the mainspring torque is removed from the great wheel and thus the escapement, and for this short period of time the watch is driven by the leaf-spring force acting on the great wheel. Watches with maintaining power can be recognised by the presence of the thin steel ratchet wheel and detent (Figs 30 and 38).

The next phase of development of the marine chronometer was more important to watchmakers in that it produced a practical device. The disadvantage of the verge escapement was that it was a frictional rest design and although Harrison had won the prize, he had not used a detached escapement but had triumphed by painstaking attention to the elimination of the effects of friction. A second fault in Harrison's work was that his temperature compensation used a curb which altered

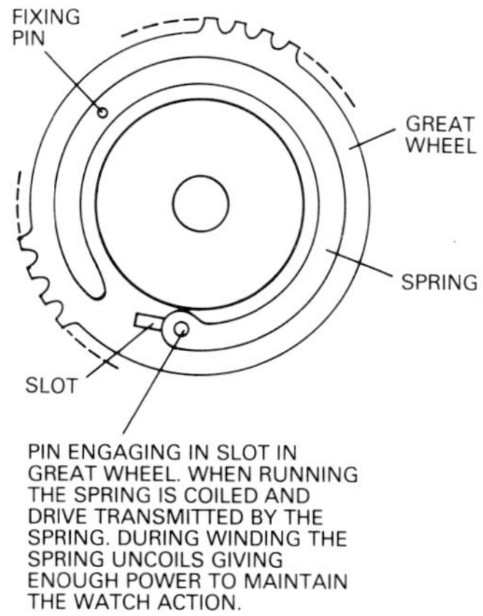

Fig 30 Fusee with maintaining power

the working of the balance spring. Since this spring is vital to timekeeping, any interference with its action was not conducive to achieving the ideal isochronous spring — 'isochronous' meaning equal vibration-time for all balance arcs of swing. Harrison's careful work and remontoire was the device which made his design successful.

The new practical timekeeper incorporated work by Pierre le Roy, who in 1765 invented a detached detent escapement with a compensation balance for a marine timekeeper. It was not fully developed as he did not pursue the design. In England, John Arnold and Thomas Earnshaw both produced detached detent escapements; the former starting with a pivoted detent, the latter with a spring version. Arnold produced a temperature-compensated balance and also found by experiment that if a specially shaped end or terminal curve was used with a helical balance spring, the vibrations came close to being isochronous. He finally adopted a spring-detent design. At about the same time Earnshaw produced a temperature-compensated balance with fused rather than riveted bimetallic layers. There was debate as to who was the actual inventor, but by the end of the century both men were producing relatively inexpensive marine chronometers in quantity, these having detached detent escapements and temperature-compensated balances which left the balance spring free to do its work. The test of time has shown Earnshaw's escapement surviving with Arnold's balance springs.

There was also work by Berthoud in France, and his products can be seen in the Conservatoire National des Arts et Métiers in Paris. The full story of the marine chronometer is told by Gould,[2] and an account of its early use by Captain Cook is interesting reading.[3] There is some contemporary writing in Rees.[4] As far as watches are concerned both Arnold, Earnshaw and other good makers produced pocket chronometers which were the ultimate in accurate watches at that time. They were rather fragile and not suited to everyday rough use, but were very attractive. The escapement is discussed in Chapter 6. All pocket chronometers used maintaining power and temperature compensation, and they continued to be made in small numbers, both in England and on the Continent, until the early twentieth century.

A closer look at the problems of timekeeping that were solved by the chronometer makers, shows that the use of terminal curves on balance springs was essential for isochronous performance and that temperature compensation was vital to allow for changes in environment. The use of terminal curves for helical balance springs was incorporated into pocket chronometer watches. Terminal curves were devised for spiral springs by Breguet. In his design the outer coil was brought up and over the rest of the spring to produce a curve with an attachment point closer to the balance centre than with the conventional flat spring (Fig 31). This is known as the Breguet overcoil, and is used in good-quality pocket watches with spiral springs. The effect of terminal curves is to

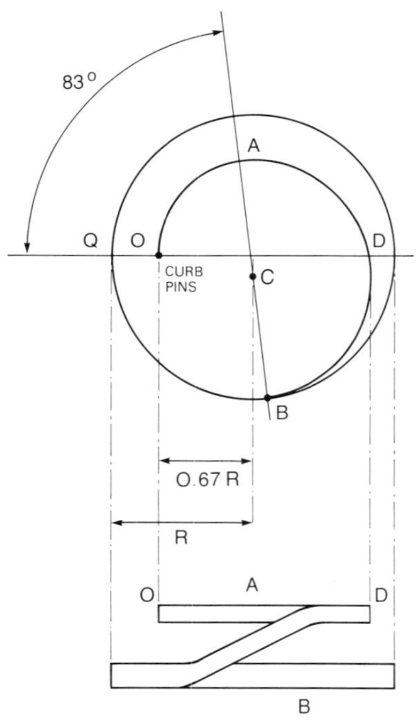

Fig 31 Terminal curves for balance springs. Arc OA is 83% of radius 0.67R. Arc ADB is 180° of radius AC. If used for spiral springs the Breguet overcoil OAD is formed above the plane of the spring.

keep the centre of inertia of the spring on the balance axis during the coiling and uncoiling motion. Visually a correctly made isochronous spring should conform to the statement[5]: 'If you cannot see the overcoil or central part, [it] will look as if the middle part is stationary whilst the outer and inner parts move in opposite directions'. Mathematical theory to justify the terminal curves developed experimentally by Arnold and Breguet was produced by Edouard Phillips in 1861, and clarified for non-mathematicians by M. Lossier in 1891[6] (Fig 31).

When the ambient temperature alters, significant changes occur in the balance and balance spring which affect the rate of vibration. First and most important, the balance-spring metal is less springy at high temperatures and more springy at low; thus a watch will lose at higher temperatures and gain when it is cooler. Secondly, temperature variation causes the balance to expand or contract. A balance that has thus expanded has its mass at a greater radius and under the application of constant torque will take longer to vibrate, so that a watch will again tend to lose at higher temperatures. Finally, expansion and contraction will affect the dimensions of the balance spring. Thus some form of temperature compensation is required.

Initial attempts at temperature compensation used bimetallic curbs, made of two thin layers — one brass and one steel. When heated or cooled, the different rates of expansion of the two metals caused the composite material to bend. One end of the curb was fixed whilst the other, the free end, was arranged so that it held the balance spring close to its point of attachment to the watch plate. If the watch got hotter and tended to slow down, the curb shortened the length of the balance spring and, hopefully, speeded the watch enough to compensate for the loss. There was another form of curb in which one (curb) pin was fixed and the other moved by a bimetallic strip in such a way as to allow the spring more or less freedom to move between the pins (Fig 32). This was equivalent to changing the spring length with a fixed gap between the pins.

Curb compensation was an improvement over no compensation, but interfering with the balance spring was not an ideal way of tackling the problem. A far better method was devised in which the balance rim was made of two different metals — the outer layer brass and the inner steel — and then cut close to the balance arms (Fig 32). When the balance temperature rose the higher coefficient of expansion of brass caused the outer layer to lengthen more than the inner one, and the cut allowed the rim to bend inwards. Thus the balance mass was moved inwards and the vibration time shortened. By carefully calculating the

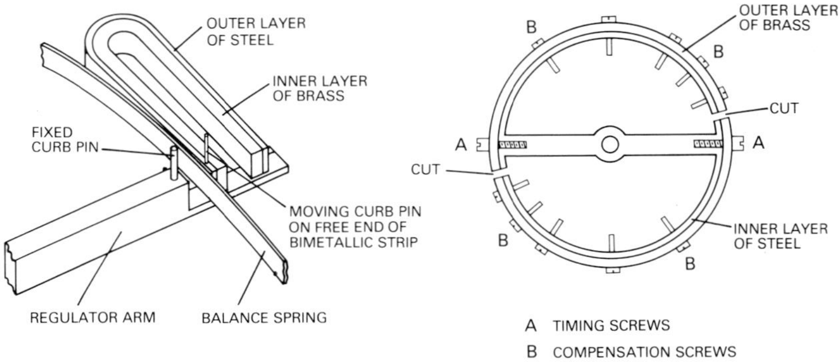

Fig 32 Compensation curb and a compensated balance

relative thickness of the brass and steel layers, the amount of compensation could be adjusted to the loss expected due to the temperature rise. Similarly, if the watch became colder the balance rim moved outwards, compensating for the expected gain.

The compensation for change of temperature obtained by this method is not exact, because the rate of variation of timekeeping due to change of elasticity is not always identical to the rate of variation due to change of balance inertia. This may be examined mathematically and the mathematically inclined reader may well find interest in thinking about timekeeping. A simple graph can be used to illustrate the effect of these different rates of change, and Fig 33 shows that it is possible for compensation with a cut-compensated balance to be correct at the two temperatures where the two curves cross. In between these two ideal situations is a small middle-temperature error, and in this area the watch will gain. Outside the two ideal situations the watch will lose.

The effects of these errors can be minimised by manipulation of the

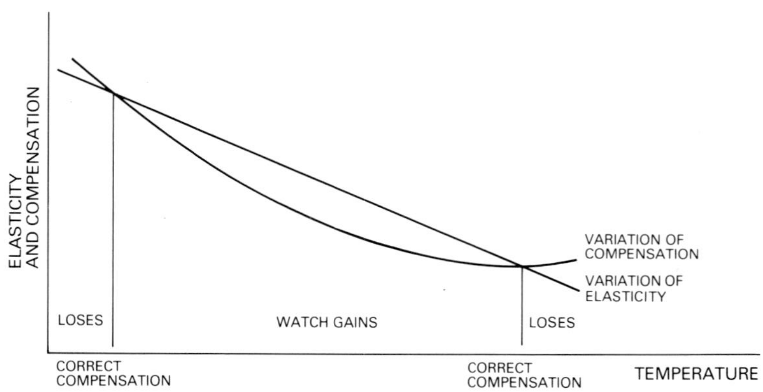

Fig 33 Middle-temperature error

mass and circumferential distribution of the compensation-screws around the rim.[7] This is a skilled task, for not only is the compensation affected by altering the mass but so is the fundamental time of vibration of the watch. However, there are two timing-screws at the ends of the arms which will not affect compensation, but which can be altered to give a basic change in mass or mass distribution. Any alterations in a balance must be made in such a way that the poise of a balance is maintained, ie the centre of gravity is retained on the balance axis so that it does not have a 'heavy' side.

Middle-temperature error is a fact of life with the cut-compensated balance. In numerous auxiliary compensations[2] additions to the balance are made in an attempt to limit excessive compensation or to bring in extra mass when temperature changes are large, but no perfect solution has been found. These refinements are usually for use in the boxed marine chronometer and are rarely found in watches. An alternative approach was a metallurgical one. In the late nineteenth and early twentieth centuries, special nickel-iron alloys were developed in Switzerland by Charles Edouard Guillaume. One of these, used in place of steel as the inner layer in a cut-compensated balance, achieved compensation which considerably reduced middle-temperature error. Guillaume also developed an alloy which did not expand or contract when subjected to changes in temperature. Known as Invar, this had considerable potential as a balance material for it would eliminate the expansion and contraction errors mentioned above.

The elasticity problems, however, remained. Guillaume took his metallurgical work a stage further and worked out the correct alloying materials for a balance spring which would have no change of elasticity with temperature, and after some years of experiment Elinvar was successfully developed. Thus from 1919 it was possible to have a watch with Elinvar spring and Invar balance which should have minimal errors due to temperature change. These alloys had disadvantages such as being prone to rust, difficult to work or susceptible to magnetic effects but, following Guillaume's lead, metallurgists have produced improved materials for use in watches — Nivarox for example. Not all watches incorporate these advanced compensation techniques.

Accuracy is affected by the rate of vibration of a watch. With a high-count train, ie one with a high rate of vibration, one faulty vibration will have less effect than with a low-count train. The 'count' is obtained by multiplying together the numbers of teeth on the centre, third, fourth and escape wheels and dividing by the product of the numbers of teeth on the third, fourth and escape-wheel pinions. This will give the number of complete vibrations per hour, since it is based on one revolution of the centre wheel. The count is usually twice the number of complete vibrations, since there are two escapes per vibration on all but duplex and chronometer watches. Bearing in mind that the fourth wheel must rotate once per minute if it is to indicate seconds, there are a considerable number of combinations of teeth on these wheels and pinions which may be used in a train. A common count is 18,000 per hour, which means that there are 5 escapes or 2.5 complete vibrations per second. Older watches will have lower counts — 14,400 per hour representing a watch beating quarter seconds is frequently used. The modern quartz-crystal electronic watches with very high-frequency vibrations have an inherently high degree of accuracy.

As accuracy increases in a watch, errors which were relatively small begin to assume a new significance. One such error results from a watch's position. A clock or chronometer can be regulated to keep good time in one situation, but a pocket watch is required to give comparable accuracy regardless of how it lies. A series of tests on a good watch, in which temperature effects have been minimised and the remainder allowed for by a rate of loss or gain, would show that this rate varies slightly, depending on whether the watch is tested with the 3, 6, 9 or 12 figure on the dial uppermost. One method of dealing with positional error is to attend to the shape of the terminal curves and the way in which the spring is pinned to the balance and the cock, all of which needs considerable skill.[8] Another method is to use a rotating escapement — the tourbillon or karrusel discussed in Chapter 7.

A good nineteenth- or early twentieth-century pocket watch with a detached escapement would be of three-quarter plate calibre using a balance mass would be adjusted with the balance timing-screws, and temperature-compensated balance. The very best watches would have a double-roller lever or detent escapement. The effective radius of the balance mass would be adjusted with the balance tuning-screws, and the compensating-screws would be set to keep correct time at two chosen temperatures — perhaps 5°C (41°F) and 25°C (77°F). The middle-temperature error would be largest at about 15°C (59°F) and there might be a rate of gain of one to two seconds per day. The watch would operate at about 25°C (77°F) in a pocket and perhaps at 5°C (41°F) at night on the bedroom stand, so that the average rate of gain would be less than this maximum.

With such a carefully adjusted watch there would be no regulator for the owner to 'play' with, and so the watch would be termed 'free sprung' (Plate 28). A regulator operating curb pins on the balance

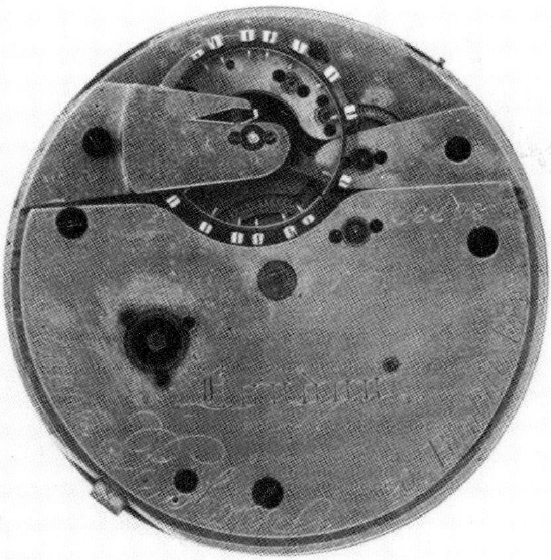

Plate 28 A free-sprung, fully jewelled, half-plate English lever movement by James Bishopp, London, *c*1870. It has a reversed fusee and an 'up and down' dial which shows the state of winding. A high quality watch so carefully adjusted as to need no regulator.

spring would only interfere with careful adjustment, though such a device is used on less finely tuned watches. Some carefully adjusted watches also have a 'reversed fusee' to reduce wear, meaning that the fusee chain is led to the *inside* of the fusee rather than the outside. This results in the net load on the pivots being proportional to the difference between the chain force and the centre-wheel pinion reaction, rather than to the sum of these two forces as in the usual fusee arrangement. Many precision watches have an 'up and down' dial to indicate the amount of time left before the mainspring is run down.

It is important to distinguish between error in a watch (or chronometer) and its rate of loss or gain. A navigator with a chronometer needs to know the latter so that he can correct the indicated time to give Greenwich Time — the actual error is of no significance. A pocket-watch owner expects his watch to indicate the correct time and is therefore interested in the error being as small as possible, preferably zero. Zero, however, is an unrealistic expectation for a mechanical watch for, even if all faults except friction could be eliminated, the variation due to friction would preclude perfection. The watch owner does not expect to apply a rate to his watch, and indeed the way it is used in his pocket would mean that the rate would vary. The watch, in fact, could lose and gain at different times and still have a net error of zero in a day.

Provided the instantaneous error at any time is small, the watch owner should be satisfied.

A simple timekeeping trial which demonstrates the complexity of temperature and positional errors was made by the author using an English lever watch with fusee, in a case hallmarked 1866. The balance was not temperature compensated. The amount of 'wind' of the mainspring was the same at the start of each trial (three-quarters full) to avoid errors in the fusee to spring matching. The results are tabulated below:

Test	*Position*	*Temperature*	*Rate in seconds per hour*
1	Dial up	15°C (59°F)	+4
2	In pocket	25°C (77°F)	−11
3	Pendant up	12°C (54°F)	−8
4*	Dial up	15°C (59°F)	+4½
5	Pendant horizontal	15°C (59°F)	0

* Test 4 is a repeat of Test 1 as a check on consistency of results

The figures show that there is a considerable change in rate as the position is changed from dial up to pendant up at approximately the same temperature. If the owner wanted good timekeeping he would be advised to keep his watch in the pendant-up position overnight (on a watch stand) and adjust the regulator so that the watch loses about 1½ seconds an hour in his pocket and gains at a similar rate on the stand. With this setting, the dial-up rate would be a gain of perhaps 15 seconds an hour.

Having solved the problem of timekeeping at sea and applied the results to the pocket watch, it might be thought that the story of timekeeping was finished. On a local basis this was true. Within a small area each person could adjust his watch sufficiently for all practical purposes. But, as we have seen, time became more important as the industrial society developed since factories worked fixed hours. It also became important as people began to travel on coaches or railways rather than use private transport (Plate 29). Timetables were required which would be in local time for each stop, but which would enable a driver to use elapsed time based on the local time at his starting place. Several solutions were possible. Timetables with starting-point time and local time for each stop is a relatively easy one, but obviously some standardisation of time was required. A letter in a newspaper of 1874 about passengers who missed their train because the local church clock was wrong, illustrates the problem.[9]

Plate 29 English lever-escapement watch with 24-hour dial, perhaps for train travel. For this, the only modification needed to a standard watch is in the motion work. The silver case is hallmarked 1884.

Organisation of time started with the establishment of Greenwich Time (colloquially known as 'railway time') in 1880 by the Definition of Time Act.[10] It is easier to enact a law than to operate it, and a communication system was needed to give regular time-checks to locations all over the country so that the value of standard time was known. Fortunately the electric-telegraph system was available and the Post Office had, in mid-century, established a limited service to transmit time and this scheme was extended after the 1880 Act. Other, private, companies also took up the challenge of transmitting Greenwich Time. In London 'Big Ben' became useful from 1859, and maps were published to show the elapsed time for its sound to reach various districts.

Similar schemes were adopted in other countries and in 1884, at an international conference in the USA, the Greenwich meridian was set up as the zero of longitude and an international time-zone system established on this basis. With the advent of wireless, the Post Office transmissions (and other similar systems in various parts of the world) became redundant, and the time was distributed by radio waves. Everyone today has access to the right time, and yet time as such has become an 'enemy' rather than a friendly ticking longcase clock or a splendid nineteenth-century watch and chain stretched over an ample stomach.

Chronology of Timekeeping in Pocket Watches

1500	Stackfreed
*c*1500	Fusee, set up and stop work
1675	Balance spring and regulator
*c*1730	Temperature compensation
1761	Harrison's 'No 4' with remontoire
*c*1770	Detached escapement
*c*1780	Compensation balances
*c*1780	Successful chronometers
*c*1780	Terminal curves
1795	Tourbillon
*c*1830	Auxiliary compensation
1870	Positional adjustment
(1880	Standard Time)
1894	Karrusel
*c*1900	Metallurgical solutions

9
COLLECTING

Collecting is a natural instinct and, if a sustained interest in pocket watches develops, collecting watches and watch-related artifacts is a likely outcome. Indeed it is very difficult to appreciate the details of a watch and its workings without having considerable numbers to examine at close quarters. Watches can be examined in museums and collections, but it is often not easy to see a particular part because the watch is closed or turned over. The real value of museums and collections is to be able to see examples of watches so rare or expensive as to be unavailable to the ordinary collector (see Chapter 12).

It is convenient to consider watch collecting in chronological groups. The first group might be pre-1600 watches which are undoubtedly museum pieces —and there could be arguments for not allowing such rare objects to rest in private hands. A second group would be post-1600 but pre-balance-spring watches are also rare and therefore already mainly in museums or private collections. This was a period of decoration, and the watches appeal also to connoisseurs of enamelling and jewellery so that prices are relatively high. A 'puritan' watch in a plain oval case of blackened, tarnished silver and probably rather battered in appearance might possibly be found, but with television giving wide publicity to all antiques it becomes less likely.

The next period offers more hope. After the introduction of the balance spring in 1675 there was a period of experiment followed by fifty years of attractive, conservative design with decorated movements, champlevé dials etc. These watches are still expensive, but plain white-enamel dialled watches in plain silver pair-cases of after 1750 are quite common. Their price invites considerable thought before purchase, but it is within the range of possibility. Thus collecting becomes viable from about 1750.

The next group, 1775–1830, offers a reasonable chance of a bargain. This is because the pair-case disappears or becomes much less common towards the end of this period, and interesting watches are contained in unimpressive, single cases (Plate 30). Similarly, watches of the next two periods — 1830–1900 and 1900 onwards — may be found at attrac-

Plate 30 A watch which could prove interesting. The period is the second quarter of the nineteenth century. It is single-cased, and could contain a duplex, cylinder or lever escapement. In this case it contains a Massey type II movement and the hallmark is 1828 (see Plate 6).

tive prices, as long as there is no gold in the case. There are, of course, expensive watches in these periods; quality influences the price.

It is difficult to discuss prices except in terms of the amount of money a collector is prepared to spend. Even for the watches that have been described as museum pieces there are a few people who will pay the enormous sums required. These are not ordinary collectors, but investors who seek expert advice from several sources before making a purchase. Such prudence is just as necessary in the more humble price ranges of the ordinary collector. Unless a watch has such special significance that the cost becomes less relevant, the collector must carefully assess its value both on the open market and as an asset to his collection. He must satisfy himself as to its genuineness and condition — whether the case belongs to the movement; whether it is in working order; the likely repairs required; the possibility of finding another if he rejects this one; and the possibility of disposing of this one if a better example is found or if he gives up collecting that period or style. At some level in the price scale, different for each collector, the cost can be considered right for a purchase. Money put into a collection should be regarded as spent; watches only have value when a customer is available and in times of recession prices may fall. A collection is not a gilt-edged investment.

The worldwide recession of the 1980s has, in fact, had a very sobering effect on what was a buoyant antiques market during the 1970s. Some of the major auction houses have had problems, and items at sales have remained unsold, to the disappointment of vendors. In March 1983 *The Times* reported a sale of clocks and instanced one which fetched £29,700 ($47,600) in 1980 but currently only £21,600 ($34,600). Bearing in mind that the vendor paid a premium plus tax on each occasion, the net loss over the three years is about £15,000 ($24,000). During this time interest rates on the capital after tax would have yielded around £10,000 ($16,000). These effects have been felt throughout the market, so that many watches selling for £40 ($64) in 1980 only fetched half this figure in 1983.

Usually, pair-case watches command a higher price than single-case ones. They are recognised as 'out of the ordinary' by the most uninformed vendor; indeed they are often over-priced because of this. Similarly, any form of decoration will increase the price since it is easily recognised by the layman. Silver cases are less expensive than gold, the price of which has varied considerably in recent years. It is a good generalisation that the ordinary collector must try to avoid gold.

If a watch comes from an eminent maker, its price can be ten times that of a similar item from a humbler craftsman. Thus the ordinary collector is unlikely to purchase watches by the greatest names but should be aware of perhaps fifty good makers so that he can recognise a bargain when confronted with one. There is not always time to go away and think about it when you discover a Graham watch, but you must be sure that it is the right Graham at the right price or the right Graham at a price for an ordinary watchmaker's product.

Rather than embark on haphazard collecting, it is worth considering the possibilities within the 1775–1945 period in more detail. The 1775–1830 group enables the collector to acquire examples of many of the escapements described in this book, although it is at the expensive end of the range of viable prices. However, it is one of the more interesting periods because of the considerable variety of watches available. Probably the best way is to start at the 1830 end and work backwards as experience and confidence increase, or when a suitably priced earlier

Elgin Nat'l. Watch Co.

U.S.A.

watch becomes available. It is important not to be over confident, and wisest to study the various types of watch in museums, collections and illustrated literature before purchasing. The style of a case may give an idea of what should be inside, and when the case is opened the style of the cock may give an idea of the type of escapement to be expected. Similarly it is advantageous to know the style of letters used in the hallmarks of the period at the London, Birmingham and Chester assay offices. The majority of available watches will be English, and will have been marked at these centres. Continental watches will not necessarily carry a hallmark.

The 1830–1900 group also offers a variety of escapements, but only in the first few years of the period. After 1840 choice practically ceases. The attractions of collection are therefore the variation in form and layout of the classic English lever; the developments in winding (although early designs are rare); balance types — brass, gold, steel, compensated etc; Swiss machine-made watches from 1840; variations in lever design; early pin-levers; fob watches etc. Each of these, with the exception of the winding types, will offer a choice of watches at the lower end of the price range. Small fob watches, however, often have attractive coloured dials and engraved cases, which tends to raise their price above their horological interest. These watches, usually with cylinder movements, are very often broken; and it is worthwhile establishing the cost of repair to the escapement before purchase.

American watches of this period (Plate 31) are another interesting field for the collector.[1,2] It is unlikely that any of the scarce pre-1850 watches will be found, for so few of these were made. There is the possibility of sub-specialisation within one company, or in the series of companies which form its history. A study of American watches for sale in Britain shows that there are plenty of the Waltham group available from the hundred-year span of its complex of companies (Plate 32). A disadvantage of this field to the British collector is that research would be largely concentrated in America, so that lengthy correspondence may be involved.

(opposite top) Plate 31 Swiss lever-escapement watch by the Elgin National Watch Company of America — an example of a factory-produced watch with gold-plated, engraved case. The movement is shown in Plate 16.

(opposite below) Plate 32 Watch made for a blind man (by Waltham) with feeling points (which can be recognised by touch) and thick robust hands. There is no glass; the hunter case protects the dial. Significantly the hallmark on the case is 1919, when such watches would have been needed by war victims.

From 1900 onwards a collector might specialise in pin-lever watches. Alternatively, an attempt could be made to acquire examples of the complex mechanisms available — repeating, chiming, moonwork, date and day, chronograph, stop etc. There is a tremendous variety of watches available in this period covering a wide range of prices, and it should be possible to build an interesting collection without difficulty.

The problem of fakes exists. It is perhaps relatively insignificant in watches costing a few pounds, but there comes a price when faking is worthwhile. Nobody is going to actually make an 'antique' verge watch in 1800 style, because the cost of making it will exceed the sale price unless the watch is inscribed with a well-known maker's name — in which case the purchaser is likely to make sensible checks to establish the genuine age and not be deceived. However, movements, dials and cases individually worth very little can be brought together and married to produce a watch which may be sold for a considerable sum.

A purchaser would do well to satisfy himself that all the parts belong together. The dial should fit snugly into the recess on the case and not be surrounded by an off-centre gap; the three-part hinge connecting movement, case back and glass bezel should match up. Often the dial, movement and case are numbered, so see if they match. The outer and inner cases should have the same maker's initials and the same hallmark (watches do exist with the marks a year apart). The style of case, dial and movement should match, although bear in mind that a 1770 verge watch could have been recased in 1840 by a relation of the original owner who wanted a more modern-looking case. It is also possible that the original cases were damaged or even so badly worn that at least the outer one had to be renewed. If the movement has been professionally recased the fit will still be perfect, which is unlikely in a marriage. The married movement may show spare holes in the dial plate when the original dial has been replaced, but if the watch has an intermediate hinge-ring between the dial and the movement these will not be visible. There may be a filled-in winding-hole in the back of the case because the married movement has its fusee winding-square in a slightly different place. Wear marks will indicate if the two cases have been together for a long time, and if the bow has been changed there should be different rubbings.

Movements are sometimes modernised. A duplex of 1810 may have broken in 1860, and the owner may have had the escapement changed to a lever which would be considerably easier to get repaired and more satisfactory to use. This work is genuine and may be worth collecting; the error would be to assume the watch to be an early lever.

However much care is taken, many collectors will find that some of their watches are not exactly what they imagined them to be at the time of purchase. This is not to suggest that they have been fooled or that there is a huge industry of putting together parts to sell, but that repairs and replacements made by watchmakers in good faith some considerable time ago are not easy to detect. The watchmaker who crudely recased or modernised a watch would not have attracted custom. A watch that is 200 years old would have to have led a very sheltered life to have survived without some repair.

For some collectors the acquisition of complete watches is unnecessary. An interest in the mechanical form of the watch rather than the complete artefact is a perfectly good reason for collecting, and in this situation the purchase of a quantity of gold and silver which hides the part of interest seems pointless. In the past, many movements have been removed (gently or roughly) from their precious-metal cases which have been melted down; the movements themselves are often available at a fraction of the cost of the complete watch. The older the movement the rarer it becomes, and the more decoration it exhibits. To many collectors this decoration is the attraction, irrespective of the movement's mechanical interest. Sometimes the only part of the movement retained in the scrapping process has been the balance cock. Cocks have even been 'faked' and used as jewellery. There is no excuse for anyone breaking up watches today, but unfortunately the practice continues and pocket-watch movements from single cases dating from 1830 onwards are still becoming available.

A collection of watches may represent an increasing investment as time passes (not necessarily by price inflation but merely because of increased numbers), and it is worth looking at the relevant clauses in the household insurance policy. The collection may need special mention in order to be covered, especially if arranged in some sort of display. Accidental damage due to dropping etc should also be considered.

Where does one buy a watch? At specialist watch dealers, general antique dealers, bric-à-brac shops, junk shops, watchmakers and jewellers. There are also street markets, stalls in market halls and, finally, auction sales. Auctions require time for viewing and assessment of the state and value of the watch (which requires confidence and experience) as well as time for bidding. The bidding can often be made on a customer's behalf by the auctioneer, given written instructions by the customer on the limit of his bidding. If you buy at an auction the watches will be largely 'as found', as will watches bought in markets and junk shops. However, if buying from a specialist watch dealer it may be possible to get a written statement about the watch. Buying from such a specialist is bound to cost more for he has had to seek out the watch, have it put into good order, and hold stock which ties up capital; but it may be a safeguard against making errors in the more expensive ranges. Another source of watches is exchange, both with dealers and friends.

Miscellaneous Items

Watch keys may be collected, but this is a very limited field for early and interesting varieties are rare. The individual key, perhaps enamelled in the same style as the watch, should of course remain with the watch; but it is possible to find a lone survivor. Watch papers are interesting in their own right. These are small, roughly cut, circular pieces of paper inserted between the pair-cases (or sometimes in the back of a double-bottom case), usually with the maker's, repairer's or seller's name and place of work printed on them, but often containing other information. They are not common for they are easily lost, or the original owner may have discarded the 'advertising'.

Watch chains are common enough to enable a collection to be viable. Seals on chains have their own following and are hardly vital to a watch although they might, if attached, provide evidence of the history of a particular watch.

When pocket watches were not in the owner's pocket they were often hung on conveniently fashioned stands (Plate 33). These were made from the sixteenth century, but it is not until the nineteenth, when watches became numerous, that they are found in any quantity. Stands are one of the most useful peripheral items to collect because they were designed to display the watch and are admirable for this purpose.[3]

Research and Records

The data available on every watch, movement etc in a collection should be recorded. A card-index system is useful, or, if you are a computer enthusiast, a disc or tape may be chosen. The watch or movement should be studied, researched and written up by drawing on the store of information in books, museums and private collections; for only by becoming more knowledgeable himself can the collector relate new and perhaps exciting facts to his own acquisitions. A watch acquired

Plate 33 Two watch stands or boxes. The *left-hand* box is made of Amboyna wood with brass inlay, *c*1830. It contains a barred-movement, Swiss-cylinder watch of the same period. There is space for a watch chain under the watch tray. The *right-hand* box is a continental folding stand made of oak, *c*1900. When it is open, the watch is held in a near-vertical position.

quite casually may have a story behind it, or its maker may have hitherto unknown connections. Although most watches will have no traceable history, it is worth making some effort to follow up any promising lead.

The card index should also record mechanical details, work done etc, so that nothing is left to memory. The simplest work done is often forgotten, yet it may prove important later when more information or experience suggests further work.

Watch literature is an enormous field. Books and journals, catalogues and patents relevant to a collection should be bought or borrowed. The use of libraries (public, reference, university, museum, polytechnic and institution) is essential; and library research facilities such as copies of old documents, out of print books and so on are usually available to the genuine enquirer. Reading about the methods used in the past by watchmakers is a help to an understanding of old watches; and the contemporary difficulties of timekeeping, regulation, balance springs and balances may be better appreciated if studied in the original documents. In this way, too, the mathematically minded collector could reach a better understanding of friction, forces and vibrations as explanation of the reasons for the success or failure of many innovations. *Antiquarian Horology*, the journal of the Antiquarian Horological Society, is worth an annual subscription to keep up-to-date with current happenings and research. The Society also holds meetings.

Photographic Records

Photography[4,5] can be used to 'collect' in normally unavailable fields. In particular, it may be possible to obtain permission to photograph watches in museums and private collections. In less-elevated fields, it may be possible to photograph quite ordinary, inexpensive watches in friends' collections or dealers' stock which cannot be purchased because they are not for sale or because of the sheer volume available. A collection representative of a period can consist of both actual watches and photographs.

If photography is to be pursued away from the home, it is necessary to have a travelling rig which can be set up and used with confidence in various locations. Most collectors will already own a camera — hopefully this has the facility to have the standard lens changed for a *macro* lens. Then, with the aid of a rigid stand and adjustable diffused lighting, a routine can be devised to maximise the chance of suitable negatives. Flash lighting is not the best since reflections from shiny metal cannot be predicted.

The picture can be composed in the 'through the lens' viewfinder before any photograph is taken. Then several shots of the watch, covering a small range of exposures, should be made; and the watch should be measured so that the final picture can be enlarged to a particular scaled size. The sequence of photographs should be noted so that no errors in identification occur at a later stage. Much of the work of producing good watch photographs is done in the enlarging by suitable choice of paper and exposure. The collector should therefore process his own work or seek the assistance of someone who possesses the necessary skills. Initially it might be wise to let a professional develop the film, to avoid error at this crucial stage. There is no doubt that it takes time and practice to produce good reflection- and shadow-free watch photographs, and evening classes in photography would be a sound investment.

Making a Watch

The manufacture of a watch is perhaps the ultimate achievement of a mechanically minded collector. It involves the deployment of a variety of skills including machining, fitting, gilding, casemaking and enamelling. It may only be suited to a collector possessing a workshop and sufficient dexterity to justify the time involved, but the skills can often be learned and the necessary equipment used at evening classes in local schools of arts and crafts. Tools may be acquired as a separate collection, for many of them are specialised and obsolete.[6,7]

Conclusion

There are many other possibilities for collectors, and it is possible to find a niche to suit the pocket of any enthusiast. And in all the emphasis on research and skills, it is important that the simple collector is not deterred. It is not necessary to seek these specialisations, for there is pleasure in finding and keeping a haphazard collection of watches simply because you like them. This is the most important aspect of collecting: the magpie instinct.

10
REPAIRS

Watchmaker's tools have been developed during the past four hundred years to solve technical problems as they arose. In the earliest days they would have been adapted from blacksmith's and locksmith's equipment, and for the problem of smaller size there may have been 'assistance' from jewellery equipment which would certainly have included hand tools for working metals into decorative wear. Apart from size, the main difference between clock- and watch-work and blacksmith's, locksmith's and jeweller's work is the use of wheels and pinions, and much of the development of tools was aimed at producing 'engines' to make satisfactory toothed wheels and dies to draw toothed pinions. Hand-cutting and filing of teeth are repetitive operations, and thus obvious candidates for replacement by less time-consuming methods. Once the engines had been devised, better and more diverse forms were possible.

A collection of watchmaker's tools is worthwhile for several reasons. Firstly, the tools themselves are interesting in their own right. Many are quite elaborately finished, whilst others are quite crude, distinguishing the well finished but ordinary bought tools[1] from the special tools made for a particular job by a watchmaker who was interested in performance rather than appearance. Secondly, the variety of engines that were developed during the eighteenth and nineteenth centuries[2] is of interest in the light of both the type and the quantity of watches made. Thirdly, a collection of tools is useful to a watch collector in that he can use them to repair his watches.

Collectable and very useful hand-tools include vices, pliers, drills, anvils, stakes, files, compasses etc. Engines are very attractive artifacts, but complex and expensive so that a large collection would require a large investment. They include designs to make wheels, pinions, fusees, escapements and tooth shapers. The most useful simple engine for a watch collector to own and use is the 'turns', on which a number of operations can be performed. A selection of drawings of tools and engines, which are probably easier to understand than photographs, can be found in Smith.[3] In this chapter, tools are considered only for their usefulness in repair work.

A watch, when found, may be in any of several states. If it is not working — due to damage such as bending or breakage of parts, missing parts, corrosion etc — its value both in terms of money and as part of a collection may be considerably reduced. On the other hand it may be so old or so rare that it has more value in an unrestored condition than a restored one. A watch may be in what can be called 'ticking order' — complete and working in a desultory and discontinuous way due to excessive wear, dirt, minor damage — but a watch in 'working order' may be expected to go continuously under reasonable conditions, though the timekeeping may be poor and unreliable. It may also be reluctant to go satisfactorily in all positions, working perfectly well on a desk when the dial is up, but soon stopping when carried about in the pocket. Finally, a watch may be in good working order, or as good as the average watch in daily use — it tells the time as accurately as its inherent capabilities allow. It is unrealistic, for instance, to expect a verge watch to give the same performance as a late-Victorian lever watch. It is also unrealistic to expect a watch to give of its best unless it regularly receives expert attention.

A collector must decide whether he requires the watches in his collection to work, or whether they can remain as he finds them. There is something to be said on both sides but it seems reasonable that, with the exception of watches so rare that restoration could be detrimental, a watch which is a device for telling the time should be able to work in some fashion. Assuming that the collector subscribes to this view, he may take his watches to a watchmaker; but this often means a long wait, for the work may involve making a missing part with time-consuming trial-and-error fitting. Also, a watchmaker is usually so busy with the regular maintenance and repair of modern watches that he has little time for investigating and repairing an antique. Besides this, the repair could be so expensive as to exceed the value of the watch to the collector. Therefore, when a damaged watch is for sale, the collector who employs a watchmaker to do his repairs would be wise to get an estimate of the cost of restoration before he decides on purchase.

Many collectors choose a more interesting alternative and repair their watches themselves. The work is extremely time-consuming, but it makes an absorbing hobby, bringing considerable satisfaction when a watch which may have been broken for a long time is finally brought to life. There are two distinct approaches — as an amateur, or as a sparetime watchmaker. The latter approach will mean tackling the work in a professional way, purchasing at considerable expense all the equipment needed to restore or renew any part of any watch. The collector taking this approach may already have the necessary skills, but if not he must teach himself or attend classes in watchmaking, silversmithing, enamelling etc. These subjects have their own literature.[4–8] Usually sparetime-watchmaker status is achieved after some years of interest, and probably after experience with the amateur approach discussed below. Eventually such a collector will seriously consider making his own watch, preferably incorporating as many complex mechanisms as he can.

The amateur approach usually starts with very limited aims: firstly, to be able to restore the majority of watches to at least ticking and preferably working order so that they will run continuously in at least one position; and secondly, to gain skill, confidence and experience so that more ambitious work can be attempted. Initially an amateur will not be capable of making new parts, but he can use ingenuity and spare parts from the other watches. His lack of skill and equipment will mean that for a while there will be watches that he will have to accept as not working, but as progress is made the problems that seemed insurmountable will become possible.

One way to start work is to acquire inexpensive broken pocket-watch movements and to repair these. Try to avoid using movements with damaged escapements, since these are not the ideal parts to tackle first. One of the most important characteristics to develop is patience. The parts are very small and continuous use of the eyeglass is tiring. Pieces have to be filed and tried for size then removed and filed again, which can mean repeated assembly and stripping. Impatience will lead to damage and lack of confidence. It is most important in repair work to think out each step carefully, especially if any cutting or filing away of material is involved. An error at this stage means a fresh start. Many jobs take a long time, and the restoration of a badly damaged movement could take months. There is no hurry, make it an enjoyable hobby.

As in any other work involving tools it is not necessary to own all those that might be useful. Only a limited number are required for most of the work and, when a special job occurs, the right tool can be purchased or devised and made. Watch repair work is an old trade; all the tools have been made before and are illustrated in books.[4–8]

Rules for the Amateur Watch Repairer

1 Never do anything permanent. It should always be possible to return the watch to its original state. Later, a better way of repairing may occur, skills may improve, more equipment may become available, or the watch may turn out to be more desirable in the original state having been discovered to be unique or rare.
2 Never start to dismantle a watch with the mainspring wound. This is extremely important because the majority of escapements will allow the watch to run at high speed as the balance staff is withdrawn. If this happens there is a good chance of damage. The mainspring should be let down.
3 Always study and, if necessary, sketch or photograph the original state before starting work. Never dismantle a mechanism that is not recognised and understood. Find out what it is and how it works, then decide how to proceed.
4 Be careful of applying force unless the construction is well understood. Unscrewing a left-hand thread with the customary anticlockwise motion will result in breaking the head from the screw — a simple example of misapplied force.
5 Always work on a clean bench and put the microscopic parts away as they are removed.
6 Always make a new part rather than cut or drill an existing one. Cutting and drilling are irreversible. Some modern glues are very strong, and parts may be glued into place rather than screwed.

Tools and Materials

These two lists can be regarded as the minimum needed to make small repairs.

Tools

screwdrivers
tweezers
pliers
needle files
broaches (cutting and polishing)
boxwood movement-stands
small vice
stake and punches
screwhead slotting-file
workbench
swivel light
centre punch
pin vices
knife
steel rule
eyeglass
Archimedean drill and drills
dividers/compasses

micrometer
hammers
dust covers
spirit lamp
scriber
calipers

Materials

small-diameter brass and steel wire for pins etc
benzine and ammonia for cleaning
lubricating oil
releasing oil
replacement glasses
replacement mainsprings
replacement staffs
glues (Araldite, shellac etc)
pegwood
Arkansas stone
fine emery paper, polishing powder
old watch movements and parts
solder (and soldering iron)

The following are tools to purchase as and when they become available or essential:

set of turns (or a lathe)
staking tool
depthing tool
arbor-drilling jig
Jacot tool
spring-winding tools

Simple turns operated by hand-held bow (Plate 34) enable a tremendous variety of jobs to be tackled — new staffs, pivots, bushes, attention to distorted wheels etc. Reference should be made to the specialist texts which describe the methods used.[4–8] Essentially the staking tool comprises a rotating platform with a range of hole sizes and a set of punches. The tool has a vertical guide through which the selected punch is inserted, the guide holding the punch so that its centre is exactly in line with the hole in the stake. Thus there is no fear of breakage and no problem of lining up and holding both work and punch. The staking tool is used for riveting, punching, staff removal, inserting of bushes, jewels etc. A depthing tool (Plate 34) enables wheels and pinions to be tested out of the movement for satisfactory performance and saves much stripping and reassembly between adjustments. The arbor drilling jig (Plate 34) holds the arbor to be drilled between centres. One centre has a hollow end which acts as a guide to the drill being offered to the arbor end. The arbor is rotated to drill the hole. A Jacot tool is a special form of turns provided with supports for small-diameter pivots. It is used for burnishing pivots to improve the surface finish and reduce friction. Spring-winders coil up mainsprings for insertion in the barrel, thus avoiding the axial distortion caused by hand insertion.

Plate 34 Three useful tools. *(Top left)* a set of turns (held in a vice). The centre slider is a tool rest, the left-hand slider is the work holder and the right-hand slider a tailstook. A bow would be used to rotate the pulley with the protruding pin rotating the work. *(Bottom left)* a depthing tool in which the meshing of wheels and pinions can be tested. The spiked ends can be used for marking out plates or checking centre distances. The *right-hand* tool is a vice-held drilling jig. The arbor to be drilled is held between the drill guide on the left and the slider on the right. The drill is offered through the guide, and the arbor to be drilled is rotated.

With these tools added to the original list, virtually the only job that cannot be tackled is the manufacture of a new escape wheel. It is possible to make an escape wheel for a verge watch and an English lever watch, but great skill and care is needed. If such a part is required it may be best to have the work done by a specialist repairer who has the necessary wheel-cutting devices. This can be expensive.

Common Faults

Examination of a considerable number of movements that are not working produces the following groups of common faults:

Worn parts	*Bent parts*	*Broken parts*	
pivot holes	pivots	pillars	pawls
jewels	wheels	pivots	ratchets
pivots	arbors	wheels	pinions
	plates	springs	verge staffs
		detents	cylinder plugs

Missing parts		*Special problems*	
motion work	cocks	balance springs	blueing
pins	dials	fusee chains	hands
wheels	hands	fusee clicks	dials
jewels		mainsprings	glasses
		Geneva stopwork	cases

Removing the Movement

The above are the parts that will need attention most frequently but before this the watch movement must be taken to pieces. This can be tricky because, even when the method of dismantling a watch is known, there may be problems caused by corrosion, rust, oil or damaged pins. It is sometimes helpful, when the movement is completely and utterly clogged with grease and dirt, to immerse the whole watch or movement in paraffin or other suitable fluid for as long as is necessary. This type of treatment should be used with care to ensure no damage can result. When the movement is ready for stripping it should (if not already out) be removed from the case. In older watches this is achieved by pushing out the brass pin through the hinge on the movement and, in more modern watches, by removing the screws securing the movement to the case and passing the movement through the case front. These are the most usual types of fixing but there are other less common varieties.

Having taken the movement from the case, the next step is to let down the mainspring.

Letting Down a Mainspring

In early verge watches the mainspring set up is by worm and wheel between the plates. A small key is required to fit the winding-square on the end of the worm shaft, and the shaft is turned until there is no tension left in the chain connecting fusee and spring-barrel. If the watch is fully wound, this will require a considerable amount of turning (Fig 34).

In later verge watches and English watches of the nineteenth century, the set up is under the dial. Remove the dial and fit a key into the square protruding from the end of the ratchet wheel. Slacken the screw which holds the pawl tight. By initially tightening the spring, the load can be taken from the pawl so that it can be pushed back with pegwood

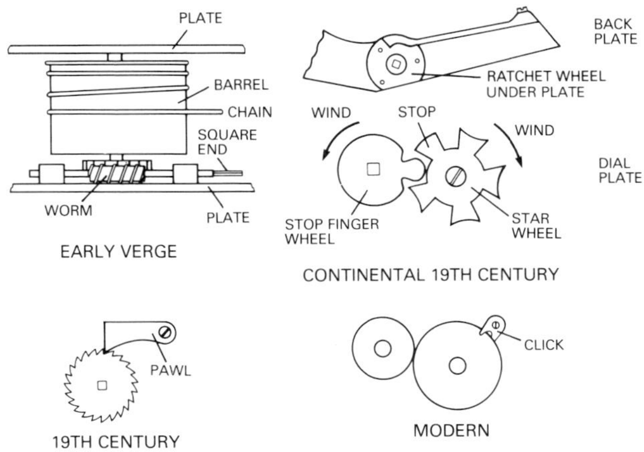

Fig 34 Mainspring set up

to free the ratchet. Hold the key firmly so that the spring does not fly undone; if there is any danger of slipping, push the pawl back and perform the operation in stages. At the end of the letting down remove the loose ratchet wheel. Sometimes the amount of square protruding through the ratchet wheel is too short for this method, in which case let the ratchet off, tooth by tooth, using a screwdriver as a detent when the pawl is out of engagement. In continental keywind watches with a going-barrel and barred movement there will be two places calling for attention when letting down the mainspring. Viewed from the back plate, the click keeping the spring wound is close to the winding-square forming a V-shaped detent integral with, and on the end of, a leaf-spring. This detent can be levered back and the spring allowed to unwind with the key held in the hand. Under the dial there will be a star wheel which is part of the stopwork fitted to limit the use of the spring to the middle portion only. Hold the lower (adjacent) square by the key and remove the star wheel. Holding the key in the hand allow the set up to unwind. Examine the action of the star wheel before removing it so that later it can be reset correctly with about three-quarters of a turn of set up. It can be seen that one arm of the star has a convex rather than a concave end, and will not pass the stop. The number of complete rotations of the winding-barrel is limited by the number of concave ends.

In modern watches the spring click holding the winding train can easily be seen above the top plate. The winding button is tensioned in the wind direction to remove the load from the click which is eased out of engagement with pegwood. The winding button must be held during this operation and then allowed to rotate slowly as the spring unwinds. It may be necessary to allow the click to re-engage and perform the letting down in increments.

There are other less common mainspring arrangements, and careful attention to Rule 3 on page 129 is advised so that accidents are avoided.

Stripping a Verge Watch and Reassembly

The movement must first be removed from the case by pushing out the hinge pin. This may be tapered and care should be taken to push in the right direction. If it is stuck apply a little releasing oil, but it is not worth using undue force as the movement can sometimes be removed without disturbing this pin. To do this, remove the hands and the dial (see below). The effect of removing the dial, if a separate dial plate is fitted, will be to release the movement from the case leaving the dial attached to the case. The remainder of the operations are presented as a list. These instructions are for the older verge watch with complete unbroken top and bottom plates and worm set up between them. Later verge watches with a bar on the bottom plate, separate barrel cover on the top plate and ratchet and pawl set up are stripped by the lever-watch method (see page 135).

Before starting to strip make sure that reassembly is possible. Put all the parts away as they are removed, labelling and sketching as necessary. Try to avoid having parts of several watches on the same bench.

1 Remove the hands using home-made levers or a puller. Protect the dial when using levers.
2 Remove the pins holding the dial or dial-backing ring from the bottom plate. There will be three feet protruding through the plate which are secured by pins. Beware of the motion work which may fall loose and get lost as the dial is removed. Lift the dial upwards off the movement to avoid this problem.
3 Remove the motion work.
4 Let down the mainspring. Support the movement on a boxwood stand whilst doing this.
5 Remove the balance cock, which is secured by a single screw.
6 Remove the taper pin holding the balance spring to the block on the plate. Remove the balance-spring end from the block and curb pins on the regulator.
7 Carefully lift out the balance complete with spring.
8 Remove the regulator mechanism and other decorative pieces from the plate.

9 Push out the four pins holding the plate to the pillars, noting the position of the short pins.
10 Carefully lift off the top plate, to which the crown wheel will remain attached.
11 Remove wheels, barrel, fusee chain and fusee. The centre wheel will remain attached to the bottom plate.
12 If necessary, remove the crown wheel by pulling out the end-bearing which is a taper fit.
13 If necessary, remove the centre wheel by removing the cannon pinion from the dial side of the bottom plate.
14 Check the action of the fusee stop-piece.

Reassembly is achieved by reversing the sequence of operations. The difficult step is replacing the top plate, which must pass over the pivots of no less than five pieces. This must be done very carefully to avoid breaking a pivot. The watch is built up on a boxwood stand and, after the top plate is replaced, assembly is straightforward. Lubricate the pivots of the watch but not the wheel teeth. Fit the balance so that the watch will be in beat. Test the running by applying a slight clockwise twisting force to the winding-square of the fusee which simulates the mainspring action. The last part to be fitted to the movement is the fusee chain. Wind this onto the fusee by the normal winding mechanism, and insert the hook at the end into the slit in the barrel (the barrel hook is the barbed one). Turn the set-up worm to apply tension to the chain and allow the watch to run until this set up is used up. Apply more set up etc until eventually the fusee chain is on the barrel with the spring unwound. Replace the motion work, dial and hands.

Stripping a Lever Watch and Reassembly

Remove the movement from the case by pushing out the hinge pin in a similar way to that described for the verge watch. Some late lever movements may be held in place with screws with either half-heads to be rotated free, or whole-heads to be removed completely. These types of movement pass out through the front of the case. If a button wind is fitted, it must be pulled back out of engagement or the small screw holding the stem in place must be slackened to allow the winding-stem to be removed. The list of instructions below applies to the nineteenth-century lever watch, but with obvious adaptations it also applies to the late verge watch and to other nineteenth-century English watches with a variety of escapements.

1–7 Remove the hands, dial and motion work. Let down the mainspring. Remove the cock, the taper pin holding the balance spring and the balance. Detailed instructions for these operations are described above under 'Stripping a Verge Watch and Reassembly'. The watch should be on a boxwood stand.

8 Remove the barrel covering-plate held by two screws. Never attempt this with the balance in place or the mainspring wound.

9 Remove the barrel and the fusee chain if on the barrel. If the fusee-chain hook is stuck in the fusee, a little releasing oil may help. The set-up ratchet wheel from the back of the plate should have been removed when the mainspring was let down. If not, it will now be loose.

10 Turn the watch over and remove the bar across the third wheel This is held by two screws. Remove the third wheel.

11 Turn the watch over and remove the four pins holding the top plate to the pillars. Note where the short pins belong.

12 Turn the watch over. Carefully separate the plates leaving the wheels on the top plate on the stand. The centre wheel will come with the bottom plate. Watch the lever very carefully as it can foul the potence.

13 Remove the wheels, fusee (and chain) and maintaining-power detent. Remove the lever, which is partly underneath the balance bottom-bearing.

14 If necessary, remove the centre wheel by removing the push-fit cannon pinion from the dial side of the bottom plate.

15 Check the action of the fusee stop-piece.

To reassemble, reverse the operations. Place the top plate on the stand, insert the lever under the balance bottom-bearing and between the banking pins, insert the escape wheel, fourth wheel, fusee and fusee detent. The dial plate with centre wheel is then placed on top and the only pivots to be fitted are the lever, the escape-wheel and the fusee-detent. Great care is still needed to avoid breaking a pivot. When inserted, turn the movement over on the stand (being careful to hold it together) and insert the four pins holding the top plate to the pillars. Again reverse the movement on the stand, replace the fourth wheel in its pivot as it will have fallen out with the reversals, insert the third wheel and fit the bar across the plate supporting the fusee, third- and fourth-wheel pivots. Reverse the movement on the stand and replace the barrel and barrel plate. Lubricate the pivots of the watch but not the wheel teeth.

The chain of a lever watch can be put back before the balance is fitted. This avoids the chance of damaging the balance; but the chain cannot be put back at this stage in any other escapement. In the lever watch the chain is wound onto the barrel using the square protruding from the dial-plate underside: hold the movement so that the barrel-arbor is horizontal and allow the chain to run under a finger which keeps a small pull on the chain. If the chain is slack it may slip off the barrel and jam on the arbor. If this happens, remove the barrel plate and barrel, then the chain, and start again. Pulling at the chain may break it. When the chain is on the barrel, continue to use the finger to hold it and hook the free end to the fusee. Place the ratchet wheel onto the square and apply set up to put the chain in tension. Push the pawl into the ratchet with pegwood and tighten the pawl screw. Replace the balance and pin so that the watch is in beat. Make sure that the impulse jewel is on the correct side of the lever-fork, or the train will be locked. Replace the cock. The running can be tested immediately as the chain is already in tension under the set up. Finally, replace the motion work, dial and hands.

In the late verge watch, and other escapements except the lever, the balance and cock must be replaced before the chain is put in. In these cases test the running by applying a small clockwise torque to the fusee winding-square which simulates the mainspring action. Then wind the chain onto the fusee using the normal winding mechanism and gradually work it back onto the barrel by applying small amounts of set up. This technique is described under 'Stripping a Verge Watch and Reassembly' above. If the watch has a dust cover this should be fitted when applying the small increments of set up; it will protect the balance.

Stripping and Reassembly of Other Escapements

Watches with other escapements will usually be of similar construction to the early verge or the lever. Thus the techniques above may be used. The most important points are to make sure that the mainspring is let down before removing the balance, and not to apply any spring tension until the balance is replaced. Pocket chronometers, unrecognised escapements, tourbillons, karrusels etc should not be disturbed by the amateur.

There will also be watches that are assembled in different ways, for example the half-plate design. These may be taken apart carefully without damage, provided that the basic methods above are used.

In key-wind watches with the set-hands-square on the back plate, both the centre wheel and the cannon pinion are push-fitted to the arbor. The arbor is removed complete with the set-hands-square from the back plate after removing the hands, dial and cannon pinion.

Cleaning a Watch

When a watch has been taken apart it may be cleaned by immersion in benzine. However, the mainspring in the barrel, the balance and the lever should not be immersed but should be brushed clean with the same liquid — prolonged immersion could disturb jewel settings. Do not be tempted to use petrol or any other solvent. Benzine immersion degreases the parts, which should then be brushed clean and dry. Holes and jewels should be cleaned out with pieces of pegwood. Pinion and wheel teeth may also be pegged clean if covered with dirt. Benzine treatment should bring the whole watch to a satisfactory state, but if the gilding on plates and wheels is not good enough it may be cleaned with a weak solution of ammonia applied with a soft brush and washed off with water. Thorough drying is essential to avoid rust in the future. The ammonia treatment should be tested on a spare part from another watch to judge the strength and result.

Pivots may be polished by using a polishing powder in a hole in the end of a piece of pegwood. This method, which will not repair damage but merely buff up the pivot which should afterwards be washed off in benzine, is of dubious merit. It could result in breaking a pivot and, in general, unless pivots show bad blemishes, they should be left alone.

After a watch has been cleaned, the parts should be touched only at their edges or held in tissue paper. This avoids transferring grease or perspiration to them. However, a fingerprint is preferable to a dropped watch, and discretion should be used.

Lubrication

Only the pivots of a watch train and escapement need to be lubricated; the wheel teeth should not be treated with any oil. The oil should be applied with a fine-wire dropper to the reservoirs in the plates (or in early watches to the pivot point). Only the smallest amount should be put on the dropper to avoid drips in the wrong places — dirt or dust will stick to oil and form abrasive mixtures. A good quality oil should be chosen and the container should be kept tightly closed as the action of the atmosphere is harmful.

Strictly speaking, different grades of oil should be used on train and balance pivots; but for the collector whose watches are not going to run continuously a single grade may be chosen. Similarly, in a lever watch, the pallets should have a microscopic amount of lubrication; but for the collector it is better to keep oil from this area. The watch is not going to run continuously and some modern watches do not use pallet lubrication at all. The impulse jewel in a lever watch should not be lubricated. Oil is, however, required in the spring-barrel. The surface of the spring should be coated to avoid rust, and the top and bottom of the inner-barrel surface on which the spring rubs need lubrication.

The following are descriptions of methods used to correct a number of faults. All the methods are suited to amateurs, and should not be regarded as the only way of tackling a job.

Putting into Beat

Often a watch will tick unevenly and stop because the neutral mid-position of the balance vibration is not in line with the correct point of the engaging lever, crown wheel or escape wheel. The watch is *out of beat*, and to set the watch in beat these points must be correctly lined up. A study of the action of the various escapements will indicate the correct position. For example, the mid-vibration position for the balance of a table-roller lever watch is with the impulse jewel in the centre of lever notch. Since the lever does not remain in this position but is to one side or the other, some judgement is required. This is true of all levers, and special care will be needed with a rack lever since there is positive engagement between the balance and the lever.

The first step in adjusting the beat is to let the mainspring down (see page 132) so that no accidents can occur. The neutral position of the balance can now be altered by unpinning the outer end of the balance spring from the post on the plate and rotating the balance the required amount in the appropriate direction. It may be necessary to remove the cock to gain access to the pin securing the outer end of the spring. If there is not enough spring available, or it has been broken off, adjustment may be gained at the other end of the spring. Remove the balance and rotate the split collet holding the inner end of the spring to provide adjustment at the outer end. The collet is a friction fit on the balance staff. Should this action be necessary it is likely that the balance spring has been broken off short, and this means that once the watch is in beat it will gain. This may be corrected by increasing the balance inertia or renewing the spring. When making adjustments to balance springs extreme care must be taken, for their shape is important in maintaining isochronous performance. Once they are bent out of shape the rate of the watch will vary, especially if used in a variety of positions.

Checking for Faults

If a watch will not tick or show any sign of motion, and there is no obvious damage, it should be carefully stripped and cleaned. The train pivots should be examined for damage and any really bad pivots straightened, cleaned, polished or renewed. The holes in the plates should be pegged out and examined for damage. Really bad holes should be cleaned up with a polishing broach, and extreme cases may be bushed. Unless accurate timekeeping is the aim, it should suffice to clean up the holes rather than rebush in cases of moderate wear. Bent or damaged wheels should be straightened or renewed. Check the action of the fusee to see that the power is being transmitted. It has been assumed that a broken mainspring is not the cause of the trouble, but the barrel cover should be removed to examine the state of the spring and to see that it is correctly attached at either end.

Reassemble the train without the fusee chain and without the escapement (balance or balance and lever), then apply a small clockwise torque to the fusee winding-square to simulate the mainspring action. The train should run freely. If it does not, there is an undetected fault. When satisfactory, fit the balance so that the watch is in beat; then again apply clockwise torque to the winding-square. The watch should run. If not, there is a fault in the escapement to be detected.

In the case of the lever watch, the fusee chain may be replaced before the balance is fitted. It will have been necessary to take the train to pieces to insert the lever, but when the chain is tensioned the action of the lever may be examined. When the lever is given a small displacement from the banking pin (by pushing the *fork* end across) and then released, the draw should snap the lever back to the banking pin. When given a larger displacement to unlock the train, the lever should snap over to the other banking pin. This action can be tested for a complete revolution of the escape wheel, ie 30 escapes for a 15-tooth wheel. Providing this action is satisfactory the watch should work once the balance is fitted. A useful fault-finding list is included in Gazeley.[4]

Balance Springs

If a balance spring is missing or damaged, it should be replaced with one of appropriate strength and size obtained either from a watchmaker or from an old watch. The count of the train will give the strength, and the spring diameter must fit the regulator curb pins. After the new spring has been fitted to the collet in the correct manner shown in Fig 35, make sure that it is central and in the correct plane. The holding pin should have a flat side against the spring and should not protrude beyond the hole through the collet. Place the collet on the balance staff in such a position that the watch can be put into beat. Next, test the rate of the new spring. Grip the spring with a pair of tweezers at the point that the curb pins will hold, and rest the pivot of the balance on a smooth surface such as a watch-glass. Set the balance vibrating and count the vibrations. Minor adjustments are possible by the putting-into-beat methods (see page 139); but if the count is obviously wrong, a different spring should be tried. The most likely counts to be found when adapting springs are 14,400 or 18,000 per hour, between which there should be no confusion. If a spring cannot be found to give the correct rate, one that is too stiff should be chosen and the height carefully and evenly reduced by rubbing on ground glass covered with grinding paste. The spring should be held embedded in a cork.

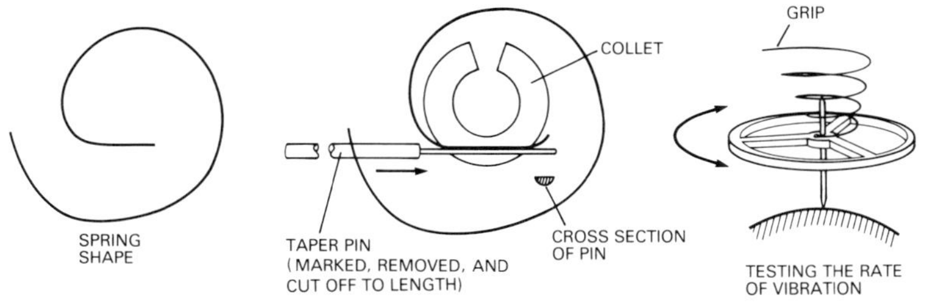

Fig 35 Balance-spring work

Balance springs are difficult to adjust accurately for all positions, temperatures, etc, and the amateur is unlikely to achieve perfect time-keeping without considerable experience. If a watch not working does so after attention to the balance spring, a big step has been taken and it is unwise to continue to seek perfection unless this is your particular interest.

Mainspring Replacement

The mainspring may be inspected after the barrel has been removed from the watch. To do this, prise off the barrel lid with a lever. If the spring is broken a new one, identical in height and thickness to the original, should be obtained from a watchmaker. The length of the new spring should be such that when it is in the barrel it occupies half the radial space available (see Fig 36). If it is too long it must be shortened, and the new end softened by being heated until red-hot and then allowed to cool. A new hook and/or hole will be required at the outer end. If a hook was fitted, a new one must be filed from a piece of steel to suit the hole in the barrel. It must be made on the slant as indicated in Fig 36, and then cut off and riveted to the spring through the new hole drilled in the end. If the spring is fitted to a hook attached to the barrel, the new hole in the spring must be cut at an angle in circular or rectangular form to mate with the barrel hook. This is also shown in Fig 36. The state of the barrel hook should be examined in case it was the cause of the spring break. If it is worn, a new hook can be made from a finely threaded steel wire and screwed into the barrel at the correct angle. If this is not possible with limited tools, an old hole may be found on the barrel which can be broached out and a spring hook made to fit.

A new spring should be fitted using a spring-winder. The amateur is unlikely to possess one, and unless a watchmaker undertakes to fit the spring it will have to be wound in by hand. This is adequate for working watches but could give erratic timekeeping, for hand-winding pro-

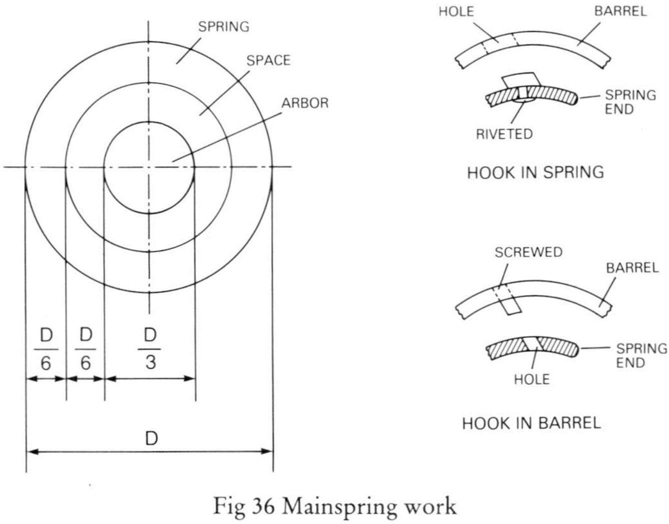

Fig 36 Mainspring work

duces a spring which, when free, is slightly helical in form rather than a true spiral. This gives a component of force acting against the barrel lid, which tends to open it; so that if the lid is a poor fit it may open and jam against the plate. This is unlikely but the opening force will cause considerable friction between the spring and the barrel, resulting in poor timekeeping. When the new spring is tested it may be found that the central hook on the arbor is not engaging with the hole in the spring. The spring centre should be bent gently inwards so that engagement is assured.

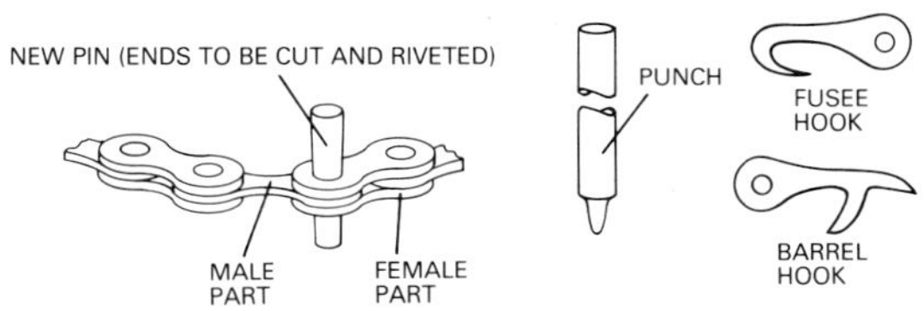

Fig 37 Fusee chain

Cleaning and Repairing a Fusee Chain

Fusee chains (Fig 37) are often found to be broken, but provided both parts are sound they may be repaired. The chain should be soaked in benzine or releasing oil and then wiped clean. A close examination should then be made to make sure that the repair is worthwhile. Large amounts of rust would make repair pointless, for breakage would occur again; but it may be possible to remove a faulty section.

A small punch is required which may be made from a needle first softened or annealed by heating and then cooled slowly. The end should then be filed to the correct size and the needle hardened by heating to red heat and plunging into water. Alternatively, an old staff may be adapted using the pivot as a punch. The broken ends of the chain are stuck in turn to a riveting stake with Sellotape, so that the rivet to be removed is over a hole in the stake. The punch is used to produce male and female parts, which are then brought together over the hole in the stake. A new rivet is made from an annealed needle or steel pin by filing the end to the correct size. This is inserted firmly and the excess length removed from both sides with a thin file such as a screwhead slotting file. The chain is replaced on the stake but not over a hole, and the ends of the new rivet are peened over with a punch to stop it falling out. A watchmaker's eyeglass will be required for most of these operations.

Should either hook from the chain be missing, a new one may be made from thin steel. The hole should be drilled (and if necessary broached) first, and then the hook filed to shape (Fig 37).

When the chain has been satisfactorily repaired or if it merely required cleaning, it should be given a thorough soaking in oil — overnight is not too long. Then run the chain backwards and forwards over a smooth, rounded surface, at the same time applying oil liberally so that all the chain joints are free and lubricated. Finally, wipe the chain clean with a benzine-soaked cloth.

Repairing a Fusee Click

If the fusee (Fig 38) rotates satisfactorily in the winding direction but fails to lock so that the spring tension immediately takes the chain back onto the barrel, it is likely that the fusee clicks are worn or broken. To strip the fusee, place the cone end in a boxwood stand and push out the pin passing through the shaft and the blued steel washer. Lift off the washer. The fusee may then be separated into the great wheel of brass, the maintaining-power ratchet wheel of steel with the two clicks or pawls, and the fusee cone with the driven ratchet wheel pinned to it. The clicks operate on this wheel and examination will show if it is wear or breakage causing the slip. If the fault is rounding off of the click points, these may be filed or stoned to give satisfactory working; but

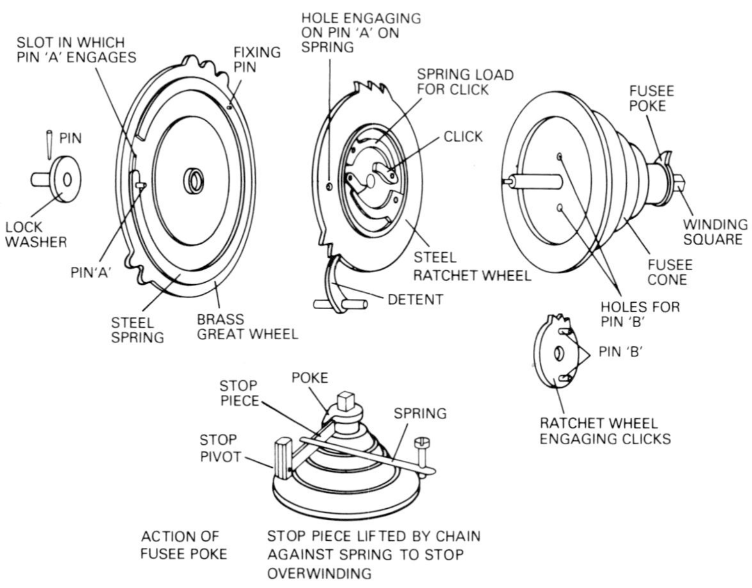

Fig 38 The fusee

excess wear or breakage will require a new click to be filed from steel. In extreme cases the brass wheel with which the clicks engage may also need attention, but damage can usually be dressed out with a file.

It is possible that the damage may not be confined to the clicks, but may also include the spring pushing the click into engagement. In this case the fusee may be persuaded to operate with only one click; but it is better to file a new spring-piece from steel. Both the clicks and the spring are secured by pins filed integral with the parts and peened over on the underside of the maintaining-power ratchet wheel. When the fusee is assembled with the new parts, the action should be tested before pushing the pin back through the blued steel washer.

The older type of fusee without maintaining power has similar clicks in its construction which will cause slipping when worn. The method of repair is similar.

In the event of a fusee being missing or damaged beyond repair, it may be possible to transfer one from another watch. The fusee must have the correct diameter and tooth spacing to mesh with the centre-wheel pinion. Differences in height can be accommodated by using a spacing bush to reduce end-shake to an acceptable amount, provided the fusee stop and maintaining-power detent will still engage.

Broken Pivot Repairs (on train wheels)

When pivots are broken there are three possible ways of repair. The best way is to make a new staff, but this may cause problems if the pinion is integral with the staff. In this case the best method is to soften the broken end of the staff by heating and then to file the end flat. The staff is then put into the pivot-drilling jig and a hole of suitable size drilled in the softened end. The new pivot is driven into this hole and finished to size, then polished (Fig 39). There is an alternative method if the broken pivot is not at the pinion end, or if it is a lever pivot that is broken. In this case, it is possible to replace half a staff by using the hub of the wheel on the staff as a joining sleeve. Fig 39 shows the principle involved. Staffs are removed from wheels, levers etc by using a punch and a stake, the punch having a suitable diameter hole to go over a pivot and deliver the blow to the shoulder of the staff. Many staffs have a taper and can only be removed in one direction, ascertainable by checking the dimensions with a micrometer. The height of the wheel on the staff should also be measured to make sure that it is correctly replaced. If a replacement-part staff is found on which the pivot is of the correct diameter, the staff diameter may be reduced by

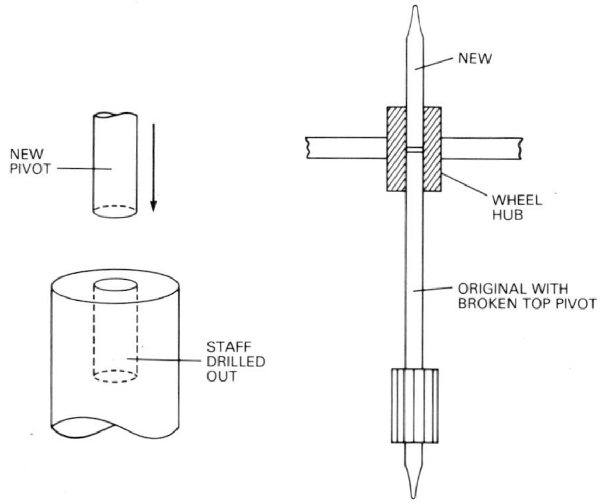

Fig 39 Staff repairs

careful filing if too large or set in with a non-permanent glue such as shellac if too small. Always modify the replacement part rather than the wheel hub or the pivot hole in the plate. Obviously the total height of the composite staff must be correct.

Verge Top Pivot and Bottom Pivot and Verge Staff

The top pivot of the verge may be repaired in a similar fashion to a broken staff. It may be found, however, that there is very little room for this technique as the verge pivot is close to the balance. In this case the brass boss on which the balance is fitted and the broken staff may be bored out to allow a new piece of staff to be fitted. This may be done with a hollow cutter which removes the soft brass and allows the thin steel of the verge to be broken off. Fig 40 shows the sequence of events

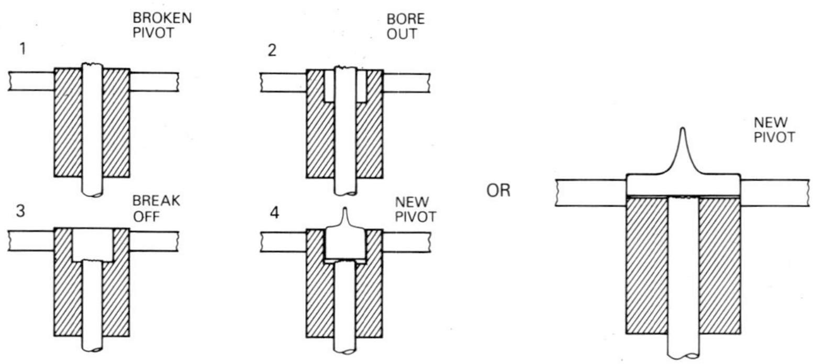

Fig 40 Verge-pivot repairs

in this repair. A simpler alternative is to remove the balance, file away half the thickness of the balance from the boss and broken verge (Fig 40), then bond on a new piece of staff. This method is not as satisfactory as the first, but is considerably easier. In either case great care must be taken to avoid damage to the rest of the verge.

If the bottom pivot is broken, the correct method is to make a new verge. This can be done with a file, but it is a lengthy process with a chance of breaking the new part at a late stage. If the verge is satisfactory except for the bottom pivot, it is possible to file away part of the shaft and solder or glue a small replacement piece of metal to the new flat surface. This can then be reshaped to form a bottom pivot.

If the verge is broken between the pallets, a thin piece of tube (hypodermic needle) may be used to join the two halves. There is very little room in this area for bulky extras, and glue or solder can be used to add strength.

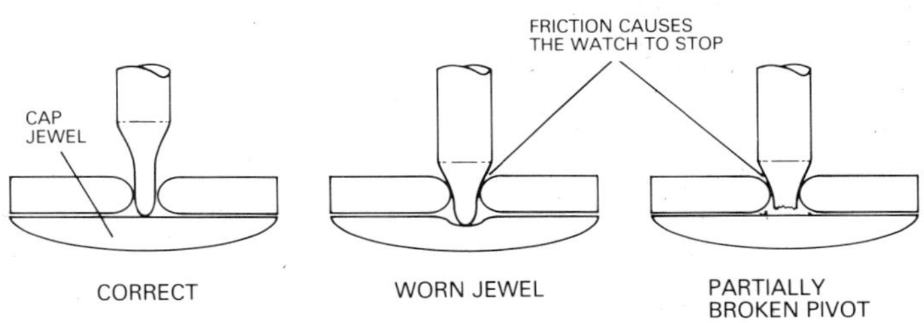

Fig 41 Balance-pivot repairs

Balance-staff Pivot

If the top pivot is completely broken it is possible to make a repair using part of another balance staff in a similar way to that suggested for train pivots. If the bottom pivot is broken it may also be possible to use this method. However, the best method is to make, or pay someone to make, a new staff. There are extra problems with balance staffs which run in jewels which are capped. The caps are the correct distance apart for the end-shake needed for free running and the balance pivots have curved sides. If the cap-jewels are worn, the balance may move in an axial direction and cause friction between the curved sides of the pivot and the pivot jewel, which will make the watch stop (Fig 41). This is a common cause of a watch, which goes when face down, stopping when moved to a face up position. One temporary solution is to fill in the wear holes in the cap-jewels with a hard glue. If the watch works satisfactorily with this done, the fault has been traced and the jewels should be replaced. These problems will also occur if a repaired staff is too short, or if the pivot is only partly broken off so that the watch will run one way up but not the other. Broken balance staffs really need replacing, and this is a skill that could be usefully acquired.

Straightening Wheels, Shafts, Pivots and Plates

If a wheel is bent, it may be straightened by pressing between two flat surfaces, heat being applied to the surfaces to ease flexing. After this has been done there will probably still be a kink at any point where the original bend was particularly sharp, and this may be removed by light taps with a small punch. The teeth should not be hit lest they spread and interfere with meshing. If the wheel is broken as well as bent, it may be soldered at the fracture. The repaired wheel should be put into its pivots or a depthing tool and examined for truth, and then tested with its pinion and any tight spots eased. If any teeth are missing a new piece of brass can be let into the rim of the wheel and soldered. Fresh teeth are filed to give satisfactory meshing.

Shafts may be straightened by tapping with the peen of a small hammer (or a similar shaped piece of metal) on the concave side. If the high convex side is hit, damage is likely to occur. Heat applied to the anvil, which will penetrate the shaft, may help the process. Pivots can sometimes be straightened by first being softened then straightened in small increments. There is a good chance of the pivot breaking, but if the watch did not work in the first place because of the bent pivot there has been no loss. In both shaft- and pivot-straightening operations there is no point in risking damage to achieve perfection if the collector is satisfied with a nearly straight part which will allow the watch to tick. As soon as this is thought possible, the train should be assembled and tested.

Bent plates can also be heated gently and hammered true. However, it may be found that the centre distances of pivot holes are no longer correct, and that considerable effort would be needed to make the watch run satisfactorily.

New Wheels and Pinions

If a wheel is so badly damaged that repair is impossible, or if a wheel is completely missing, it is possible to transfer a suitable replacement from another movement. The number of teeth and diameter will be known, or can be calculated by counting the teeth and measuring the size of the meshing pinion and the distance between the two shafts. The correct meshing of teeth is important but, if it is a case of making a watch go, trial and error can be used. If a wheel appears to be a satisfactory substitute, it should be mounted on the staff and a trial made with the appropriate pinion. If the wheel is too small it may be possible to spread the teeth outwards by tapping with a hammer; the tooth sides will probably need easing with a file after this treatment. If the wheel is too large the diameter may be reduced with a file; again the tooth sides may need easing. All modifications should be made to the replacement wheel, not to the original watch pinion, so that in the event of failure the watch is still intact and a fresh start can be made. Once the wheel runs satisfactorily with its pinion, the train should be assembled and tested before the whole watch is rebuilt.

If it is an escape wheel that is missing, the problem is more difficult, and with a cylinder, duplex or detent escapement the task is one for a professional antique-watch repairer. The amateur, however, should be able to make or adapt a crown wheel for a verge watch. Careful examination of a complete verge escapement will make the scope of the work clear; it is a task for patient filing. With a lever watch it may be possible to take the escape wheel from a scrap movement and fit this in the damaged watch, but if an escape wheel of the correct size cannot be found both escape wheel and lever may be planted in the damaged watch. The lever may need some adapting at the fork end. This transfer should only be attempted in a watch of little value, for new pivot holes may have to be drilled in the plates to accommodate the new escapement — an irreversible step. This technique was used by professional watchmakers in the latter part of the nineteenth century when cylinder or duplex watches had their escapements changed to lever.

If a pinion is missing or broken, the only satisfactory repairs are to file a new part to mesh correctly with the wheel, to find a new pinion on a staff and adapt the staff to suit, or to get a professionally made pinion and staff. The loads on pinions are too great to be able to repair a tooth satisfactorily, and the effort is hardly worth making.

Filing Out New Parts

The file should never be underestimated. Provided that the work can be held in some way or a jig made to support it, and provided that adequate patience and time are available, a considerable range of replacement parts can be filed out. Bearing in mind that the conversion of a broken watch to a ticking watch is a considerable achievement, the fact that a part made by amateur hand-filing may leave much to be desired in timekeeping or continuous reliable running is trivial. As experience is gained, handmade parts will improve in quality and it may be possible to return and improve earlier work. Parts made in this way include pinions, hands, clicks, hinges, balance wheels, cocks, staffs, a verge-bearing bracket, verge etc. When confronted with a seemingly impossible task, consider the possibilities of a file.

Bushing

If the pivot holes in a plate are so badly worn that bushing is required, a decision has to be made, for holes in the plate will have to be enlarged — an irreversible step. If the watch is of no great value, however, bushing can be attempted without fear. The bushes can be purchased from a watchmaker and they come with an extended piece which can be broken off after the bush is fitted. The old hole will need to be broached out to give a good tight fit on the bush.

An alternative but bad practice sometimes seen in watches is to spread the metal around the pivot hole by using a punch around the perimeter. The hole is then broached to size. Although this is a habit to be avoided, it cannot be denied that it may achieve some success.

Pivot holes which are jewelled may also need repair. Replacement jewels are available from a watchmaker, but the design will be different from the jewels which were set in with screws. If the original jewelling is complete but damaged, it is possible to effect a repair with glue which will enable the watch to run. It is also possible to transfer period jewels from an old movement.

Impulse Jewels

These are sometimes found broken in an otherwise perfect lever watch. If a replacement jewel is not available, a piece of steel wire may be used. The pin or jewel is not normally circular, but an ellipse or D-shaped as shown in Fig 7. The D-shape is the easier to form, but the hole in the roller should be the guide to the shape required. The 'D' should be formed by removing one-third of the circular profile, leaving a flat surface. Some early lever watches appear to have been fitted with circular jewels, and many watches function quite adequately fitted thus.

The replacement pin should be a sliding fit in the hole in the roller, and the length just adequate to operate the lever without fouling the bottom pivot. The hole in the roller is filled with a non-permanent glue (shellac, varnish etc), the new pin is introduced and adjusted, and then the whole system is put aside so that the glue sets.

Motion Work

It is disappointing to find all, or part, of the motion work missing from an otherwise complete watch; but it is a not uncommon fault. If one wheel only is missing, it is possible to find a correct replacement in an old movement. The teeth numbers should be such that, when combined with the two remaining wheels, a 12:1 gear ratio is obtained. The diameter of the replacement wheel must also be correct. The wheel centre may need broaching out to fit the pin or the cannon pinion on which it revolves.

In the absence of a suitable matching wheel, it is better to take a complete set of motion work from another watch movement. This may require one hole to be made in the underside of the dial plate to take the pin on which the idler wheel rotates. It may also be necessary to broach out (having first softened) the centre of the replacement cannon pinion. The parts removed should be retained so that when a suitable matching wheel is found they can be replaced.

Hands

Replacement hands are available from watchmakers but they will be modern, pressed-out ones suitable only for post-1800 watches. Older hands such as beetle and poker designs were hand-filed from steel and this is how replacements should be made. First, drill the holes through the hands and broach or file the centre to the correct square or round size. Then file the hands to shape. These designs are not simple one-plane affairs but are contoured in three dimensions. A contemporary pair of hands should be used as a pattern. Finally, polish, degrease (with benzine) and then blue the hands.

Blueing

Steel screws and hands etc are usually blued in pocket watches. To achieve successful blueing, polish and degrease the parts in benzine. They must not then be touched by hand. Place the parts on a tray and heat the tray with a spirit lamp. The heating will cause the polished steel to change through a range of colours passing through pale straw, dark straw, brown-yellow, yellow-purple, purple, dark blue, pale blue, until the steel is finally colourless. The technique of blueing is to stop the process so that the steel remains dark blue with perhaps a tinge of purple. One of the main problems is to obtain a uniform colour, which means a uniform temperature. If the tray is filled with brass filings and tapped during the process, it facilitates the even distribution of heat. It is also possible to use a heated metal block for thin objects, and to slide the part about to achieve the uniform colouring.

If the result is not satisfactory, the part can be made colourless by repolishing and the process repeated. If all else fails there are blueing solutions available. These are useful for 'repairs' to blued steel cases of the early twentieth century. However, the treatment is not 'invisible' to the expert.

Case Work

The amateur cannot afford to work on gold cases, for new material is too expensive. Even silver is surprisingly costly when purchased new. The silver used in watch cases is not pure but is alloyed with 75 parts per 1,000 of copper. However, the use of silver from scrap cases and case parts reduces the cost, and can be chosen so as to be of the correct antiquity. There are laws about repairs to hallmarked goods which should be studied if the watch is to be sold.

Silver soldering requires either a butane blowlamp or mouth-blowing from ordinary gas. Care must be taken to avoid melting adjacent joints, and the lowest-melting-point solder available should be chosen. Wet rags placed on adjacent joints help to keep them cool. Parts to be soldered should be clean and grease free, and the correct flux should be used — borax crushed in water is usual.

New pendants etc can be cast from old case metal, but the melting temperature of silver is just too high for a small butane lamp and a large torch or kiln is better. New bezels can be made from silver strip, but considerable skill is required to achieve satisfaction. New backs can be adapted from old cases. Dents in cases can be beaten out using hardwood backing pieces of the correct contour, and then the beaten surface can be polished smooth.

For movements without cases, it is possible to adapt empty cases or to make a new one. The best way to tackle the problems of major case work is to attend a jewellery class at a local art and craft school. They will charge for the course and for the materials used, but the experience and skills of a professional silversmith will be available.

Watch Glasses

Watch glasses, as opposed to plastic ones, should always be fitted to old pocket watches. Many watchmakers still carry stocks of glasses and will fit them when purchased. The older type of glass fitted to watches before 1800 which had a flat in the centre (bull's-eye glass) is less common, and should be purchased and held as stock against future needs. Watches which should have these glasses are often found with a more modern glass fitted. These replacement glasses will still have a very high dome and should not be lightly discarded, but should be replaced with the correct glass and stored for later use.

Dials

Dial repairs are rarely completely satisfactory, for all fillers seem to have a different colour or texture to the original. An alternative, interesting approach to a watch with a badly damaged or missing dial, is to make a new one. Again the local school of art and craft will be able to help if it has a jewellery class where enamelling is practised. It is, however, possible to teach oneself to enamel successfully because the materials are cheap and the temperatures involved are within the range of a small butane blowlamp.[9]

The new dial should be made from copper sheet about 25 gauge for domed dials and 20 gauge for flat dials (which tend to flex and crack the enamel if made of thinner metal). Mark out the dial, cut to size and drill for hands. Annealing is achieved by heating to red heat and then plunging into cold water. Use a small bolt to hold the dial in the chuck of a power drill, and press the dial to a dome shape as the drill rotates. Use a piece of wood to bring pressure to bear on the dial and expect that annealing will be required part-way through the doming process. Smooth and clean the domed blank to a good finish and then place in dilute sulphuric acid for a quarter of an hour. After this only handle it with tweezers to avoid grease contamination. Wash the acid-treated blank with water. The acid process can be omitted provided that the blank is completely scale and grease free.

Coat the blank with gum tragacanth (mixed from powder to paste with methylated spirits and diluted with water, 13g (½oz) gum to 1 litre (1qt) water), place it on a coarse metal mesh and sieve white enamel powder through 60-gauge mesh onto the face. Treat both sides with gum and powder to avoid edges but the butane method burns most of the enamel off the back. Apply the butane lamp to the back of the dial until the enamel fuses at about 820°C (1,508°F). Repeat this process until a satisfactory white finish is obtained. Then draw or paint the numbers with black painting-enamel mixed with water to a suitable consistency. Considerable trial and error will be needed until satisfactory draughtsmanship is achieved, but the black enamel can be washed off and a new start made as often as required. When you are satisfied with the lettering, the painting-enamel must be fired. Painting-enamel fuses at a lower temperature than the white enamel (about 730°C or 1,346°F) so that there is no problem with the white base. The dial is again heated from the back, for at no time should the lamp be played directly onto the face. Sometimes the enamel ground cracks at this late stage in the treatment, but in some cases it is possible to salvage the work by fusing new layers of white on top of the numbers and then to paint new ones.

New feet can be fitted to the back of the dial using glue to bond them on or, if preferred, they can be brazed on before enamelling. Enamel repairs to chipped dials are not satisfactory, for the new enamel does not have the same whiteness as the original which, in any case, tends to be damaged by the butane treatment. The original dial should be put to one side and preserved as part of the watch, and a complete replacement made.

Dials may be cracked but complete. The cracks are usually black with trapped dirt, but a vast improvement can be achieved by washing the dials in ammonia solution or some other bleach. Experiments are best made on old severely damaged examples before using the cleaner on a valuable good dial.

11
INVESTIGATION AND RESEARCH

Anyone who collects or has an interest in watches will sooner or later be involved in investigation or research into some topic which comes his way and excites his curiosity. It may be a learned investigation which will result in publication in some journal, but more often than not it will be in lighter vein. Nevertheless even simple research will involve visits to collections, libraries and museums, and perhaps the making of simple experiments. A number of examples together with their intermediate results are described in this chapter, the term 'intermediate' being deliberate, as an investigation is rarely completed — the leads come to a temporary end and the project is filed until new information appears and the file is reopened. The examples given are of several types involving different techniques; some may not appeal to the less scientific reader, others will not appeal to those not concerned with history. Everyone, however, is likely to be concerned with the first step: research into watchmakers.

Watchmakers

A watch comes into someone's possession or is seen in a museum and the top plate has a 'maker's' name engraved on it. The word 'maker', as already mentioned, is spurious; however, there is a name and you consult Baillie[1] or Loomes[2] who give lists of names, places and dates, together with other interesting information about the maker. A typical example of the sort of information obtained is 'Smith, Joseph, London, a[pprenticed] 1805', but with luck there may be more: 'Smith, Samuel, London and Coventry, 1812, patented the use of the stone pallets, Pirouette watch Ilbert coll[ection].' There are also lists for various areas which continually extend the information on makers as more are published.[3] These are all the results of someone's research.

Any dates obtained from an entry are highly important, otherwise the date of the watch may be estimated from the style and possibly the case hallmark (though it could be base metal, pre-hallmark or recased). A date narrows the search area. In the United Kingdom, recourse can now be made to trade directories in the town or area in which the maker worked; for example, *Pigot's Directory*[4] covered London and the South East of England. Start at your local library or museum and progress to the Guildhall Library (see Chapter 12) which holds many directories. Most directories start about 1780, but there are a few earlier ones.

If dates and addresses are known, family history may be traced through record offices or church records. There are also census results, but these are only released 100 years after the event so that 1881 is the latest presently available. If there is nothing else to hand, a visit to the local newspaper office (of the maker) might help, although this is only worthwhile if you have reason to believe that there is something special about the watch or maker. If there is, look through the old files at the relevant period and see if there are advertisements etc.

Another lead is the examination of patents which can be seen at the Patent Office Library (see Chapter 12), the Science Museum Library and the Guildhall Library. Often a watch is marked 'patent'. This may mean nothing, especially in the early nineteenth century; but if the patentee is named, there is real hope (not always fulfilled). To find a patent, number and date are almost vital; but the name of the patentee and the approximate date can be used as a starting point. Copies of patents can be purchased from the Patent Office. There is also a book listing all horological patents up to 1853.[5]

The following three examples show how these various sources can be drawn on in an attempt to build up a viable picture.

Morton's patent

The first example concerns an elegant, plain watch with 'Chronometer' printed on the dial. This word does not always mean what it seems — some pin-lever watches have this feature. This watch was not a pin-lever, but appeared to have an ordinary lever of post-1860 shape. When wound, the watch seemed out of beat, and the escape wheel looked rather odd. The case was hallmarked 1862 and the movement engraved 'Morton's Patent'. Removing the balance enabled the arrangement shown in Fig 42 to be seen: the lever-pallets were set differently and the escape-wheel teeth backs were different. The safety action was similar to the Massey lever and the unlocking jewel looked similar to a Massey, Type V. There was also a jewel to impulse the balance as in a chronometer; in fact the watch was a cross between a lever and a chronometer

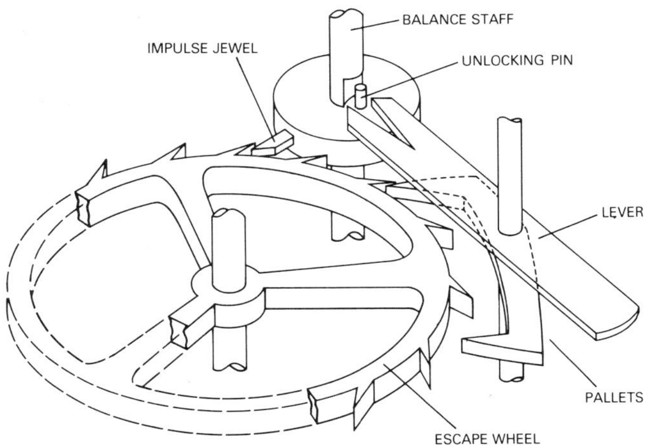

Fig 42 Morton's patent escapement

using the lever for unlocking but a jewel for impulsing the balance direct from the escape wheel every other beat. The watch had a low number so perhaps Morton's patent was about 1860. Baillie had nothing about this particular Morton and Loomes was not yet published, but Baillie did have: 'Morton, Thomas, St Helens, ca 1820', who could be a relative. Nothing could be found in local libraries, but a letter written to a museum elicited the following information:

(a) George Morton's patent is No 2432 of 1856
(b) A similar escapement was patented in 1859 by Charles Kelvey and William Holland of Birkenhead. They called their instrument the Patent Union Chronometer. Their escapement is described and drawn by Chamberlain in 'It's about Time'. You will see Chamberlain makes a slight slip in describing the patent as 'a simplification of one granted to George Marton'. However it would appear that the general principle of the escapement was not original even to Morton, since it was described by Robin in 1792.

The important piece of information is the reference to Chamberlain who gives details of many escapements.[6] The patent list[5] had not been published at the time of this investigation, but the patent was purchased and Chamberlain's book obtained by the local library (Inter-Library Loan Service) so that notes could be made. The patent is to 'George Morton of Keighley in the County of York' for 'Improvements in escapements for chronometers and other timekeepers'. In the description Morton clearly states that impulse is given as in the ordinary chronometer, but that he is replacing the detent locking-spring with an alternative system.

It would be interesting to know if Morton had studied Robin's work or whether he was looking for a simple chronometer escapement. The latter is a more attractive idea and is backed by a quotation: 'This is a combination of the lever and the detached escapement which has been several times reinvented although or because it has never turned out as good as it looks.'[7]

A second watch, with Morton's Patent on the back plate and 'J Bull, Bedford' as maker, had been converted to an English lever. The movement number is similar to that of the watch above. Loomes gives 'John Bull, Bedford 1830–54' which is a bit early, and 'Bull & Son 1869' and 'Bull Brothers 1877' which are a bit late. However, further research might show a suitable member of the Bull family. A possible connection between Morton and Bull could be investigated; Morton may have sold his movements to various 'makers' including Bull, or Bull may have made the conversion.

This piece of research relied on outside assistance, it brought the work of Chamberlain to the fore and it showed how helpful museums can be to genuine enquiries. The work could be continued to try and find out something of Morton in Keighley.

Thomas Yates

Watches that beat slowly or indicate seconds (see Chapter 6) seem to turn up at regular intervals. The watch in this investigation (Plate 35) had 'Yates Patentee' written on the dial, the movement was engraved 'Thomas Yates, Patentee, Preston', and the case was hallmarked Chester, 1853. It had a heavy gold balance and made two beats per second. Yates is not an unknown maker and the information could be gathered relatively easily without recourse to museums. Baillie gave 'Yates, Thomas, Preston, ca 1825, lever watch beating seconds'; Loomes gave 'Yates, Thomas, Preston, 1851–58. W[atch]'; Britten[8] gave 'Yates, Thomas, Preston. In 1846 he patd (no 11443) . . . having few teeth in the escape wheel so that the watch balance would vibrate only twice per second.'

The patent is for 'Improvements in Timekeepers' and proposes to reduce friction, use a mainspring of less power and use a balance of greater weight to 'propel the balance a less number of beats to the minute and at a much slower and more regular speed'. He suggests a balance of nearly three times the normal weight. The watch needed wider pallets on a longer lever, a 12 (or 10)-tooth escape wheel with options to use other numbers, and a rearranged train to give correct motion to the hands. The escapement was made dead beat. The Yates under investigation had an arrangement using a 15-tooth escape wheel

Plate 35 A Thomas Yates (Preston) half-seconds-beating, lever-escapement watch (No 2034), case hallmarked 1853. Yates's patent (No 11443 of 1846) allowed for various combinations of train wheels to achieve the slow beat. This watch has a heavy gold balance and no train jewels. It goes satisfactorily on the desk but not when worn — a common failing of this unsuccessful design.

with 14-tooth pinion, 56-tooth fourth wheel with 8-tooth pinion, 60-tooth third wheel with 8-tooth pinion, 64-tooth centre wheel with 10-tooth pinion and 75-tooth great wheel.

Under test, the watch worked well on the mantelpiece but it behaved erratically in the pocket. Was this due to wear or to the design? Further investigations showed that information had been published about Yates which also mentioned erratic performance.[9,10] Carrington, in fact, had done much of the research necessary to answer the question. In particular, he quotes from an advertisement in which Yates suggests that the watches 'are specially adapted for persons who have violent exercise, as they are not so liable to get out of order as ordinary watches'. Yates must have had a number of dissatisfied customers since no modern writer appears to find a watch of his that performs satisfactorily. Carrington also cites prices ranging from £6 6s to £12 in 1850–60, and gives much other interesting data including the fact that Yates's shop at 12 Friargate, Preston, was still in existence in 1975 with the original patent still on display.

The information was so readily available and other investigators were pursuing the same line, so the Yates file was temporarily closed It might be expected that Yates's half-seconds-beating watches would survive in some quantity since as poor performers they would tend to be put on one side rather than be worn out. The next report from the investigators should be interesting.

Wall and Frost

After a visit to a collection where a potentially interesting but uncatalogued watch was seen locked in a glass case, arrangements were made to examine it more closely. The watch had been recased or married into an 1843 case, but had obviously been made much earlier in the nineteenth century. The sequence of events of the next year is described below, together with thoughts at the time and a statement of the present state of the investigation. This is really a set of notes relevant to the research which is not yet concluded.

1 *Watch-inspection notes, bracketed items are comments:*
Movement recased; movement engraved 'Wall and Frost, Wandsworth, No 14, Patent' (this gives hope); fusee without maintaining power (early, strange); wheels have curved crossings (early); two escape wheels geared together with top bearings in blind holes (hard to assemble); four-wheel train; stop device; probably pre-1820, English; original hands; white dial inscribed 'patent' (this is why it looked interesting in the glass case); two beats per second, uneven, one ¾ second, one ¼ second rather like a duplex (probably out of beat); sluggish action (poor performer?); flat verge-type balance; action by impulse via slot in balance staff from alternate escape wheels which are rotating in opposite directions as they are geared together (make a sketch). This appears as Fig 43.

2 *Check of makers:*

Loomes	Wall, William, Coventry, 1828; Wall, William, Wandsworth, 1828–39; Wall, William A, New Bedford, USA, Early 19C. Frost, Jonathan, Exeter, 1785, W; Frost, Jonathan, Reading, USA, 1798–1881.
Baillie	Wall, William, Putney, 1791, C & W; Wall, William, Putney and Wandsworth, 1796–1817, Patented an esc. with two esc. wheels. Frost, Jonathan, Exeter, before

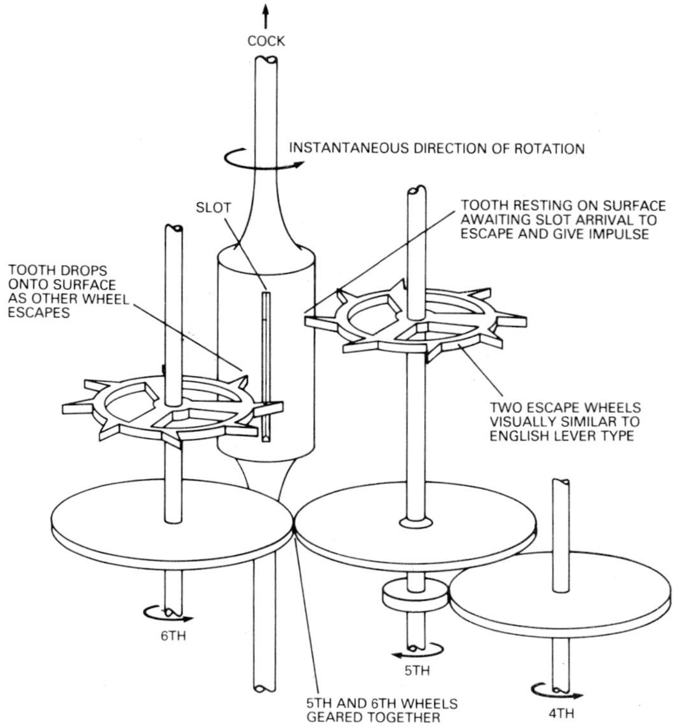

Fig 43 Wall escapement

1783, W; Frost, Henry, London, 1805–08; Frost, John, London (Clerkenwell) a 1799, CC1809, 1 CC 1816; Frost, Thomas, London, a 1772; Frost, William, Liverpool, 1796, W.

Britten — Wall, William, Wandsworth, patented an esc. in 1817 (No 4097). Frost, Exeter, put Lovelace's clock in order 1833 (clock now (1911) in Liverpool museum).

Comments — Nothing about Wall and Frost. Wall identified if this is the right patent. Any significance in a Wall and a Frost both in USA?

3 *Check of patents:*

No 4097 of 1817 is for 'A new or improved horizontal escapement for watches'. The description is that shown in Fig 43. It is the right Wall.

Comments — The Wall and Frost movement uses Wall's patent, perhaps Wall needed Frost to make it or finance it?

4 *Consulting of various museums for information and other examples:*

No other examples located. Key words from replies: Risdon duplex and conceptually similar to Flamenville. Baillie; Risdon, Francis before 1744 but Britten; Risdon, Francis, Ca 1790; Flamenville, Paris 1727, devised a modified verge escapement. Flamenville's escapement shown in Chamberlain.[6]

5 *Letter to specialist journal with diagram asking for information, three replies:*

a Gives another two escape-wheel watch by Swiss maker, again this looks a Flamenville-derived concept.
b Vaguely remembers seeing a movement some time ago.
c Gives useful comments covering makers involved.

6 The owner took the watch to a museum but no further information was obtained. Photographs supplied to me.

7 A description of Mr Lovelace's clock was obtained which is complicated and Frost must have been a skilled man to put it in order.[11] Perhaps he did make Wall's escapement for him, perhaps Wall found it hard to make it work!

Conclusion: The watch movement is English, made *c*1820 and uses Wall's patent. It may be unique. Certainly there are few about, probably because it was not successful. The Ilbert Collection (British Museum) does not have one and most watches can be found there. The file is now closed but has potential. The work needs another watch or movement from Wall or Frost to help. It would also help to identify Frost. Several watchmakers did emigrate to America and Canada in the early nineteenth century and there is the slight possibility that Wall and/or Frost did. Some of the dates make this difficult, Lovelace's clock is 1833 and Wall in Wandsworth till 1839 does not agree with the US dates. Some trade directory and record office work would help here. The file needs reopening.

File reopened, 1983

1 An earlier watch with similar escapement auctioned in Paris, escapement attributed to Volet *c*1745.
2 A second movement has been located, No 156, but has not yet been inspected.

This last piece of research illustrates the importance of making notes and copying from all relevant books and documents in order to build up evidence. This saves repeated visits to the same sources as more data becomes available. The watch should be photographed and the escapement, or any other special parts, sketched. Patience is also necessary, this file started in 1977!

Conclusions

The three examples illustrated have each provided interest and the results have been different. In the case of Morton, the watch part is conclusive although little appears to have been written about him — there is potential for an article. Regarding Yates, the work is in hand and the new data has been passed on to the investigators. The final example, Wall and Frost, has great potential and hopefully more information will accrue from this presentation.

Hand Repeating

A box containing what was obviously part or all of a watch of some complexity, provided the next interesting problem. The parts contained a gong so that striking or repeating was suggested. However, there was no guarantee that everything in the box belonged to the same watch. There was no repeating-drive spring-barrel, no chain, no sign of any hammers, so it seemed unlikely that the pieces were complete.

After several evenings' work the whole was assembled to produce a hand repeating watch which certainly did have one part missing, but it was not crucial to understanding the working, as it was a locking device. The whole watch needed a considerable amount of professional work to put it into good order, and the owner had to make a decision regarding the cost. Fig 44 shows the essential parts.

The action (Fig 44) is achieved by unlocking the pivoted arm D by

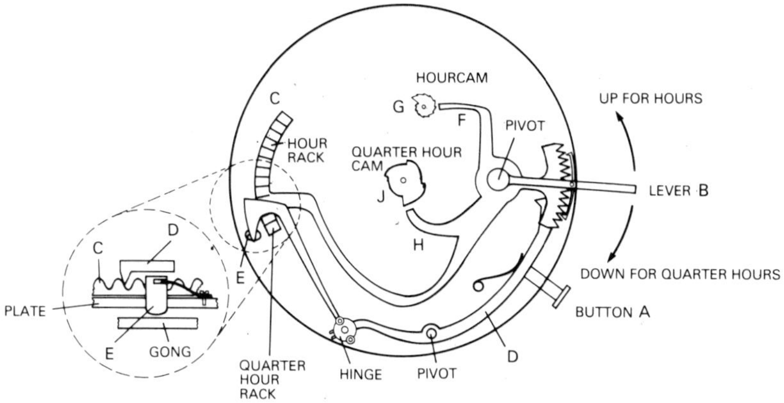

Fig 44 A hand-repeating mechanism

pushing button A, and then moving lever B upwards towards the 12 mark. This causes rack C to lift the pivoted arm D one step at a time and strike the sprung hammer E onto the gong at each step. The number of strikes is dictated by the feeler F contacting the stepped hour snail-cam G. Button A is pushed again so that springs can re-centre the rack C and lever B. The button A is again pushed and lever B moved towards the 6 mark. This again causes rack C to lift the pivoted lever D one step at a time and strike the hammer E onto the gong at each step. The number of strikes is dictated by the feeler H on the stepped quarter-hour snail-cam J. Finally button A is pushed to reset the mechanism. The sequence of operation — button, lever, button; button, lever, button — sounds complex but is not difficult when one becomes familiar with it.

Examination of the remainder of the watch suggested that, with some simple modifications, the repeating action could be powered from the mainspring so that the watch could have been marketed in two forms.

The watch had a Swiss lever escapement with a barred movement and going-barrel and was engraved 'Patented 6 July 76, P V F, Ste Croix, No 35325'. It was housed in a silver hunter case similarly numbered. The dust cover was marked 'T A Jones, 352 Essex Road, London, N' and had a trademark 'Flood and Field' with a logo consisting of a whip, stirrup and rifle. The quality of workmanship was not high.

Loomes gives 'Thomas Alfred Jones, London, 1881' which is the right period, but the patent and identification of P V F have not yet been pursued. Ste Croix, a Swiss town twenty miles north of Lausanne, was a centre for the manufacture of repeating work (cadrature), the earliest record being that of Junod who set up there in 1752. The work steadily increased and, by 1834, 164 repeating workers were centred in the town; by 1860 there were perhaps 900 although by then not all were engaged in repeating work for the musical box and musical watch industry was also centred at Ste Croix.[12]

Other hand-repeating mechanisms, notably by Berollas and Elliot, were made in the early years of the nineteenth century and are described by Rees.[13] They bear little resemblance to this watch, being operated by a button passing through the pendant. In the Elliot design, the button shaft carries cams to operate the repeating work when the button is rotated. In the Berollas design the button unscrews as it is rotated, drawing the repeating mechanism into action.

Simple Scientific Analysis of Watches

Fusees and springs

The fusee has been in existence for 500 years, with the object of obtaining constant torque from a variable spring force. The mathematical equation to the shape has been produced at intervals for at least 250 years, but there has recently been debate as to the validity of the approach. It is doubtful if the early clock and watch makers worried too much about equations, although the real masters would no doubt have made their own calculations and experiments. They fully realised that to succeed they could not spend all their efforts on the escapement and ignore the fusee.

Fusees are made with fusee engines,[13] early examples of which were basically tapering devices and, even if equations had been available, were not capable of producing exact shapes. After an approximate shape had been cut, the fusee had to be crudely tailored to its mainspring. Later engines were more advanced, and finishing was achieved by testing the fusee with an adjusting rod. The rod was clamped to the fusee axis and a sliding weight moved along it until it sat in the horizontal position with the spring force just balanced. As the fusee was wound, the weight would have to be moved if the torque changed. Using this trial and error method, the necessary corrections to the profile could be made by putting the fusee into a fusee frame and removing excess metal. If a spring was replaced it was quite possible that the new one would not match the fusee. As the numbers of clocks and watches increased and mainsprings became more consistent in their performance, it was to be expected that there would be standard fusees associated with standard springs. Ordinary watches would not then need fine tuning, but only correct set up, to give adequate timekeeping.

The start of this investigation was to make what is known as a 'literature survey', in other words to 'seek out all the references to fusee equations'. The earliest readily available, dated 1748,[14] produced an erroneous theory that the shape of a fusee was a special curve known as a rectangular hyperbola. This curve is described by an equation — fusee radius multiplied by angle of spring rotation is constant ($X\,\Theta =$ constant). This form of equation is also produced in Rees (1820)[13] and in Haswell (1928).[15] It therefore seems likely that any fusee met in any watch would use this form with some fine tuning. Presumably the tuning would result in a shape more like that suggested by the better equations published since 1928.

The first approximately correct statement was by Rawlings (1948)[16] who showed that the equation should read

$$X^2 \Theta = \text{constant}$$

(X is the fusee radius and Θ the angle of spring rotation)

Unfortunately he did not fully explain how it should be applied, although he no doubt knew, which led to some further work by Powell (1975)[17] and Preisendorfer (1977).[18] At about this time an article was published[19] which interested a number of people including the author. Whilst the work described below was taking place in response to this article, Honig[20] produced another approximate relation, and Weaver[21] produced a proper theory for an ideal fusee which should close matters for some time. (Weaver in fact reopened his fusee file when he read the article[19] and sorted out the problem.)

The action of a fusee is complex and all published theories prior to Weaver make assumptions to simplify analysis. His ideal solution gives a maximum torque error of about 5 per cent more than Rawlings's approximate theory. A derivation of an equation using a similar method to Rawlings's is shown below.

To see how the equation works it was necessary to test a fusee and spring and, because watch work is so small, the work was done with an 8-day-dial clock movement of about 1900. The fusee and barrel were removed and set up between plates, and a fusee rod with sliding weight was made in order that the torque produced could be measured as the spring was wound. One result is shown in Fig 45. A parallel-sided 'fusee' was also made and tested to see what the spring performance was without a fusee. This enabled the spring-torque constant to be calculated. The spring dimensions were measured and the spring-torque constant was calculated from the theory below. The experimental value and the theoretical value were in reasonable agreement, and could be used in the equation to predict the necessary fusee profile. The actual fusee profile was measured and both are shown in Fig 45.

It can be seen that the fusee fitted gives constant torque for most of the seven days that this movement would normally be expected to run between windings, so that the poor part of the torque curve is not in fact used. It would also seem that if the fusee were adjusted by cutting metal off towards the base, the torque on the eighth day would be improved. This does not account for the extra metal needed in the centre of the predicted shape. The work is not complete and the next stage should be to make the predicted fusee and test it. Some set-up changes were

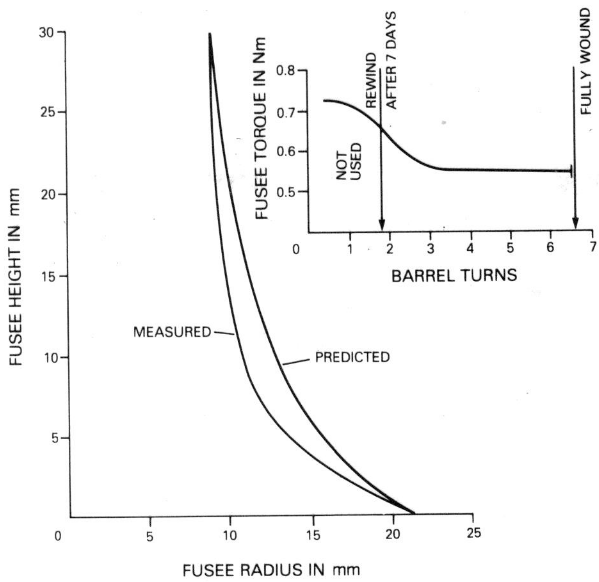

Fig 45 Fusee test result and profiles

made with the existing fusee to see if performance on the eighth day could be improved, but to no avail. When the new fusee has been made and tested it is proposed to refurbish the clock movement and observe its timekeeping ability with the original fusee, the new fusee and with the parallel-sided 'fusee'. A home computer has also been used to plot fusee profiles for various spring constants, fusee pitches etc (Fig 46).

Fusee theory and measurement

1 *Calculation of spring-torque stiffness:*

From the equation for bending[22] we obtain $M = \frac{EI}{R}$

(R = radius of curvature)

But $R\Theta = L$

hence $\frac{M}{\Theta} = \frac{EI}{L}$

for a rectangular cross-section of spring[22] $I = \frac{bd^3}{12}$

hence $\frac{M}{\Theta} = \frac{Ebd^3}{12L}$

where $\frac{M}{\Theta}$ = bending moment or torque per radian of winding

E = Young's modulus = 207000 N/mm^2

b = spring height (measured as 36mm)

d = spring thickness (measured as 0.45mm)

L = spring length (measured as 2400mm)

$$\frac{M}{\Theta} = \frac{207000 \times 36 \times (0.45)^3}{12 \times 2400 \times 1000} = 0.0236\text{Nm/rad}$$

This can be compared with the value measured with the parallel-sided 'fusee' of 0.023Nm/rad.

Note: 1 Newton (N) is equal to 0.225lb.

2 *Analysis to determine profile:*

Assume 1 The torque exerted by fusee = wire tension x fusee radius = $(A + K\Theta)X$. Where X is the fusee radius at any point, Θ is a cumulative barrel rotation, K is the spring constant and A is the initial wire tension.

2 A fusee consists of a series of circles of radius X, so that in one turn of the fusee the length of groove is $2\pi X$.

3 The length of chain in the space between the barrel and fusee is constant.

4 The fusee pull is not inclined to the fusee axis.

Assumption 1 is unlikely to be true, assumptions 2, 3 and 4 are false.

Referring to Fig 46

$$R\,d\Theta = X\,d\phi$$

but $$d\phi = \frac{2\pi\,dy}{p}$$

hence $$R\,d\Theta = \frac{2\pi X\,dy}{p} \qquad (1)$$

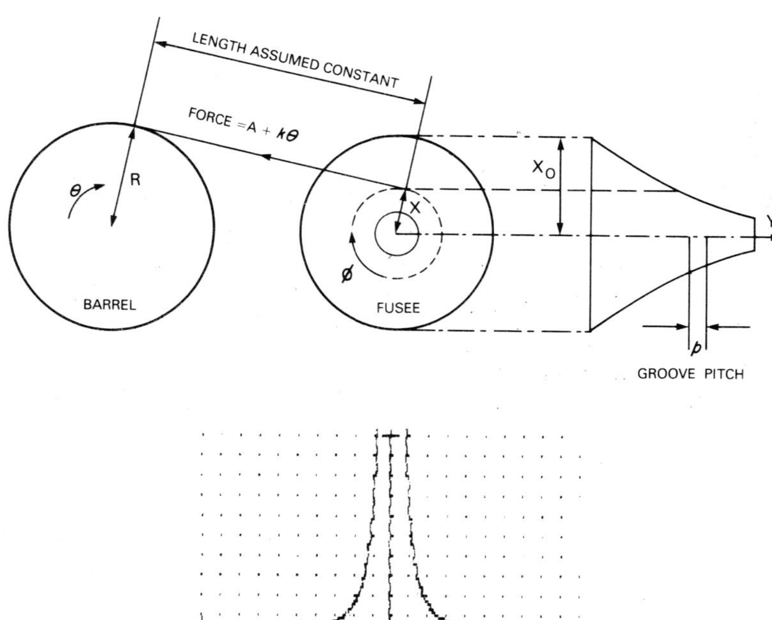

Fig 46 Fusee equation and profile

We require the fusee torque to be constant so that

$$(A + K\Theta)X = C$$

Differentiate $$K d\Theta = \frac{-C}{X^2} dX \qquad (2)$$

and from 1 and 2 — $$\frac{RCp}{4\pi K} \frac{dX}{X^3} = dy$$

Integrate to obtain y $$= \frac{RCp}{4\pi K} \frac{1}{X^2} + F$$

where F is the integration constant found from the initial conditions, ie when $y = O$, $X = X_0$, where X_0 is the base radius of the fusee.

giving $$F = -\frac{RCp}{4\pi K} \frac{1}{X^2_0}$$

and thus the fusee profile equation is

$$y = \frac{RCp}{4\pi K} \left[\frac{1}{X^2} - \frac{1}{X^2_0}\right]$$

For the fusee under investigation the measured values were

R	=	barrel radius	28.5mm
C	=	constant torque	0.55Nm
p	=	fusee groove pitch	1.9mm
K	=	spring constant	0.83N/rad
X_0	=	fusee base radius	21mm

The calculated fusee profile is given in the table below together with the measured profile of the fusee in the clock.

Fusee Height Measured y mm	Fusee Height Calculated y mm	Fusee radius X mm
0	0	21
1.83	2.34	18
2.72	4.68	16
4.45	8.10	14
6.91	13.36	12
12.05	22.08	10
26.00	28.78	9
30.00	30.40	8.8

Balances, balance springs and timekeeping

It is interesting to speculate on how the design of the interior of a pocket watch has crystallised into a particular form. Consider the conventional nineteenth-century English lever watch which uses a four-wheel train with fusee and runs for thirty hours. The centre-wheel pinion takes the drive from the great wheel on the fusee; the size (calibre) of the watch therefore fixes the size of the great wheel and hence the fusee-base diameter. The size also determines the maximum barrel diameter and hence the spring length and thickness as a pair. The spring height can be chosen. The shape of the fusee depends on the spring strength and the fusee pitch can be chosen to fit the distance available determined by the spring height. The spring is critical—what determines its strength?

For this we look to the balance end of the train where the balance spring rather than the mainspring is in charge. The balance and balance spring can be compared to a mass on the end of an ordinary coil spring or piece of rubber band. Simple experiment shows that if the mass is increased, the time of vibration increases. It is also easy to demonstrate that the vibration dies out due to friction. Similarly if a stronger balance spring is used, the time of vibration decreases. Thus the time of vibration depends on spring strength and the mass, and tends to die out. Because it tends to die out, the balance needs impulse every vibration and this is ultimately obtained from the mainspring. This can lead us to the necessary mainspring height, because we need just enough impulse to keep the balance moving through the correct arc and this impulse may be determined by replacing the mainspring with a dead-weight system attached to the train. It will in fact tell us the torque to be given to the train by the great wheel. By varying the dead weight and having different arcs of vibration, it would be possible to find out how isochronous the balance spring and balance were, and to determine the maximum and minimum permissible spring torque for isochronous behaviour. This would give us an indication of how tolerant the watch is to imperfection in the fusee.

A little more information is really necessary because we are considering an existing balance and balance spring, choice of which is dictated by the train-wheel gear ratios. The vibration rate must be set so that, with these ratios, the hands move at the correct speed and the watch runs for thirty hours. (In the late nineteenth century the lever-watch rate of vibration was chosen to give five 'ticks' per second.) In our 'rubber-band experiment' the time of vibration depended on the mass vibrating and the strength of the spring (rubber). In watch terms this is the balance mass and radius at which the mass is concentrated (rim radius), and the balance spring strength. The balance mass and radius give the balance inertia approximately equal to mass times rim radius times rim radius or $I = mr^2$.

To solve this problem, balance mass and radius and balance springs were again chosen and made in standard sizes, which meant that a given balance spring, balance, train, mainspring and fusee could be chosen to suit each other from standard stock and only fine adjustment would be required. The mathematical equations for the balance and balance spring calculations are shown on page 172. If the mass is large and the radius large then the balance spring will need to be strong to keep the correct vibration rate. This can be seen on Harrison's (Chapter 8) third timekeeper in the National Maritime Museum, Greenwich, which has a massive balance and spring. It is also mentioned earlier in this chapter that Yates used a heavy balance to reduce the rate of vibration.

Balances must also be poised, ie the centre of gravity of the balance should be on the staff centre-line. This avoids positional errors, rapid pivot wear and unbalanced centrifugal forces. If the underside of a solid balance is examined, filed or drilled away, portions can be seen which are associated with getting the balance mass correct and the balance poised. When a compensation balance is fitted all the screws must be placed and adjusted for total mass and poise in addition to correct compensation. This is a complex problem and it is doubtful if many antique compensated-balance pocket watches are still correctly set up. Few owners would be able to check this. The fine tuning of an existing balance and spring is normally achieved with the regulator, which allows some scope for error in the initial setting up as well as for large environmental changes.

Experiments on the sensitivity of a watch to these factors may be made if an old movement is available. Small masses can be added to the balance which should cause it to lose. The balance spring could be shortened by regulator or resetting to compensate, but this should also alter the positional errors (see Chapter 8). If a movement gains and the balance spring is too short, the balance mass could be increased to compensate. The mainspring could be changed in a watch within the limits of the barrel capability, thickness being the most effective dimension to change since it has a cube effect on strength. But before going too far with these modifications it would be as well to study Rawlings[16] for theory and De Carle[23] for practice.

This 'research' is planned for the future as a routine has yet to be established for the results to be meaningful. It is vital to vary only one item at a time and therefore a constant-temperature box will be needed to be sure that only the chosen variable is examined. A watch to be tested should first be put into good working order, but trials before and after restoration would be interesting. It is also useful to have a 'regulator' as a control device — a modern quartz watch rated against radio signals would be quite sufficient. The remaining problems are the length of the trials and how to analyse the data which will accrue.

So far some simple tests in a pilot scheme have confirmed the fact that positional error exists in watches with various escapements. All the watches lost pendant up as compared with the dial up position. The results — which indicate there is a great deal of work still to do — are shown below.

Temp 15°C (59°F)	Rate of loss or gain in seconds per hour		
Escapement	Dial up	Pendant up	Comment
Verge 1	−120	−80	Shorten the balance spring
Verge 2	+25 to −27	Regulator pin broken	Repair regulator pin and retest
Verge 3	+48	+7	Regulate with pendant up for no loss or gain
Rack lever	+45	0	
English lever 1	+4½	−8	Regulate with pendant up for no loss or gain
English lever 2	−1	−4	Regulate with pendant up for no loss or gain
English lever 3	−3	−8	Regulate with pendant up for no loss or gain

Balance and balance-spring theory

Balance-spring bending is governed by the same equation as that for the mainspring

$$M = \frac{Ebd^3\Theta}{12L}$$

where M = bending moment or torque
Θ = angle of twist
E = Young's modulus
b = spring height
d = spring thickness
L = spring length

This torque is applied to the spring by the balance and then applied to the balance on the return swing. The motion of the balance is governed by the equation[22]

$$M = I\alpha$$

where I = inertia of balance
α = angular acceleration of balance

If the slight effect of losses due to internal friction and air resistance are ignored, the oscillation of the balance is found to have a periodic time of free vibration[22]

$$T = 2\pi\sqrt{\frac{\Theta}{\alpha}}$$ which becomes $$T = 2\pi\sqrt{\frac{12LI}{Ebd^3}}$$

This is the time that has to be arranged as correct by the choice of balance-spring dimensions (b,d,L), material (E) and balance mass and size (I). Note that temperature compensation is necessary on balances to allow for changes in E, I, and d with temperature. (The ratio $\frac{L}{b}$ should be constant.)

Railway Watches

A watch which caused an interesting diversion appeared in 1979 in a London market (Plate 36). It was very large, weighed 230g (8oz), and the movement was signed 'John Walker, 77, Cornhill St, London'. (Neither Baillie nor Loomes gives this John Walker.) The dial was inscribed 'Natal Government Railways' and the German silver case-back was numbered. Inside the case was a full-plate fusee lever movement. The plates were twice as thick as those of a normal watch and the winding-square was about 3mm (1/8in) across, wound by a key rather like a pre-war clockwork toy. Some months later another similar but damaged watch from the same source was seen, so that possibly a whole batch was sold off.

The first approach was to look at the railway history of Natal and the results showed that in

1860 A standard-gauge railway was started
1881 The railways became state owned
1910 Natal became part of the Union of South Africa

This dated the watch between 1881 and 1910 and its appearance suggested about 1880 to 1890. It was also possible to construct a map of the railway showing how it grew from 1881 to 1883, when it was centred on the port of Durban with coastal-strip development and an inland line to Pietermaritzburg. By 1900 the inland line had extended to Ladysmith where it forked, giving lines to the Transvaal and the Orange Free State. By 1910 there was a line to Cape Colony.

Natal has a savage history involving the Zulus (Chaka in 1818–20 and Dingaan in 1837–8). In 1838 it became a Boer Republic, but this was short-lived for the British made it a colony in 1845. The Zulu war of 1879 is well known, and an uneasy relationship with the Boers erupted into the Boer War of 1899 to 1902, starting with the Boer invasion of Natal and the siege of Ladysmith. In this war railways were an important factor involving armoured trains and strong points to counteract track demolition, for they were the only means of

Plate 36 A massively constructed full-plate English lever watch which weighs 230g (8oz). It is in a German silver case and was made by John Walker, Cornhill, London, c1885. The winding key is also shown.

moving supplies over long distances. This watch, therefore, was almost certainly involved in military events.

The other interesting feature of the watch was its massive construction. When railways were developing rapidly at the end of the nineteenth century, Standard Time was introduced (see Chapter 8) and the reliability and accuracy of the watches carried by railway employees was important. Signalling systems and communications were relatively crude, and a correct knowledge of time was vital. Thus early railway watches are, in general, robust and well made. Some British railways chose factory-made American watches, but others chose traditional fusee watches made in England. In the USA, to ensure that good time-keeping was observed, a railway watch specification was drawn up at the turn of the century. This demanded positional and temperature errors of not more than 30 seconds per week in an environment of between 4 and 31°C (40 and 90°F). Such watches were usually certified by stamping on the plates.

A Return to the Early Nineteenth Century

A watch paper printed with an 'equation of time' table was found in the usual place — between the pair-cases — of an 1808 verge watch. The watch and paper both had the same maker's name, and the paper had a repair date (1849), which might signify a later owner. The discovery seemed an opportunity to turn the clock back 150 years and see how a watch owner lived in the days before radio time-signals.

The first requirement was to build a sundial, and an interesting book[24] describing the construction of various types was consulted. Two were made — one a horizontal and one an equatorial dial. The latter is easier to make as it has equal hour-divisions, but it is harder to set up than the horizontal dial which has unequal ones. The watch was cleaned and set up on a watch stand to keep reasonable time in the pendant-up position.

The trials were made between mid-June and August, when hopefully the sun would shine and the equation of time is large enough to be noticed. The watch was checked daily at noon (if the sun was out) with due allowance for British Summer Time. This meant reading the sundial at 1300, consulting the watch paper and, since the sun is slower, adding the equation of time to obtain the correct time. The watch was then set correct. The results were confusing for there was an error which could not be explained by the watch performance, which was satisfactory. The sundial was checked for siting and seemed correct. In terms of life in the early nineteenth century the errors were not significant, but as a trial it was disappointing. The solution was to return to the twentieth century and use radio time-signals to sort out the problem. In due course it was concluded that there was an error in the equation of time on the watch paper.

An almanack[25] was consulted to obtain other values of the equation of time and the experiment was repeated. The results were satisfactory — the watch paper was the problem. The table on the paper was compared with the almanack values and it was clear that the paper was for a Julian Calendar (see Chapter 8). It was eleven days in error. The abstract below shows the comparison; the figures are minutes.

	June				July					August			
Date	4	11	18	25	2	9	16	23	30	6	13	20	27
Paper	0	1	4	5	5	6	6	6	5	4	2	0	
	SUN ←										→ SLOWER		
Almanack	2	1	0	2	3	5	5	6	6	5	4	3	1
			SUN ←										→ SLOWER

There were several possibilities:

1 That the date on the repair paper was 1749, not 1849; but this looked unlikely although Britten[8] and Loomes[2] do suggest that the maker had a long family history in this area.

2 The paper was old stock, but this would make it a hundred years old as the Gregorian Calendar was introduced in 1752.

3 The paper was a reprint of old data by a country watchmaker who did not know of the eleven-day change in 1752. The paper certainly looked a nineteenth-century product. This seems the most likely explanation.

Looking further into equation tables it would appear that in London, as opposed to the country, people were aware of the difference. A table printed for Tompion in 1690[26] added to the confusion in that the dates here would be expected to agree with the watch paper. However, this table used Gregorian dates and must have been printed for continental use where the change took place from 1582. This is borne out by a friend who kindly translated the table's Latin rubric:

> Table of equations of natural days showing the time intervals between the hours shown from equally moving oscillatory clocks and from accurate sun dials, for any single day in the year 1690, in the New Style: being useful even for future years in this century without a sensible difference.

The words 'New Style' are the significant ones. Tompion also produced equation tables for clocks and watches used in Britain based on the Julian Calendar and one dated 1683 is reproduced in an article about equation clocks.[27] Both Tompion tables are produced in minutes and seconds for each day, suggesting use for longcase clocks rather than watches.

At this stage the purpose of the original experiments had become obscured, but the trials were repeated in a later summer. The results were confirmed, and the daily rate of loss of the verge watch was about five minutes. It then became apparent that, if regular noon checks are made, it is possible to accumulate several days of error if the sun is not conveniently out. Timekeeping in the early nineteenth century involved observation when the sun came out, *not* at the owner's convenience. Thus if the sun was out whilst a person was passing a public sundial, his watch could be checked if he had a special portable 'equation of time' watch paper kept in the case.

Newspapers and Watches

A Christmas gift of a 1788 copy of the *Edinburgh Advertiser*, which contained an advertisement about watches, started another line of investigation. Part of the advertisement reads:

> GEORGE MONRO, WATCH MAKER AND WATCH JEWELLER, in the fourth side, Canongate Head, Edinburgh has practised watch jewelling for nearly 40 years . . . The parts of the wheels moving in these jewels or hard bushes, are never corroded nor impaired; go with much less friction, and greater velocity, than a wheel moving in brass, for brass corrupts and putrifies the oil, and turns it sometimes in half a year to a thick substance which clogs the wheels and roughens the pivots.

Baillie shows 'Munro, b 1724, d 1804, good watches in V and A, L C clock, a maker of repute'; this advertisement, however, is optimistic in its claims although it does bring out the problem of lubrication in this period — a useful piece of contemporary information.

A later gift of the *Northampton Mercury* of 6 August 1765 reports the arrival in 'Barbadoes' of Admiral Tyrrel:

> . . . sent by the Board of Admiralty to try some schemes for ascertaining the Longitude at Sea; among them is one Mr Harrison who has invented a Time Piece to tell Navigators true time at an absent Place.

This was the end of the voyage of HMS *Princess Louisa* which carried Maskeleyne and Green, the official observers for the schemes for marine timekeepers that were undergoing their trials. Harrison was in HMS *Tartar* with his No 4 timepiece and this voyage in 1764, leaving Portsmouth on 28 March and arriving in Barbados on 14 May, was its second trial before being accepted by the Board as having proved its timekeeping capabilities.

A few more extracts from newspapers are quoted to show the sort of information that is available. The *Illustrated London News* of 13 June 1857 carried the advertisement:

> On board HMS *North Star* in the Arctic Regions, for two years the Ship's time was kept by one of Jones's levers, all other watches on board having

> stopped. In silver £4 4s; in gold £10 10s at the Manufactory, 328 Strand (opposite Somerset House). Read Jones's 'sketch of watch work' sent free for 2d stamp.

From the *Northampton Mercury*, 6 August 1764:

> On Tuesday last in the dusk of the evening, as a shop keeper at Newbury was going to Reading, he was stopt near that town by a single footpad who robbed him of £163. The villain returned him his watch.

St James' Chronicle and British Evening Post, Tuesday 6 October to Thursday 8 October 1795, carried the notice:

> Bankrupt (Dividends to be paid) December 10th (and not on 10th instant as before advertised) William Swanson of Banner Street, Bunhill Row, Middlesex, Watchmaker at Guildhall.

Thus old newspapers are obviously a fruitful source of contemporary horological data. Evidence[28] shows that the earliest publication in England was *Coranto* of 1621; but the *London Gazette*, started in 1666, was probably the real beginning of newspapers, for it survived. Over the next hundred years newspapers increased and from perhaps 1760 there were large numbers, so that any amateur survey to extract their horological information could be a lifetime's work. Indeed the Guildhall Library contains some of the work of F. and G. B. Buckley[29], brothers who made a considerable effort between the wars to correlate the available information into lists of eighteenth-century watchmakers. But they disregarded other horological snippets such as those quoted above, so that there is a vast amount of data available and great scope for research for anyone who has a local newspaper office or archive near his home.

Running a Market Stall

Buying and selling is a fascinating idea. If a watch can be purchased and then sold retail for twice the purchase price, an interesting sideline of watch collecting might be to become a spare-time dealer. This section describes an investigation into the feasibility of this course of action.

Having an idea and putting it into practice are entirely different things. Initially, consideration of possible sales outlets included shops, indoor markets and street markets in various towns. Visits and further consideration suggested that the one-day street-market stall was the easiest outlet to try, and London was chosen as having the biggest potential clientele. The day had to be a Saturday or Sunday as these were the only ones available. Sunday was not really served by suitable London markets and thus the possibilities were reduced to a stall in Islington or in the Portobello Road, Notting Hill.

Islington has been associated with markets since the eighteenth century.[30] Initially it was an area producing vegetables, later it became a resting-place for cattle en route for Smithfield. When Smithfield became a meat market rather than a cattle market in *c*1860, Islington became the site of the replacement market for live cattle and this lasted until 1939. Smithfield had also had the Pedlars Market for clothes which moved to the Caledonian Road in Islington at the same time as the cattle market. By 1900 the Caledonian Road had become a centre for antiques, but this was closed in 1939 as the whole area was required by the army. The antique traders moved to Bermondsey and the New Caledonian, or Bermondsey, market still operates on Fridays. After the war the army's need disappeared, and Islington was re-established as an antique centre around Camden Passage which is open on Wednesdays and Saturdays.

The name Portobello Road derives from the successful capture of Porto Bello in Panama in 1739 during the War of Jenkins' Ear,[31] which started when a merchant sea-captain lost his ear to Spanish coastguards. The market for fruit and vegetables developed in the 1860–70 period and is still there encapsulated by antique and bric-à-brac stalls which are a post-1945 phenomenon. It is now a larger Saturday market than Islington, but its goods are more diverse and it attracts large crowds of British and foreign visitors.

A survey showed that more people visited Portobello Road than Islington, so the former seemed the better prospect. To secure a stall it is best to enter a renting contract rather than rely on casual vacancies, and to avoid commitment every Saturday a group of people on a duty rota is advantageous. A group was formed and a stall rented, and various goods were bought for sale by the group members. All attended the opening day, full of hope. A long day from 0700 to 1700 produced virtually no sales! The reason was simple. An inside stall had been chosen and the number of people finding their way to it was too small. Fortunately, a month later an outside stall became free at a much higher rental and a move to this site improved sales to an acceptable level. This was the first lesson learned.

The second lesson concerned prices. It had always seemed that dealers made large profits when buying privately or at auction and selling retail at perhaps twice the purchase price. A day in the market revealed that life is not so easy. To pay rent, fares and other overheads and earn fourteen hours' pay (for time worked actually at the stall isn't the whole story) requires a considerable turnover. This can only be achieved by having well-chosen desirable goods, well displayed and competitively priced. A sixth sense has to be quickly acquired as to the amount the customer will really pay in any haggling situation.

The third lesson was to do with the amount of stock held. It was absolutely necessary to have adequate fresh stock available to replace items that were sold. A half-empty stall is wasted rent — you are renting display area and it must be used. This means that, as well as selling on Saturday, buying has to be done in the week by attending local auctions for viewing and leaving bids, or by buying in bulk from another dealer which, in the watch trade, means 'buying a parcel of watches'. A parcel is a job lot taken together, good and bad, its attraction being that a reasonable outlay followed by investment in repairs provides reasonably priced stock plus a 'scrap bin' of oddments which attracts collectors looking for spares. Surprisingly in the whole time of operation, very few items were bought over the stall counter for resale. Quite a few were bought from other dealers by walking the length of the road, but few 'hawkers' had items which offered much profit or were of value to the personal collector. The only item kept was a Waterbury watch box. A further problem with stock requires decisive action: as the stall runs, it will be found that certain items do not sell and that capital becomes tied up in this unsaleable stock. This dead stock is best put to auction to release the capital.

The fourth lesson concerned transportation of stock — not a great problem with watches and other jewellery which can be easily carried, but if other items are to be sold as well there may be problems. Porcelain can be easily damaged, needs careful packing and is bulky; books are heavy and can be damaged; furniture is large; metal objects are heavy etc. With the outside stall, the goods were carried to and fro each week; but with the inside stall they could be left, at the owner's risk, in the stall. The only real way to move bulky goods was by car or van which had to be parked close to the stall for loading and unloading. Most of the market area is a 'no parking' zone and to secure one of the few places available meant arriving at 0500 so lengthening the working day. Watches and jewellery do in fact present an alternative problem by their very portability. They must be in a locked box to stop theft ('leakage') and the box must be large or secured or the whole thing will disappear! Locking the box stops browsing and must result in loss of custom, but it is essential. Similar precautions must be taken with money, which must be put into a secure zipped-away concealed waist-bag or similar safe place. Pockets, purses and wallets are useless.

The final thought on sales concerns the ratio of sales to enquiries, which may be 1 to 30. If you think about the number of watches you look at before you buy one, it is probably a similar ratio. As in repair work, so with sales, patience is a virtue; and each potential customer must be treated well for that person may be a real buyer, not a browser.

All this sounds fairly dismal but, for four years, on a rota basis, the running of the stall was enjoyable — especially on fine, warm days. There was the pleasure of meeting lots of interesting people from various countries, the pleasure of making a sale, the market atmosphere, the food and drink. Above all the amount of knowledge, information and experience gained was beyond belief, and running a stall was a great eye-opener on life. The final question of course is 'Was it profitable?' The answer is a qualified 'Yes'. For those members of the group living within car-driving distance of the market there was definitely a profit, but for those who came from a long distance by train or car and had an overnight journey or a hotel stop, there was usually a loss. To make a long journey profitable it is necessary to adopt a different approach and make considerable purchases of stock in the week for resale to the trade in parcels. This is not easy for the regular part-time dealer, but could be practised on an intermittent basis by attending the market as a hawker only when sufficient stock has been acquired. This is not an attractive alternative, for the whole thing becomes a purely financial consideration rather than an interesting hobby.

After four years, the experiment was judged to have reached the end of its useful life. Changes in the economic state of the Western World meant that the number of customers with money to spend diminished and the profits were reduced to unacceptably low levels. There were also other aspects of watch collecting to be pursued. The conclusion arrived at was that the best way to be involved in buying and selling watches as a hobby would be to rent a small inside stall as a specialist in watches. The stall would only need to open for a few hours, which regular customers would learn. It would be necessary to be able to produce interesting watches for sale, but if the sales were slow it would not matter because it was a hobby not a commercial enterprise. It would be best to live within an hour's journey by train to avoid the problems of using a car. The conversations and occasional successes would make this a pleasant involvement with watches and hopefully, in due course, interchange of items would improve one's personal collection.

A final remark on accounts and UK taxes. Obviously these spare-time activities should appear in annual income tax returns but, if the turnover is small, VAT should not be involved. In order to be able to justify such tax returns as are made, accounts must be kept. Such accounts are very useful in showing how much the exercise is really costing, because the overheads tend to get forgotten by the amateur in the excitement of selling at an apparent profit.[32]

12
MUSEUMS

In most European cities there are museums featuring watches, and some in Britain and Switzerland have very comprehensive collections. This is not to disparage the exhibits of other countries, but it is possible in these two locations to see an enormous quantity and variety of watches within a comparatively small area. There are also collections in the USA, but because they are so far apart it is not easy to see so much. Museum personnel are experts in their subject and give help and advice to realistic enquiries. But remember, they are *not* a valuation agency.

This chapter outlines the contents of museums, collections and libraries which have been visited mainly in Britain, but including a few in Switzerland, France and the USA. This is followed by references to unvisited museums. Guide books[1,2,3] can help in locating collections in Britain, and travel guides to other countries[4] list museums. National Tourist offices are also able to supply relevant brochures. It should be realised that museum displays may change and confirmation of the display would be wise if a special journey is contemplated.

GREAT BRITAIN: LONDON MUSEUMS AND LIBRARIES

Guildhall Library Clock Room, Aldermanbury, EC

Open: 0930–1645 Monday to Saturday. Underground: Bank, St Paul's or Moorgate

The Clock Room within the Guildhall Library contains the collection of the Worshipful Company of Clockmakers comprising about three hundred watches chronologically arranged from 1600 to 1930 and grouped by escapement. The lever watches include examples by Emery, Leroux, Grant and Breguet. There is also a selection of chronometers, clocks, books and over a thousand watch keys. The watches show cases and/or movements in what is probably the clearest display in London. However, the escapement you wish to see may not be one of those selected for an open-case, as opposed to a closed-case, view. The London Museum (qv) is close by.

Science Museum, Exhibition Road, South Kensington, SW

Open: 1000–1800 Monday to Saturday; 1430–1800 Sunday. Underground: South Kensington

This museum displays watches from a technical viewpoint, thus movements rather than cases are on view. The collection includes escapement models, table clocks from 1550 and watches from 1600 to the twentieth century. The arrangement is not chronological but according to similar technical features; for example, stop-watches are grouped. There are also clocks (including the Wells Cathedral clock), chronometers and other clock-based devices. Also on the same floor, there is a display of tools including a wheel cutting engine of about 1672 and other lathes.

The museum is very close to the Victoria and Albert Museum which displays watches as jewellery.

Victoria and Albert Museum, Exhibition Road, South Kensington, SW

Open: 1000–1730 Monday to Thursday and Saturday; 1430–1730 Sunday. Underground: South Kensington

This museum displays over two hundred watches in the first bay of the jewellery cage. No movements are shown; but for the collector interested in style and design of case work, the collection is excellent. The display is arranged to show separately German, English, Dutch, French and Swiss watches of the sixteenth and seventeenth centuries; but collectively for later styles. Cocks, keys, seals and châtelaines are also shown.

The museum is very close to the Science Museum which displays watches from a technical viewpoint.

National Maritime Museum, Romney Road, Greenwich, SE

Open: 1000–1700 Tuesday to Saturday; 1400–1700 Sunday. British Rail: Charing Cross to Maze Hill (15 minutes)

A visit to this museum is essential for anyone interested in the solution of the longitude problem in Britain at the end of the eighteenth century. In the main building, Harrison's four marine timekeepers can be seen *working* and these alone make a visit worthwhile and are a tribute not only to Harrison but to their restorer, R. T. Gould. Out of the main building, in Flamsteed House in the Old Observatory, there is a collection of watches, pocket chronometers and marine chronometers, including watches belonging to various sea-captains such as Nelson, Hardy and Collingwood. The chronometers include work by Arnold, Earnshaw, Breguet and Mudge (Pennington). There is also a display of auxiliary compensation. An Emery lever watch and the 1552 Jacques de la Garde clock, similar to the 1551 Louvre watch (see Chapter 1), are also on view.

British Museum, Great Russell Street, Bloomsbury, WC
Open: 1000–1700 Monday to Saturday; 1430–1800 Sunday. Underground: Russell Square or Tottenham Court Road

The British Museum holds the renowned Ilbert collection, which has examples of most watch or movement types but is not on view. Part of the collection is, however, often used for temporary displays arranged to illustrate a particular theme. The museum also has an early English watch by Randolph Bull dated 1590. A telephone call to find out what is displayed may be helpful (01–636–1555). Part of the British Library (qv) is housed in the same building.

London Museum, London Wall, EC2
Open: 1000–1800 Tuesday to Saturday; 1400–1800 Sunday. Underground: St Paul's or Moorgate

This museum is not arranged by items but chronologically, the indicated route beginning in pre-history and moving on to twentieth-century London. If the visitor is sharp-eyed, watches can be seen together with other objects relevant to a period; in particular, small groups can be seen in 'Late Stuart London' and 'Georgian London'. The museum is not recommended specifically for watches, but is interesting in that it puts the watch into contemporary surroundings. It is very close to the important Guildhall Library Clock Room (qv), and the two visits could conveniently be combined.

Science Museum Library, Imperial Institute Road, South Kensington, SW
Open: 1000–1730 Monday to Saturday. Underground: South Kensington

The library is close to both the Science and the Victoria and Albert Museums. It contains a considerable number of horological books and patents and should be regarded as a prime source of data. Books cannot be borrowed except through the Inter-Library Loan Service, but are available for study during opening hours.

Guildhall Library, Aldermanbury, EC
Open: 0930–1700 Monday to Saturday. Underground: Bank, St Paul's or Moorgate

This library has a collection of horological books and is a prime source of data. It does not lend books, nor can they be obtained through the Inter-Library Loan Service; the library is purely for reference. The Clock Room in the same building contains the watch collection of the Worshipful Company of Clockmakers.

The British Library, Great Russell Street, Bloomsbury, WC
Open: 1000–1700 Monday to Saturday; 1430–1800 Sunday. Underground: Russell Square or Tottenham Court Road

The reference section of this library arranges book and manuscript exhibitions on various topics, and in the student's room genuine researchers can gain access to any documents relevant to their work. It is not a library for casual use, but one which may have a rare work needed for special study. It is necessary to make appointments to discuss problems.

The British Library (Science Reference Library) and The Patent Office Library, 25 Southampton Buildings, Chancery Lane, WC2A 1AY
Open: 0930–2100 Monday to Friday; 1000–1300 Saturday. Underground: Holborn or Chancery Lane

The library holds British and foreign patents and a useful selection of horological material. Publications earlier than 1965 are in store and may take up to 3 hours to retrieve. Books are not loaned but there is a quick photocopying service. There is another Science Reference Library at 9, Kean Street, Drury Lane, WC2B 4AT which has material of peripheral interest to horologists.

GREAT BRITAIN: PROVINCIAL MUSEUMS

Basingstoke: The Willis Museum, New Street
This museum contains an interesting horological collection of clocks, watches, tools, dials, chains, etc. There are not a vast number of watches, but there is a fine early German clockwatch. The tools are very good.

Birmingham: The Museum of Science and Industry, Newhall Street
The museum contains clocks, watches and tools. The watches on display are only accompanied by limited information, but the staff are helpful with queries. The clock display is more comprehensive and the tools are well worth studying.

Bournemouth: Russell-Cotes Art Gallery, East Cliff
The gallery has about thirty watches, so it is worth a visit if one is in the area, though the information about the watches on display is limited.

Bury St Edmunds: Gershom Parkington Memorial Collection, 8 Angel Hill
This is a major provincial collection and contains clocks, watches, chains, dials and quadrants. The earliest items date from the sixteenth century, the watches from about 1600 to 1850. The emphasis is on decoration rather than technical merit and there are no early lever or chronometer exhibits. The museum is about thirty miles from Cambridge and could be combined with a visit to that city.

Cambridge: Fitzwilliam Museum, Trumpington Street
About a hundred watches are displayed with the emphasis on decorative rather than technical aspects so that no movements are shown. The collection spans the seventeenth, eighteenth and nineteenth centuries, and includes examples reputed to have been owned by Gainsborough and Beethoven. There are many enamelled cases and continental exhibits outnumber English ones. There is also a display of clockwatches and of miniature, enamelled panel carriage clocks. The museum is worth a visit and is thirty miles from the Bury St Edmunds museum. There is no catalogue.

Canterbury: Beaney Institute, High Street
A collection of about thirty watches with a local bias, and worth a visit if in the area.

Cardiff: Welsh Folk Museum, St Fagans
This museum of modern layout has a considerable number of watches which were not on display. Now that there is a Welsh section of the Antiquarian Horological Society, it is likely that some watches will be shown.

Exeter: Royal Albert Memorial Museum, Queen Street

The museum has an excellent collection of about seventy pocket watches attractively displayed and well arranged, together with a few tools and clocks. The watches include local work, but the emphasis is on good lever watches and pocket chronometers of which there are ten. There are also chronographs and a tourbillon by Smith. Other makers represented are Mudge, Arnold, Earnshaw, Barraud, Kullberg, Haley, Viner, Dent, Frodsham and McCabe.

Hove: Museum of Art, 19 New Church Road

The hundred or so watches in this museum include examples by Ody, Molyneux (and Cope), Arnold, Mudge and Dutton, Ellicott, Litherland, Roskell, McCabe etc. Not all are displayed but the staff are very helpful, especially if an appointment is made. There is also a large collection of keys.

Lancaster: Lancaster Museum, Market Square

This museum with its display of verge movements signed by local 'makers' is worth a visit if one is in the area, but not a special journey. It is close to the Lake District, and Preston Museum.

Leeds: Abbey House Museum, Kirkstall

This museum is arranged in 'streets' and one of the 'shops' is that of John Dyson, Clock and Watchmaker. Its contents include many clocks and watches and bits and pieces, which must be examined carefully so as not to miss anything. The emphasis is on local industry. The whole museum is very enjoyable in concept (the Castlegate Museum in York is also arranged in this way).

Leicester: The New Walk and Deacon's Workshop, Newarke Houses

The New Walk Museum contains about twenty-five watches and around the same number of clocks. The emphasis is on local makers, the most famous probably being Loseby who moved to London and is known for chronometer work. Most of the clocks are eighteenth-century longcase examples.

Deacon's Workshop is a fascinating late eighteenth-century clockmaker's workshop which was moved bodily to the site in 1951.

Lincoln: Usher Gallery, Lindum Road

This collection of about seventy English and continental watches, from the mid-seventeenth to the mid-nineteenth century, emphasises their role as jewellery and is one of the best provincial collections of continental watches in Britain. It does, however, have a notable English ring watch by Arnold dated 1764, with a movement less than 10mm (0.4in) in diameter, which was made for George III. There are also a few interesting clocks.

Liverpool: Merseyside County Museum, William Brown Street

This museum has about four hundred well-displayed watches of which a large proportion are from Liverpool since this part of England was an important watchmaking centre. There are also examples by well known makers from London and the Continent, including Ellicott, Emery, Graham, Lepine, le Roy, Mudge, Quare and Tompion. The collection of tools that used to be housed here has been largely transferred to the museum at Prescot a few miles distant (qv). These two museums combined make a special visit worthwhile.

Oxford: Museum of the History of Science, Broad Street

This museum displays about a hundred watches from England and the Continent dated between 1600 and 1850; a reserve collection (not displayed) contains another two hundred. This — one of the major British collections containing examples by many significant makers — is an essential visit, and the displaying of the examples on mirrors so that both sides can be seen is excellent. The catalogue is very good. There are also clocks and a large collection of sundials.

Prescot: Prescot Museum, 34 Church Street

A visit to this small museum is vital for anyone interested in watch manufacture. The exhibits are on two floors, the upper of which is devoted to clock and watch making history from a table clock of 1440 and a watch of 1590 through to electronic watches. There is information about tools, toolmaking and processes used in making clocks and watches; also a watchmaker's workshop with various engines and parts. Last, but by no means least, is the Lancashire Watch Company exhibit which includes watches, tools, machinery and documents connected with a pioneering attempt to make watches in a factory in England from 1889 to 1910. A visit to Prescot can be combined with a visit to the museum at Liverpool a few miles distant (qv).

Preston: The Harris Museum and Art Gallery, Market Square

This museum's collection of about forty pieces is not displayed, but appointments can be made to view. In general the watches are of local interest. There are interesting pieces by Yates, Emery (cylinder) and Thomas Hatton. It is hardly worth a special trip, but worth a visit if one is in the area.

Snowshill Manor, near Broadway, Worcestershire
This National Trust property houses a small collection of verge-watch movements and cocks, clocks and a few tools. Although not of great horological significance, the Manor and its collection of artifacts are well worth a visit and the staff are very enthusiastic. (No public transport, variable opening hours, telephone 852410.)

FRANCE

Paris: Conservatoire National des Arts et Métiers
This museum contains a large horological collection and is well worth a visit, though the watch section is not the most important. The main features are early marine timekeepers by Berthoud, le Roy and other French makers, some excellent regulating clocks and a large collection of horological tools. The watches, mainly uncased movements of the eighteenth and early nineteenth centuries, are displayed in wall-mounted cases.

Paris: Petit Palais
A display of about fifty enamelled-case watches makes this an essential point of call for the student of this field when in Paris. There are few other watches, but a number of interesting clocks.

SWITZERLAND

Chaux de Fonds: Musée International d'horlogerie
Open: 1000–1200 and 1400–1700 daily except Monday

This purpose-built museum has an impressive collection which includes watches, clocks, chronometers, astronomical instruments and musical boxes, the watches forming a major part of the exhibits. English watches by Arnold, Graham, Harrison, Quare, Tompion and others are included; the continental examples are of similar quality with examples by Berthoud, Breguet, le Roy, Robin, etc. The catalogue is expensive but is beautifully produced and well illustrated, with minimal descriptive text. The two opening sessions each day are all too short. The museum has repair, library and advisory facilities. Le Locle museum is nearby.

USA

San Francisco: California Academy of Sciences, Golden Gate Park
This is a large museum with an interesting selection of watches including some early American and interesting European examples. It is the only museum visited in which exhibits have been sectioned (or had new cut-away plates made) to display significant parts of their mechanism — an interesting method of display provided the original parts can be replaced. The watches are hung in glass cases to enable all-round viewing.

The following museums have not been visited but are on a 'personal list' of those considered interesting or large enough to merit attention when time and money permit.

Great Britain: Bath, Carlisle, Edinburgh, Hastings, Ipswich, Norwich, York

Austria: Innsbruck, Salzburg, Vienna

Belgium: Brussels

Canada: Calgary, Toronto

Denmark: Aarhus, Copenhagen

France: Besançon, Ecouen, Paris (Louvre), Strasbourg

Germany: Dresden, Kassel, Munich, Nuremburg, Pforzheim, Schwenningen, Stuttgart, Wuppertal, Würzburg

Holland: Amsterdam, Leiden, Rotterdam, Utrecht

Italy: Milan

Norway: Oslo

Sweden: Lund

Switzerland: Basle, Geneva, Le Locle, Neuchâtel, Winterthur, Zürich

USA: American Clock and Watch Museum, Bristol, Conneticut
Metropolitan Museum of Art, New York City
Time Museum, Rockford, Illinois
Smithsonian Institute, Washington DC

GLOSSARY

Arbor A shaft or axle
Arcaded dial A dial on which the minute ring has arches between the numerals rather than a circular form
Automatic Self-winding
Auxiliary compensation Additional compensation added to a bimetallic balance to reduce middle-temperature error
Back plate The plate of the watch furthest from the dial
Balance The oscillating spoked wheel which controls the rate at which the mainspring is allowed to unwind
Balance spring The spiral or helical spring controlling the balance vibration
Balance staff The axle on which the balance is fitted
Banking A system to control the arc of vibration of a balance or, in the lever watch, the motion of the lever
Barrel The cylindrical container for the mainspring
Beat The audible tick of the watch. A watch that is in beat has an even tick
Beetle hand The hour hand used on eighteenth-century watches in combination with the poker minute hand
Bezel The ring-shaped piece of case holding the glass
Bimetallic balance A balance wheel whose rim is made of two metals such that the differential expansion rate counteracts the effects of temperature changes on the rate of the watch
Bottom plate The plate of the watch nearest to the dial
Bow The hanging ring of a pocket watch
Bull's-eye glass A high-domed watch glass with a flat centre piece
Button The winding knob of a keyless watch
Calibre A term used to denote the size (and shape) of a watch
Cam A contoured shape which rotates to give a special motion to a follower resting on the cam
Cannon pinion The pinion driving the motion work with a long hollow arbor which fits over the extended centre-wheel shaft between the dial and the plate
Centre wheel The second wheel of the train rotating once per hour
Chaffcutter A Debaufre-type escapement described in Chapter 6
Chapter ring The ring marked on the dial with hour divisions
Chinese duplex A duplex escapement watch with double-locking teeth so that two complete balance vibrations are required for escape. The watch advances in increments of one second
Chronograph A watch with a seconds hand capable of being started, stopped and reset independently of the mean-time hands
Click A pawl or detent inhibiting motion in one direction
Club-foot verge A Debaufre-type escapement
Club-tooth lever A lever escapement with the type of escape wheel known as the Swiss lever described in Chapter 3
Cock A bracket supporting the pivot of a wheel. Usually the term refers to the

balance cock for the top balance pivot
Compensated balance A bimetallic balance designed to counteract the effect of temperature change on the rate of a watch
Contrate wheel A wheel with teeth at right angles to the plane of the wheel. The fourth wheel in a verge watch is an example
Coqueret A hard steel bearing on the balance cock of continental watches
Crank lever escapement A Massey lever escapement described in Chapter 3
Crank roller escapement Another name for the crank lever escapement
Crown wheel escapement The verge escapement described in Chapter 2
Curb pins The pins attached to the regulator which loosely hold the balance spring so that its working length can be varied as the regulator is adjusted
Cylinder escapement The first successful alternative to the verge escapement introduced in 1726. Described in Chapter 6
Dart The safety pointer below the lever-fork in the double-roller lever watch
Dead beat escapement An escapement without recoil
Dead beat verge A Debaufre-type escapement
Debaufre-type escapement An escapement based on an invention by Peter Debaufre in 1704
Deck watch An accurate watch used aboard ship during astronomical observations; it is usually contained in a wooden box
Depth A term to describe the amount of penetration between two meshing gears
Detached escapement An escapement in which the balance vibration is free from friction except during the unlocking and impulse action
Detent A holding piece which stops movement in one or two directions
Detent escapement The (pocket) chronometer escapement. Described in Chapter 6
Divided lift An escapement in which the lift giving impulse is partly a result of pallet slope and partly as a result of the escape-wheel tooth shape
Double bottom case A case in which the back opens to reveal a second bottom pierced by a winding hole
Double roller A lever escapement with two rollers. One roller is for impulse action and the second (smaller) for safety action
Draw The shaping of the escape-wheel teeth so that the lever-pallets are drawn into the escape wheel and the lever on to the banking pins to prevent friction due to accidental lever motion
Drop The free travel of the escape wheel between escape and locking
Duplex escapement An escapement based on a design by Dutertre described in Chapter 6
Dust cap A cover placed on the movement in keywind watches
Dutch forgery A term used to describe watches with a bridge-type balance cock, an arcaded dial with or without a scene and often with a repoussé case. The work is of mediocre quality and marked with an English 'maker'. Probably made partly in England and partly on the Continent
Ébauche An unfinished movement supplied by a factory to the watchmaker who finishes and signs it
End-shake The axial clearance between a shaft and its bearings
Endstone A disc-shaped jewel on which the end of the balance pivot rests
Engine turning The common form of nineteenth-century case decoration
English lever escapement The escapement used almost exclusively by English watchmakers from 1850 till 1920; described in Chapter 3
Entry pallet The pallet on a lever which receives impulse as the escape-wheel teeth enter
Equation of time The relationship between solar time (based on the position of the sun) and mean time (based on averaged solar motion)

Escapement The part of a watch movement which constrains the train motion to small increments. It consists of the escape wheel, (lever) and balance
Escape wheel The wheel in the movement connecting with the lever or balance
Exit pallet The pallet on a lever which receives impulse as the escape-wheel teeth leave
Figure plate The small dial indicating the amount of regulation fitted to watches with Tompion regulation
First wheel The great wheel on the fusee or going-barrel
Fourth wheel The fourth wheel of the train which rotates once per minute if a seconds hand is fitted
Free sprung A watch with no regulator and curb pins. Regulation is achieved by the timing screws on the balance
Frictional rest escapement An escapement in which the balance motion is affected by friction during the major part of the vibration
Front plate The plate of the watch nearest to the dial
Full plate A watch in which the top plate is complete or has a barrel plate. The balance is fitted on top of the plate
Fusee The conical-shaped piece with a spiral groove for the fusee chain which equalises the mainspring torque
Going-barrel A spring-barrel driving the watch train without the use of an intermediate fusee and chain
Great wheel The first wheel of the train on the fusee or going-barrel
Greenwich time The local mean time at Greenwich used as a basis for longitude and world time-zones
Guard pin The vertical pin (at the base of the fork on the lever of an English lever escapement) which gives safety action on the roller
Hairspring The balance spring
Half plate A watch in which balance, lever, escape wheel and fourth wheel have separate cocks
Hallmark The assay mark on English silver and gold indicating date and quality
Heart piece The cam used in a chronograph to reset the centre seconds hand
Hog's bristle regulator Flexible bristles arranged to limit the arc of vibration of a pre-balance-spring watch
Horizontal escapement The cylinder escapement described in Chapter 6
Horns The tips of the forked end of a lever
Hunter A watch case with a hinged solid cover over the glass. If fitted with a small glass it is called a half hunter
Impulse The push given to the balance by the escapement
Index The regulator pointer
Isochronism The property of taking the same time for a balance vibration independent of the arc of vibration
Jewels Bearings made of precious stones such as ruby. Modern jewels are synthetic
Karrusel A rotating escapement designed to avoid positional error. Described in Chapter 7
Kew Certificate A rating certificate (A, B and C grade) given by Kew Observatory from 1884
Keyless A watch that is both wound and hand set without a key
Lancashire size An English scale for the size of a movement
Land of a cam A flat portion on the cam profile during which the follower does not move
Lever escapement A detached escapement described in Chapter 3
Lift The angular motion of the lever
Ligne A continental unit of measurement of watch size

Mainspring The spiral spring in the barrel providing power
Maintaining power An arrangement in the fusee to keep power on the train whilst the watch is being wound. This avoids the watch stopping or faltering during the operation
Massey lever escapement A detached lever escapement described in Chapter 3
Mean time The conventional time shown by clocks and watches based on average solar motion
Middle-temperature error A residual timekeeping error in watches with a compensated balance
Motion work The gearing under the dial used to make the hour hand rotate at one twelfth of the speed of the minute hand
Movement The watch works without case, dial and hands
Oil sink The small depression in the watch plate around a pivot hole designed to hold oil in place
Ormskirk escapement A Debaufre-type escapement described in Chapter 6
Overcoil The last coil of a balance spring which departs from the spiral by being bent above the spring to give a better approach to isochronism. Invented by Breguet
Pair-case A watch with an inner case and a separate outer case. It was in general use until about 1800; uncommon after 1830
Pallet The part of the escapement through which impulse is transferred from the escape wheel to the balance wheel or lever
Passing crescent The indentation in the roller in a lever watch to allow the guard pin or dart to pass at the instant of impulse
Pendant The part of the watch case to which the hanging bow is attached
Pillars The distance pieces separating the watch plates
Pillar plate The plate of the watch nearest to the dial
Pinion A small steel gear wheel (6–12 teeth) driven by a larger brass wheel
Pin-lever escapement An inexpensive lever escapement described in Chapter 4
Pivot The small diameter part at the end of a shaft which is supported in a bearing
Plates The flat brass discs supporting the train of the watch. The plates are separated by pillars
Poker hand The minute hand used on eighteenth-century watches in combination with the beetle hour hand
Positional error An error due to the variation in the rate of a watch in different positions: pendant up or down, etc
Potence A hanging bearing such as the lower balance pivot on a full-plate watch
Rack lever escapement An early lever escapement described in Chapter 3
Ratchet wheel A wheel with saw-shaped teeth which will rotate in one direction. Rotation in the other direction is impeded by a pawl
Rate The daily rate of loss or gain of a watch
Recoil The backward motion of a watch when the escapement is unlocked
Regulation The term used to describe the adjustment of the timekeeping of a watch
Repeater A watch which gives audible indication of the approximate time by sounding gongs when a push piece is operated
Rocking bar A device used to change from winding to hand-setting mode (or vice versa) in keyless watches
Roller The disc fitted on the balance staff in a lever watch to receive impulse and give safety action
Roskopf escapement A pin lever escapement
Safety roller The smaller roller for safety action in a double-roller lever watch
Savage two-pin escapement An early lever escapement described in Chapter 3
Second wheel The centre wheel of the train
Self-winding A watch with an eccentric weight pivoted so that it will always swing

to the low position. The swinging motion winds the watch
Set hands square The square on the end of the cannon pinion used to set the hands on a keywind watch
Set up The initial adjustment of tension in a spring
Shifting sleeve A device used to change from winding to hand-setting mode (or vice versa) in keyless watches
Single roller A lever watch with a single roller fulfilling both impulse and safety requirements
Solar time The time indicated by solar position. A day is the time elapsed between two transits of the sun. This is not a constant
Spade hand An hour hand with an enlarged end of similar shape to the spade symbol on a playing card
Split seconds A chronograph with two independent seconds hands, each of which can be operated separately
Stackfreed An early regulation device based on the friction between a cam and a spring-loaded follower
Stem wind Keyless winding and hand setting through a button
Swiss lever escapement The continental form of lever escapement described in Chapter 3
Table-roller lever escapement The English lever escapement described in Chapter 3
Temperature compensation Compensation for the changes in timekeeping caused by changes in temperature, usually by bimetallic balance
Terminal curve The special end shape given to a balance spring to give isochronous motion
Third wheel The third wheel of the train
Three-quarter plate A watch in which the balance, lever and escape wheel have separate cocks
Timing-screws The two (or four) screws at the ends of the balance arms (if four, also at right angles to the ends of the arms). They are not compensation screws
Top plate The plate of the watch furthest from the dial
Tourbillon A rotating escapement designed to avoid positional error. Described in Chapter 7
Train The series of meshing wheels and pinions connecting the fusee or going-barrel to the escapement
Up-and-down dial An extra indicator on a watch dial to show the state of mainspring winding
Verge The vertical staff below the balance wheel carrying the pallets of the verge escapement
Verge escapement Early escapement described in Chapter 2
Watch paper A circular piece of paper or cloth often carrying printed information or advertising placed between pair-cases by the seller or repairer. The paper takes up play and inhibits rubbing
Wheel A large, brass, train wheel which drives a smaller steel pinion
Winding-square The square end on the fusee or barrel arbor used for winding a keywind watch
Worm An 'endless' screw which is rotated to turn a gear placed tangentially to the worm surface. The plane of the gear is that of the worm axis

APPENDIX: USEFUL INFORMATION

There are specialist horological dictionaries available in reference libraries which should be used to clarify terminology, mechanisms, etc.[1,2]

Hallmarks on Silver Cases

Subsequent to the passing of the Plate Duty Act of 1719, silver cases of English origin, and those of European origin that have passed through an English assay office, have carried a hallmark indicating the metal and the place and year of assay. This system of marks may be used as a guide to the date of a watch. However, watches can be recased and marks can be faked, so the information must be treated with care and used in combination with that obtained from other sources. Casemaker's marks, usually consisting of initials, also appear on some cases and this may help in dating. European marks are not so easily interpreted but may be used as a guide to the metal quality: the number 800 or 925 indicates the parts per thousand of silver in the case alloy.

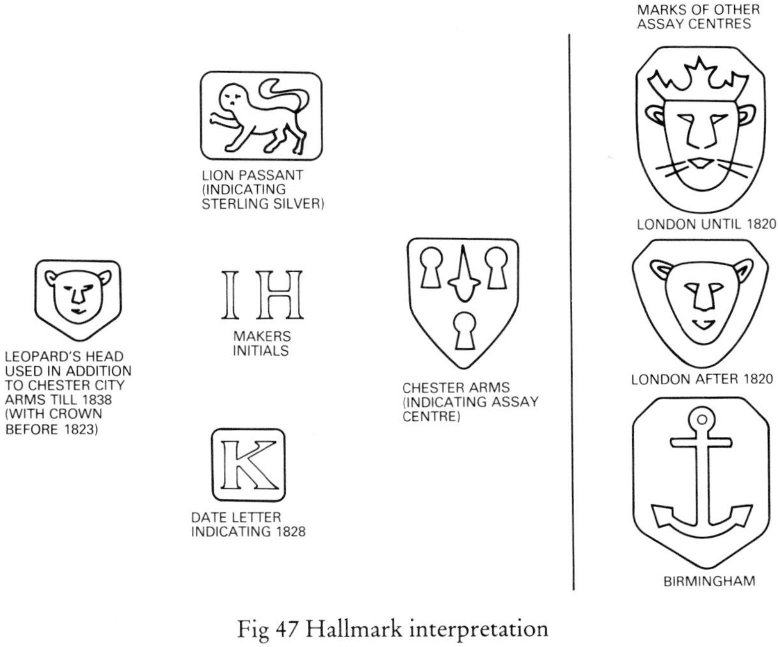

Fig 47 Hallmark interpretation

On English hallmarked silver, the indication of sterling silver (92.5 per cent pure) is a lion passant. There were a number of assay offices, but in the period covered by this book the majority of cases were assayed in London, Birmingham or Chester, represented by a leopard's head, an anchor and the Chester arms respectively (Fig 47). Alphabetical letters used in sequence A–Z (with some letters occasionally missed out) represent the year of assay; however, they were not changed on the first day of January but some time in mid-year so that dating is not precise. The date-letter style lasts from twenty to twenty-six years and then the style is changed, so that with the aid of an inexpensive book on silver marks, or a good memory, dating should present no difficulty. Marks are often worn and not very clear, but the fact that they should appear on each part of the case goes some way to obviate this difficulty. On pair-cases, difference in marks may indicate a new or married case. Fig 47 shows typical marks found inside the case of a watch, and gives the method of interpretation.

Weights and Measures

Jewellers and silversmiths measure in troy weight in which:

24 grains make 1 pennyweight (dwt)
20 pennyweights make 1 ounce troy (oz troy)
12 ounces troy make 1 pound troy (lb troy)

Thus 1oz troy is 480 grains and 1lb troy 5,760 grains. In the normal avoirdupois system, 1lb is 16oz or 7,000 grains; so that 1oz avoirdupois is 437½ grains.

In metric measurements 1lb is 453.6 grams (g) and 1in is 25.4 millimetres (mm).

Watch Sizes

Some watch movements of English makers have carried a size indication stamped on the underside of the dial plate since the second half of the nineteenth century. This consists of a single number between 0 and 40 possibly followed by two numbers written over each other, eg 12^{0}_{2}. The first number is the Lancashire watch size which gives the overall movement diameter. Size 0 represents 1in and the diameter is 1in plus the number of 1/30ths of an inch given by the number, plus 5/30in of 'fall' (the allowance for the larger size of dial plate to allow the top plate to hinge into the case). Thus in the example above, the dial plate diameter is (1 + 12/30 + 5/30) = 1.567in. The numbers written over each other give the pillar height. Size $^{0}_{0}$ is 0.125in and if the top number is altered the height is 0.125in plus the number of 1/144ths of an inch indicated by the top number. If the bottom number is altered the height is 0.125in less the number of 1/144ths of an inch indicated by the bottom number. Thus in the example above, the pillar height is (0.125 − 2/144) = 0.111in. The range of pillar heights is from $^{0}_{6}$ to $^{30}_{0}$, ie from 0.0833in to 0.333in.

Consideration of the history of these sizes would indicate that the sizes were for use with gauges rather than in the awkward decimals produced above and that the gauges were based on fractional figures obtained on a system based on twelfths.

Continental watch sizes are based on lignes — a system of units in which 1 ligne = 2.255mm.

Markets

Local markets

Many places have markets weekly or daily, eg Bath has a Wednesday market.

Noted London markets

Bermondsey (Caledonian) Market, Tower Bridge Road, SE1. Opens 0600 on Friday: Tube station, London Bridge.

Cutler Street, E1 (now moved to nearby Goulston Street). Opens on Sunday morning: Tube station, Aldgate.

Portobello Road Market, Portobello Road, W10. Opens on Saturday: Tube station, Notting Hill Gate.

Camden Passage, Islington, N1. Opens on Wednesday and Saturday mornings: Tube station, Angel.

Paris market

Marché aux Puces, Porte de Clignancourt. Opens on Saturday, Sunday and Monday: Metro, Clignancourt.

Where to buy Watch Materials

Parts, tools, fluids, etc

Local watch-repair, tool and chemist shops.

Southern Watch and Clock Supplies Ltd, 48–56 High Street, Orpington, Kent.

A. G. Thomas (Bradford) Ltd, 50–2 Heaton Road, Bradford 8, West Yorkshire.

Enamels

W. G. Ball Ltd, Anchor Road, Longton, Stoke-on-Trent, Staffordshire.

Silver etc

Johnson, Matthey Metals Ltd, 73 Hatton Garden, London, EC1.

Sheffield Smelting Co Ltd, 134 St John Street, London, EC1.

Patent Copies

Photocopies of British Patent Specifications may be obtained by post from: Patent Office Sale Branch, Orpington, Kent, BR5 3RD, or at the Sale Counter, Patent Office, 25, Southampton Buildings, London, WC2A 1AY.

REFERENCES

AH denotes *Antiquarian Horology,* the journal of the Antiquarian Horological Society, New House, High Street, Ticehurst, Wadhurst, Sussex, TN5 7AL

Chapter 1

1 *The Concise Oxford Dictionary,* Oxford, 1934
2 Michel, H. 'Some new documents in the history of horology', AH, 3, March 1962, 288–91
3 Drover, C. B. 'The Brussels Miniature', AH, 3, September 1962, 357–61
4 *Horological Journal,* 89, August 1947, 398
5 Correspondence, AH, 4, June 1965, 348–9
6 Thomas, C. 'George Newton, Blacksmith, turned Clockmaker', AH, 12, Winter 1980, 420–7
7 *Encyclopedia Britannica,* 12 and 21, fourteenth edition 1930, 650 and 369
8 Ward, F. A. B. 'A 15th Century Italian "Clockmaker's" Workshop', AH, 12, Summer 1980, 172–4
9 Symonds, R. W. *A Book of English Clocks,* Penguin, 1947

Chapter 2

1 Caillard, B. 'The history of the pendulum watch', AH, 3, March 1960, 41–3
2 Rees, A. *Clocks, Watches and Chronometers (1819–20),* David & Charles, 1970
3 Jaquet, E. and Chapuis, A. *Technique and History of the Swiss Watch,* Hamlyn, 1970
4 Peate, I. C. *Clock and Watch makers in Wales,* National Museum of Wales, 1960, 9
5 Alan Lloyd, H. 'Samuel Watson', AH, 1, December 1954, 60–1
6 *American Watch Historical Information with Serial Numbers and Dates,* Minnesota Watchmakers Association, USA c1970
7 Dawson, P. G. 'Verge Watch Movements in Wood Cases', AH, 12, June 1981, 604–8
8 Burchall, A. 'Pitt's clock and watch tax: a reassessment', AH, 13, September 1982, 454–61

Chapter 3

1 Allix, C. 'Mudge Milestones', AH, 12, Summer 1981, 627–34
2 Daniels, G. 'Thomas Mudge, the complete horologist', AH, 13, December 1981, 150–73

3 Daniels, G. 'Mudge's lever escapement', AH, 5, June 1968, 396–407, 420
4 Clutton, C. 'The second Mudge lever watch', AH, 3, March 1960, 47–8
5 Clutton, C. 'Josiah Emery and John Leroux', AH, 13, December 1981, 145–7
6 Turner, A. J. 'New light on George Margetts', AH, 7, September 1971, 304–16
7 AH, 14, September 1983, 231
8 Rees, A. *Clocks, Watches and Chronometers (1819–20),* David & Charles, 1970
9 Miles, R. H. A. 'Did Julien le Roy make the first detached lever escapement?', AH, 3, September 1961, 224–30
10 Clutton, C. 'Julien le Roy's lever revived', AH, 4, September 1963, 108–9
11 Correspondence, AH, 4, December 1963, 154, and March 1964, 184; 5, September 1968, 464
12 Clutton, C. 'Le Roy and the lever escapement. Some new evidence?', AH, 5, March 1966, 53–4
13 Clutton, C. and Daniels, G. *Watches,* Batsford, 1965
14 Clutton, C. 'Collection of the Clockmakers' Company', AH, 1, June 1956, 165–6
15 Clutton, C. 'Two early lever watches', AH, 3, December 1960, 127–9
16 Clutton, C. 'Visits to Collections', AH, 2, December 1957, 86–8
17 Clutton, C. 'Collection of the Clockmakers' Company', AH, 1, September 1956, 181–2
18 Allix, C. 'Another "new" lever watch, Ellicott No 9927', AH, 4, June 1965, 335–7
19 Chapiro, A. 'Lepine, Breguet and the origins of the lever escapement in France', AH, 14, December 1983, 369–96
20 Chapiro, A. 'Two interesting watches of the late 18th century', AH, 8, September 1973, 412–15
21 Jagger, C. 'Robin's "revolutionary" lever watch No 3', AH, 5, December 1965, 21–3
22 Jaquet, E. and Chapuis, A. *Technique and History of the Swiss Watch,* Hamlyn, 1970
23 Mercer, R. V. 'Peter Litherland & Co.', AH, 3, June 1962, 316–23
24 Gould, R. T. *The Marine Chronometer,* Holland Press, 1960
25 AH, 10, Spring 1977, 225–6
26 Correspondence, AH, 9, March 1976, 705
27 Kemp, R. 'The Massey Watch Escapement', AH, 13, December 1982, 558–64
28 Kemp, R. 'Watch movement making in Prescot', AH, 13, September 1981, 77–83
29 Private communication
30 Gazeley, W. J. *Clock and Watch escapements,* Heywood, 1956
31 Chamberlain, P. M. *It's about Time,* Holland Press, 1964
32 *Antique Watches,* Collector Books, USA, 1979

33 Carrington, R. F. and R. W. 'Pierre Frederic Ingold', AH, 10, Spring 1978, 698–714

34 *The Lancashire Watch Company, Prescot, Lancashire, England, 1889–1910*, Ken Roberts, USA, 1973

Chapter 4

1 Jaquet, E. and Chapuis, A. *Technique and History of the Swiss Watch*, Hamlyn, 1970

2 Tshudy, R. F. 'Ingersoll' *Bulletin of the National Association of Watch and Clock Collectors*, 5, April 1952, 97–110

3 *The Lancashire Watch Company, Prescot, Lancashire, England, 1889–1910*, Ken Roberts, USA, 1973

4 De Carle, D. *Practical Watch Repairing*, NAG Press, 1947

Chapter 5

1 'The Worshipful Company of Clockmakers', AH, 13, December 1981, 140–2

2 Torrens, D. S. 'Nail and Cork', *Horological Journal*, 80, February 1938, 22–3

3 Symonds, R. W. *A Book of English Clocks*, Penguin, 1947

4 Rees, A. *Clocks, Watches and Chronometers (1819–20)*, David & Charles, 1970

5 Jaquet, E. and Chapuis, A. *Technique and History of the Swiss Watch*, Hamlyn, 1970

6 Kemp, R. 'Watch movement making in Prescot', AH, 13, September 1981, 77–83

7 *Horological Journal*, 9, April and May 1867, 85–8, 101–4

8 Torrens, D. S. 'Some notes on the history of machine watchmaking', *Horological Journal*, 89, April 1947, 177–84

9 Carrington, R. F. and Carrington, R. W. 'Pierre Frederick Ingold', AH, 10, Spring 1978, 698–714

10 *The Lancashire Watch Company, Prescot, Lancashire, England, 1889–1910*, Ken Roberts, USA, 1973

11 Indermuhle, 'Precision Engineering in the horological industry', *Horological Journal*, 89, February 1947, 74–6

12 *Encyclopedia Britannica*, 23, 14th edition, 1930, 406

Chapter 6

1 Peate, I. C. *Clock and Watch makers in Wales*, National Museum of Wales, 1960

2 Rees, A. *Clocks, Watches and Chronometers (1819–20)*, David & Charles, 1970

3 Gould, R. T. *The Marine Chronometer*, Holland Press, 1960

4 Foster, G. 'The De Baufre genre', AH, 7, September 1971, 337–9

5 Gazeley, W. J. *Clock and Watch escapements*, Heywood, 1956

6 Jaquet, E. and Chapuis, A. *Technique and History of the Swiss Watch*, Hamlyn, 1970

7 Mauss, J. 'The Independent jumping seconds mechanism of Jean Moise

Pouzait', AH, 12, Spring 1980, 30–5
8 Chamberlain, P. M. *It's about Time,* Holland Press, 1964

Chapter 7

1 Rees, A. *Clocks, Watches and Chronometers (1819–20),* David & Charles, 1970
2 Wadsworth, F. 'A History of repeating watches' (four parts), AH, 4, September 1965, 364–7; AH, 5, December 1965, 24–7; AH, 5, March 1966, 48–52; AH, 5, June 1966, 90–2
3 Haswell, J. E. *Horology,* EP Publishing, 1976
4 Gazeley, W. J. *Watch and Clock making and repairing,* Newnes, 1980
5 Britten, F. W. *Horological Hints and Helps,* Baron, 1977
6 Good, R. 'Watch by Thomas Mudge, London, No 574 with perpetual calendar mechanism', AH, 13, December 1981, 178–87
7 Von Bertele, H. 'Equation clock inventions of Joseph Williamson', AH, 1, December 1955, 123–7
8 Wenzel, J. 'Equation Clocks', AH, 13, September 1981, 24–43
9 AH, 13, June 1982, 411
10 Mercer, V. M. 'Some early keyless mechanisms', *Horological Journal,* 126, November 1983, 14–18
11 Jaquet, E. and Chapuis, A. *Technique and History of the Swiss Watch,* Hamlyn, 1970

Chapter 8

1 Wenzel, J. 'Equation Clocks', AH, 13, September 1981, 24–43
2 Gould, R. T. *The Marine Chronometer,* Holland Press, 1960
3 Howse, D. 'Captain Cook's marine chronometers' (two parts), AH, 6, September 1969, 190–205; AH, 6, December 1969, 276–80
4 Rees, A. *Clocks, Watches and Chronometers (1819–20),* David & Charles, 1970
5 Swinburne, J. 'The isochronous spring', *Horological Journal,* 89, January 1947, 36–7
6 De Carle, D. *Practical Watch Repairing,* NAG Press, 1947, Chapter 13
7 Mercer, V. 'The Penningtons and their balances', AH, 12, Spring 1981, 514–22
8 De Carle, D. *Practical Watch Repairing,* NAG Press, 1947, Chapters 12, 14
9 Correspondence, AH, 14, March 1983, 87, 90
10 Davies, Alun C. 'The adoption of standard time', AH, 11, Spring 1979, 284–9; 'The story of Greenwich Time', AH, 6, December 1969, 302–3

Chapter 9

1 Townsend, G. *Almost everything you wanted to know about American Watches and didn't know who to ask,* G. E. Townsend, USA, 1971
2 Townsend, G. *Encyclopedia of Dollar Watches,* G. E. Townsend, USA, 1974
3 Street, E. 'Watch Stands', AH, 12, Spring 1981, 504–13; 'More About Watch Stands', AH, 14, September 1983, 298–306

4 Randall, A. 'The technique of photographing watches', AH, 10, Summer 1978, 835–42
5 Walters, T. T. 'An aid to depth of field determination in horological photography', AH, 11, Spring 1979, 280–3
6 Smith, A. *Clocks and Watches,* Connoisseur, 1975
7 Crom, T. R. *Horological Wheel Cutting Engines, 1700 to 1900,* T. R. Crom, USA, 1970

Chapter 10

1 Smith, A. *A catalogue of tools for watch and clockmakers by John Wyke of Liverpool,* University of Virginia, USA, 1978
2 Crom, T. R. *Horological Wheel Cutting Engines, 1700 to 1900,* T. R. Crom, USA, 1970
3 Smith, A. *Clocks and Watches,* Connoisseur, 1975
4 Gazeley, W. J. *Watch and Clock making and repairing,* Newnes, 1982
5 De Carle, D. *Practical Watch Repairing,* NAG Press, 1947
6 Saunier, C. *The Watchmaker's Handbook,* Technical Press, 1948
7 Britten, F. W. *Horological Hints and Helps,* Baron, 1977
8 De Carle, D. *The Watchmaker's Lathe,* Hale, 1980
9 Swinkels, B. *Enamelling,* Hale, 1975

Chapter 11

1 Baillie, G. H. *Watchmakers and Clockmakers of the World,* Vol 1, NAG Press, 1976
2 Loomes, B. *Watchmakers and Clockmakers of the World,* Vol 2, NAG Press, 1976
3 Area lists are known for Buckingham, Channel Isles, Colchester, Cornwall, Cumberland, Devon, Dorset, Durham, Essex, Ireland, Kent, Lancashire, Leicestershire, Middlesex, Norfolk, Northamptonshire, Northumberland, Oxford, Scotland, Somerset, Stafford, Stamford, Suffolk, Sussex, Tiverton, Wales, Westmorland, Yorkshire, eg Daniel, J. *Leicestershire Clockmakers,* Leicester Museum, 1975. Others may now be available.
4 *Pigot's Directory* (also *Hunt's, Kelly's, Slater's, Worrell's* etc)
5 Aked, C. *Complete list of English Horological patents to 1853,* Brant Wright, 1975
6 Chamberlain, P. H. *It's about Time,* Holland Press, 1964
7 Grimthorpe, Lord. *A rudimentary treatise on Clocks, Watches and Bells for Public Purposes,* EP Publishing, 1974
8 Britten, F. J. *Old Clocks and Watches and their Makers,* 8th edition, Eyre Methuen and Son, 1973
9 Carrington, R. F. 'Thomas Yates of Preston', AH, 9, June 1975, 317–19; September 1975, 472
10 Correspondence, AH, 10, Spring 1978, 741; 11, Autumn 1979, 522
11 Smith, A. 'The Exeter Lovelace Clock', AH, 5, June 1966, 78–85
12 Jaquet, E. and Chapuis, A. *Technique and History of the Swiss Watch,* Hamlyn, 1970

13 Rees, A. *Clocks, Watches and Chronometers (1819–20)*, David & Charles, 1970
14 Philo Chronos, 'The art of making clocks and watches', *Horological Journal*, 117, March 1975, 7–12 (reprint of 1748 material)
15 Haswell, J. E. *Horology*, EP Publishing, 1976
16 Rawlings, A. L. *The Science of clocks and watches*, Pitman, 1948
17 Powell, F. 'The form of the fusee', *Horological Journal*, 118, August 1975, 10–11
18 Preisendorfer, R. W. 'Fusee Theory', *Horological Journal*, 120, November 1977, 65–7
19 Martin, H. G. 'A fuss around a fusee', AH, 10, Winter 1977, 573–9
20 Honig, P. S. 'History and mathematical analysis of the fusee', Paper 10 in *Clockwork Universe*, Adam Hilger, USA, 1981
21 Weaver, J. D. 'The theory of the fusee', *Journal of Physics E: Scientific Instruments*, 13, April 1980, 396–402
22 Bacon, D. H. and Stephens, R. C. *Mechanical Technology*, Butterworths, 1977
23 De Carle, D. *Practical Watch Repairing*, NAG Press, 1947
24 Herbert, A. P. *Sundials Old and New*, Methuen, 1967
25 *Whitaker's Almanack*, 13, Bedford Square, London
26 Welch, K. F. *Time measurement*, David & Charles, 1972
27 Wenzel, J. 'Equation Clocks', AH, 13, September 1981, 24–43
28 Chappell, W. *A short history of the printed word*, André Deutsch, 1972
29 Guildhall Library Ms 3338/1–2 and 3355/1–2
30 Roberts, S. *The story of Islington*, Hale, 1972
31 Evans, E. *Kensington*, Hamilton, 1975
32 Rawlings, R. *Making and managing: Antique Shop*, David & Charles, 1979

Chapter 12

1 Stevens, J. C. and Aked, C. K. *Horology in provincial and rural museums*, Antiquarian Horological Society, 1974
2 *Museums and Galleries in Great Britain and Ireland*, ABC Historic Publications (annual)
3 *Historic Houses, Castles and Gardens*, ABC Historic Publications (annual)
4 *Fodor's Guides* (to various countries), Hodder & Stoughton

Appendix

1 De Carle, D. *Watch and Clock Encyclopedia*, NAG Press, 1975
2 Britten, F. J. *Watch and Clockmaker's Handbook, dictionary and guide*, Baron, 1976

BIBLIOGRAPHY

Readers who do not wish to pursue the detailed chapter references will find that this bibliography includes the more useful quoted sources. The books are not rare and should be obtainable through a local library. There is also a vast amount of horological literature in the Guildhall and Science Museum libraries, London.

Baillie, G. H. *Watchmakers and Clockmakers of the World*, Vol 1, NAG Press, 1976 (For Vol 2 see Loomes, qv)

Britten, F. J. *Old Clocks and Watches and their Makers*, 8th edition, Eyre Methuen and Son, 1973

—— *Watch and Clockmaker's Handbook, dictionary and guide*, Baron, 1976

Camerer-Cuss, T. P. *The Camerer-Cuss book of Antique Watches*, Antique Collectors' Club, 1976

Chamberlain, P. M. *It's about Time*, Holland Press, 1964

Clutton, C. and Daniels, G. *Watches*, Batsford, 1965 (or 3rd edition, 1979)

Cutmore, M. *The Watch Collector's Handbook*, David & Charles, 1976

Daniels, G. *English and American Watches*, Abelard Shuman, 1967

De Carle, D. *Practical Watch Repairing*, NAG Press, 1947 (early editions are best for pocket watches)

Gazeley, W. J. *Watch and Clock making and repairing*, Newnes, 1980

Good, R. *Watches in Colour*, Blandford, 1978

Gould, R. T. *The Marine Chronometer*, Holland Press, 1960

Haywood, J. F. *English Watches*, HMSO, 1969

Jaquet, E. and Chapuis, A. *Technique and History of the Swiss Watch*, Hamlyn, 1970

Loomes, B. *Watchmakers and Clockmakers of the World*, Vol 2, NAG Press, 1976 (For Vol 1 see Baillie, qv)

Rawlings, A. L. *The Science of clocks and watches*, Pitman, 1948

Rees, A. *Clocks, Watches and Chronometers (1819–20)*, David & Charles, 1970

Smith, A. *Clocks and Watches*, Connoisseur, 1975

Thomson, R. *Antique American Clocks and Watches*, D. Van Nostrand Co, USA, 1968

Weiss, L. *Watchmaking in England, 1760–1820*, Hale, 1982

INDEX